EXETER MEDIEVAL TEXTS AND STUDIES
General Editors: Marion Glasscoe and M.J. Swanton

The cover illustration is a line-drawing from a late 10th-century manuscript
(British Library, Additional MS 24199, f. 18) and shows men abandoning
themselves to Luxuria. Used by permission of the British Library.

THE OLD ENGLISH LIFE OF ST MARY OF EGYPT

An edition of the Old English text
with modern English parallel-text translation

by Hugh Magennis

UNIVERSITY
of
EXETER
PRESS

First published in 2002 by
University of Exeter Press
Reed Hall, Streatham Drive
Exeter, Devon EX4 4QR
UK
www.exeterpress.co.uk

Printed digitally since 2010

British Library Cataloguing in Publication Data
A catalogue record of this book is available
from the British Library.

ISBN **978 0 85989 672 6**

Printed and bound by CPI Group (UK) Ltd, Croydon, CR0 4YY

For Anna, Ruth and Rozzie

CONTENTS

ACKNOWLEDGEMENTS

I wish to express my thanks to Queen's University Belfast for funds awarded in connection with my research for this book and for a grant towards its publication. For help and advice on particular points, grateful thanks are due to Linda Cantara, Ivan Herbison, Peter Jackson, Bruce Mitchell, Margaret Mullett, Don Scragg and Estelle Sheehan. My greatest debt is to my partner Helen for her support and patience.

LIST OF ABBREVIATIONS

ASE   *Anglo-Saxon England*

BHG   *Bibliotheca Hagiographica Graeca*, 3rd ed., ed. François Halkin, 3 vols, Subsidia Hagiographica 8a (Brussels: Société des Bollandistes, 1957); *Auctarium Bibliothecae Hagiographicae Graecae*, ed. François Halkin 47 (Brussels: Société des Bollandistes, 1969)

BHL   *Bibliotheca Hagiographica Latina Antiquiae et Mediae Aetatis*, ed. Socii Bollandiani, 2 vols, Subsidia Hagiographica 6 (Brussels: Société des Bollandistes, 1893-1901); *Supplementi Editio*, Subsidia Hagiographica 12 (Brussels: Société des Bollandistes, 1911); *Novum Supplementum*, ed. Henricus Flos. Subsidia Hagiographica 70 (Brussels: Société des Bollandistes, 1986)

BT; BT, *Suppl.*
        Joseph Bosworth, *An Anglo-Saxon Dictionary*, ed. and enlarged by T. Northcote Toller (Oxford: Oxford University Press. 1898); *Supplement*, ed. T. Northcote Tollei (Oxford: Oxford University Press, 1921). reprinted with *Enlarged Addenda and Corrigenda to the Supplement*, ed. Alistaii Campbell (Oxford: Clarendon Press, 1972)

C-C   Cotton-Corpus Legendary

CSASE
      Cambridge Studies in Anglo-Saxon England

DOE   *The Dictionary of Old English*, ed. Angus Cameron, Ashley Crandell Amos, Antonette diPaolo Healey, Joan Holland *et al.*, *A-E* (Toronto: Pontifical Institute of Mediaeval Studies, 1986-)

EETS   Early English Text Society
            OS Original Series
            SS Supplementary Series

LWS   Late West Saxon

MS(S)   manuscript(s)

NM   *Neuphilologische Mitteilungen*

OE   Old English

PG   *Patrologia Graeca*, ed. J.-P. Migne (Paris: J.-P. Migne, 1857-67)

PL   *Patrologia Latina*, ed. J.-P. Migne (Paris: J.-P. Migne, 1844-91)

R   *Vita Sanctæ Mariæ Ægyptiacæ*, ed. H. Rosweyde, *PL* 73, 671-90

For grammatical abbreviations, see below, p. 210.

MANUSCRIPT TEXTS

(i) *Old English*:

B   London, British Library, Cotton Julius E. vii, ff. 133v-134r: second iteration of passage in J copied twice

G   Gloucester, Cathedral Library 35, ff. 4-6

J   British Library, Cotton Julius E. vii, ff. 122v-

136r

O   British Library, Cotton Otho B. x, ff. 26, 56,
       16, 17 and 15

(ii) *Latin*:

C   British Library, Cotton Claudius A. i, ff. 76v-
       84v

N   British Library, Cotton Nero E. i, Part I, ff.
       179r-184v

S   Salisbury, Cathedral Library 221 (formerly
       Oxford, Bodleian Library, Fell 4), ff. 195v-
       204v

INTRODUCTION

THE LEGEND OF ST MARY OF EGYPT

The Old English text edited in this volume represents the earliest Western vernacular version of the edifying, though, in parts of its content, very scandalous, legend of St Mary of Egypt, a legend that fascinated audiences both in the Middle Ages and later. The story of St Mary of Egypt presents a powerful and unusual image of female sanctity. It is the story of a woman who repents her early life of immorality and withdraws to the desert to live a life of extreme penitence. Her period of immorality had lasted for more than seventeen years, which she had spent mostly in Alexandria, though she was in Jerusalem at the time of her conversion, after which she crossed east over the River Jordan into the vast deserts lying beyond. She lived alone as a hermit in this wilderness for forty-seven years, before, just prior to her death, recounting her story to a monk and priest, Zosimas (Zosimus in the Old English version), who had come across her in his own solitary wanderings in the desert. According to the legend, Zosimas was attached to a monastery near the Jordan distinguished for the perfection of its spiritual life. One of its traditions was that the monks should each spend Lent alone in the desert. In his Lenten wanderings Zosimas had been hoping that he might possibly find some wise desert father who could provide further spiritual enlightenment for him. In meeting the saintly *woman* Mary and hearing her remarkable story, he encounters in the innermost desert a degree of holiness far above anything he had experienced or imagined in his own life of prayer and striving. Through Mary, Zosimas learns humility and advances in spiritual understanding.

In translating this legend from Latin into the vernacular the anonymous Old English writer was making available to a wider audience of Anglo-Saxon men and women material that would otherwise have remained the preserve of those in religious life. Though translation inevitably introduces change into that which it transmits,[1] the St Mary of Egypt translator is remarkably faithful to the Latin source, displaying nothing of the tendency of other Old English hagiographers, notably Ælfric of Eynsham (the most celebrated and prolific of them), to tone down – or ignore altogether – material that might have been deemed problematic for a vernacular audience. Old English hagiographers are notably very protective of the sensibilities of lay readers,[2] but the Old English *Life of St Mary of Egypt* betrays no indications of anxiety or reticence in transmitting the saint's sense of her own sinfulness or in detailing the extent of that sinfulness, nor does it seek to downplay the gender issues that are inherent in the received legend, in which Mary, a woman, is presented as a figure of authority and a teacher to Zosimas, while he, though a priest, defers to her spiritual superiority. The *Life of St Mary of Egypt* portrays a spiritually-empowered female, who has lived independent of the guidance of men to an extent unparalleled

---

[1] On this point, see Colin Chase, 'Source Study as a Trick with Mirrors: Annihilation of Meaning in the Old English "Mary of Egypt"', in *Sources of Anglo-Saxon Culture*, ed. Paul E. Szarmach, Studies in Medieval Culture 20 (Kalamazoo, MI: Medieval Institute Publications, Western Michigan University, 1986), pp. 23-33.

[2] The reticence of Ælfric in transmitting problematic material in his Old English saints' lives is discussed by E. Gordon Whatley, *'Pearls Before Swine*: Ælfric, Vernacular Hagiography, and the Lay Reader', in *Via Crucis: Essays on Sources and Ideas in Memory of J. E. Cross*, ed. Thomas N. Hall, with assistance from Thomas D. Hill and Charles D. Wright (Morganstown, WV: West Virginia University Press, 2002), forthcoming; elsewhere Whatley discusses writers other than Ælfric: see his article 'Lost in Translation: Omission of Episodes in Some Old English Prose Saints' Legends', *ASE* 26 (1997), 187-208; see also my essay, 'A Funny Thing Happened on the Way to Heaven: Humorous Incongruity in Old English Saints' Lives', in *Humour in Anglo-Saxon Literature*, ed. Jonathan Wilcox (Cambridge: D. S. Brewer, 2000), pp. 137-57.

elsewhere in Old English writings about saints.[3]

The Old English version of the legend of Mary of Egypt is a translation of the influential ninth-century *Vita Sanctae Mariae Egyptiacae* (*BHL* 5415) of Paul, a deacon of Naples.[4] Paul's Latin version is itself a generally faithful translation of a Greek original (*BHG* 1042), which dates probably from the late sixth or early seventh century and has traditionally been attributed to Sophronius of Jerusalem (ca. 560-638), though this attribution is regarded by modern scholars as very questionable.[5] The Greek original refers in its prologue to the events of the story as having occurred in the writer's own time, but it is apparent that the author has reworked existing

---

[3] One comparable figure appears in the Anglo-Saxon vernacular tradition, Pelagia, whose story is briefly summarized in the ninth-century *Old English Martyrology*: see *Das altenglische Martyrologium*, ed. Günter Kotzor, Bayerische Akademie der Wissenschaften, Philos.-hist. Klasse, Neue Forschung 88, 2 vols (Munich: Bayerische Akademie der Wissenschaften, 1981), II, 233-35. Like Mary of Egypt, Pelagia is a 'repentant harlot' (on repentant harlots, see further below, p. 4) who withdraws from the world; however, unlike Mary of Egypt, she is converted through the preaching and guidance of a bishop, and though she lives as a recluse, she is not entirely cut off from human society, inhabiting a cell at the Mount of Olives outside Jerusalem.

[4] A text and translation of Paul's version is provided below, pp. 139-209. The 'standard' edition is nearly four hundred years old: Heribertus Rosweydus (Rosweyde), *Vitae Patrum* (Antwerp, 1615), 381-92, reprinted *PL* 73, 671-90; there is a free translation of this by Benedicta Ward, *Harlots of the Desert: A Study of Repentance in Early Monastic Sources* (London and Oxford: Mowbray, 1987), pp. 35-56; the recent edition and translation of the Latin by Jane Stevenson in *The Legend of Mary of Egypt in Medieval Insular Hagiography*, ed. Erich Poppe and Bianca Ross (Blackrock, Co. Dublin: Four Courts Press, 1996), pp. 51-98, are not reliable.

Paul of Naples is recognized as not being the same person as the famous eighth-century historian and homilist Paul the Deacon, though some commentators continue to insist on equating the two. On Paul of Naples, see Konrad Kunze, *Studien zur Legende der heiligen Maria Aegyptiaca im deutschen Sprachgebiet*, Philologische Studien und Quellen 49 (Berlin: Erich Schmidt, 1969), p. 26, n. 5; P. Albert Siegmund, *Die Überlieferung der griechischen Christlichen Literatur in der lateinischen Kirche bis zum zwölften Jahrhundert*, Abhandlungen der Bayerischen Benedictiner-Akademie 5, (Munich: Filser, 1949), p. 269.

[5] *PG* 87.3, 3697-726; trans. Maria Kouli, 'Life of St Mary of Egypt', in *Holy Women of Byzantium: Ten Saints' Lives in English Translation*, ed. Alice-Mary Talbot (Washington, DC: Dumbarton Oaks Research Library and Collection, 1996), pp. 65-93; on the attribution to Sophronius, see Kouli, p. 66; see also Kunze, *Studien*, pp. 20-22.

hagiographical material and traditions, going back at least to the fifth century, to produce a carefully-wrought narrative centred on what is in fact a composite heroine. It is a narrative with an inspiring spiritual message but no demonstrable historical basis. We know of no public cult of Mary, and supporting evidence of her existence is entirely lacking.

The Greek *Life of St Mary of Egypt* is one of a number of Byzantine saints' lives of 'repentant harlots', a type of exemplary narrative which, as Maria Kouli points out, 'found particular favor in the milieu of Syro-Palestine and Egypt in the fourth to seventh centuries'.[6] Two notable antecedents of the Mary of Egypt legend from the Byzantine world are drawn upon in the 'Sophronian' version. In both of these the saint is presented as virtuous throughout – in one she is a former nun, in the other a former pious church singer – but flees to the desert because she fears that her beauty is too ensnaring for men.[7] In introducing the theme of conversion and repentance, the author of the *Life* turns the story of his hermit into a dynamic narrative of process and progress, rather than presenting a static image of achieved sanctity.

The 'Sophronian' version combines its focus on conversion and repentance with a commitment to the monastic path and a veneration of the powerful ideals of desert spirituality (which had themselves been inspirational in the development of monasticism), as propagated in hagiographical and other writings from the fourth century onwards. It has long been recognized, indeed, that one of the seminal lives of the desert fathers, Jerome's *Life of St Paul of Thebes*, provided a direct model

---

[6] 'Life of St Mary of Egypt', p. 65; on repentant harlots, see Benedicta Ward, *Harlots of the Desert*; Lynda L. Coon, *Sacred Fictions: Holy Women and Hagiography in Late Antiquity* (Philadelphia, PA: University of Pennsylvania Press, 1997), esp. pp. 84-94. Another repentant harlot from the Byzantine tradition who is referred to by an Old English writer is Pelagia: see above, n. 3.

[7] See Efthalia Makris Walsh, 'The Ascetic Mother Mary of Egypt', *Greek Orthodox Theological Review* 34 (1989), 59-69, at pp. 60-61; see also Kouli, 'Life of St Mary of Egypt', pp. 65-66. For texts, see, respectively, *PG* 87.3, 3049-50 (by John Moschos), and *PG* 115, 939-42 (by Cyril of Scythopolis). See also Kunze, *Studien*, pp. 17-20.

for the *Life of St Mary of Egypt*,[8] and parallels with other works in the desert tradition are also evident in the *Life*.[9]

The Greek *Life of St Mary of Egypt* is most remarkable for the compelling central image of female sanctity it provides, an image that would have been seen as deeply challenging in the patriarchal context of late antique and early medieval Christianity. Mary's conversion has come about without the agency of the institutional church or its ministers, and in her life of holiness she displays a striking degree of personal autonomy, as she had also in her earlier life of sexual activity. Her very appearance when Zosimas meets her contradicts all conventional images of femininity.[10] She is an aged woman who wears no clothing (that which she had when she fled to the desert having long since worn away) and her body is blackened from the extremes of the climate; her short hair is as white as wool.

Meeting her is for Zosimas an overwhelming experience, which has strong overtones of love. He addresses her in terms of fervent affection and thinks longingly of her when not with her, and his interaction with her has a distinctly physical dimension, as he looks upon her body, embraces her feet, shares the kiss of peace with her, and finally tends her naked corpse; as he anxiously searches the desert for her two years after their first meeting, he is referred to, in a familiar erotic

---

[8] See F. Delmas, 'Remarques sur la vie de Sainte Marie l'Égyptienne', *Échos d'Orient* 4 (1900-1), 35-42. For the *Life of St Paul of Thebes*, see *PL* 23, 17-30; trans. Carolinne White, *Early Christian Lives* (Harmondsworth: Penguin, 1998), pp. 76-84. On desert spirituality, see further Derwas J. Chitty, *The Desert a City: An Introduction to the Study of Egyptian and Palestinian Monasticism under the Christian Empire* (Oxford: Blackwell, 1966); Peter Brown, *The Body in Society: Men, Women and Sexual Renunciation in Early Christianity* (London: Faber and Faber, 1989), pp. 213-40; Andrew Louth, *The Wilderness of God* (London: Darton, Longman and Todd, 1991), pp. 43-61.

[9] See Jane Stevenson, 'The Holy Sinner: The Life of Mary of Egypt', in *The Legend of Mary of Egypt in Medieval Insular Hagiography*, ed. Poppe and Ross, pp. 19-50, at pp. 30-35.

[10] Joyce E. Salisbury, *Church Fathers, Independent Virgins* (London and New York: Verso, 1991), discusses ancient female dress codes, including reference to St Mary of Egypt, pp. 70-73 and *passim*.

image, as a hunter seeking his prey (see Old English text, lines 873-5). Mary, on the other hand, does not display a sense of personal attachment to Zosimas, though she is in awe of his priestly powers.

Though a challenging figure (as is suggested in a later section of the Introduction, she might have been seen by someone like Ælfric as *too* challenging for an Anglo-Saxon vernacular audience), Mary is not ultimately a subversive or institutionally threatening one, however. The *Life of St Mary of Egypt* venerates the priesthood and, as explained below (pp. 8-9), it proclaims the centrality of the priestly sacrament of the eucharist to Christian life. As Lynda Coon suggests, Mary is essentially the product of a male discourse, a fictional construct of the patriarchal tradition of Byzantine hagiography, and her function is to provide a spiritual lesson for the audiences of that hagiography.[11] She can be viewed as a stereotypical figure of the sexually voracious female, who leads men astray. Interestingly, the excesses of the men who use Mary, particularly on their religiously-inspired voyage to Jerusalem, are not commented on in the *Life*, nor is there any suggestion that, like Mary, they are divinely prevented from entering the temple because of their sins.

The immediate, 'internal', audience of Mary's story is, of course, the male Zosimas, a fallible figure with whom the 'external' audiences of the *Life* can strongly identify. Zosimas may even be seen as the real protagonist in the narrative, with Mary as an instrument rather than a 'subject', by which Zosimas's spiritual progress is brought about. The story of Mary has a particular significance for those engaged (like

---

[11] Coon, *Sacred Fictions*, pp. xx-xxi; Coon draws upon Kate Cooper, 'Insinuations of Womanly Influence: An Aspect of the Christianization of the Roman Aristocracy', *Journal of Roman Studies* 82 (1982), 150-64; Cooper argues that in late antique hagiography, 'Narrative treatment of the actions or intentions of women did not straightforwardly represent flesh-and-blood women themselves, but rather served to symbolize aspects of the tension to be found among men' (p. 151; quoted by Coon, p. xx). On the 'binary opposition' in the legend between the ascetic masculine body and the sexual feminine body, see Andrew Scheil, 'Bodies and Boundaries in the Old English *Life of St Mary of Egypt*', *Neophilologus* 84 (2000), 137-56.

Zosimas) in monastic life; it has been argued indeed that the *Life of St Mary of Egypt* 'was first understood strictly as a monastic document, written not to convert or to edify the masses but to teach monastics true humility'.[12] But the exemplary appeal of the *Life* clearly extended beyond the monastery to the wider community of the church, for, as Coon puts it, hagiographical texts such as the *Life of St Mary of Egypt* 'affirm the possibility of universal salvation'; she writes, 'By transforming profane female flesh into a vehicle of grace, women's conversion extends the hope of universal salvation to sinful humanity.'[13] The story of Mary was soon absorbed into the mainstream of the life of the eastern church, where it acquired a place in the liturgy of Lent (see below, pp. 9-10).

Among the distinctive features of the *Life of St Mary of Egypt* are its emphasis on the veneration of the cross and the central position it allocates to the Virgin Mary in its narrative of a holy woman (who begins as the antithesis of all that the Virgin epitomizes). The occasion of Mary of Egypt's conversion is the Feast of the Exaltation of the Holy Cross (14 September), when she is in Jerusalem and finds that some mysterious power prevents her from entering the Church of the Resurrection (Holy Sepulchre) along with the throngs of people who have come there to honour the cross. It is a miraculous icon of the Virgin, which she sees in the courtyard of the church, that helps Mary at this time. The icon of the Virgin is instrumental in her conversion,[14] and after her conversion she adopts the Virgin as the 'guarantor' of her repentance, praying to her in times of crisis. The 'Sophronian' text, and subsequent versions of the legend based on this original, can be seen as having a role in propagating the cult of

---

[12] Walsh, 'Mother Mary of Egypt', p. 60.

[13] *Sacred Fictions*, p. xvii. Referring to the exemplary nature of such lives, Kouli comments that St Mary 'offered reassurance to every Christian: if such a licentious woman could find forgiveness, surely ordinary sinners could hope for salvation' ('The Life of St Mary of Egypt', p. 65).

[14] The conversion of Mary of Egypt is cited by John of Damascus in his *De imaginibus* as an instance of the efficacy of icons (*PG* 94, 1415-18).

the Virgin,[15] as well as reflecting the attachment to the Virgin that was characteristic of Palestinian monks.[16]

The Greek writer also associates Mary's conversion with that other participator in Christ's redemptive plan, the cross. Veneration of the cross had developed from the fourth century and it is thought that it was fully established by the early seventh century, the period from which the Greek *Life of St Mary of Egypt* probably originates. Veneration of the cross had a particular focus in Jerusalem, where the True Cross was housed at the Church of the Holy Sepulchre (in 614, however, it was carried off by the Persians, before being miraculously rediscovered and returned to Jerusalem, and then brought triumphantly to Constantinople by the emperor Heraclius).[17] Mary tells Zosimas that after she had prayed to the Virgin, 'I was deemed worthy to see the life-giving cross, and saw the mysteries of God' (ch. 24; *PG* 87.3, 3713; trans. Kouli, p. 83).[18] In the narrative as a whole the sign of the cross is much in evidence, for example when Mary blesses the River Jordan with it before miraculously walking across the water to meet Zosimas (Greek version, ch. 35; Latin and Old English versions, ch. 22).

Even more striking than the integration of the cross and the Virgin Mary into the scheme of the narrative of the *Life* is the author's emphasis on the saving mystery of the eucharist. This emphasis on the eucharist plays a decisive part in countering any possible anti-institutional thrust or suggestion of spiritual

---

[15] See Henri Barré, *Prières anciennes de l'Occident à la mère du Sauveur* (Paris: P. Lethielleux, 1963), p. 60 and *passim*; Mary Clayton, *The Cult of the Virgin Mary in Anglo-Saxon England*, CSASE 2 (Cambridge: Cambridge University Press, 1990), pp. 257-58; Kunze, *Studien*, p. 40.

[16] See Stevenson, 'The Holy Sinner', p. 33.

[17] For a concise account of the development of the cult of the cross, see Michael Swanton, *The Dream of the Rood*, 2nd ed. (Exeter: University of Exeter Press, 1996), pp. 42-52; see also H. Leclercq, 'Croix et crucifix', in *Dictionnaire d'Archéologie chrétienne et de Liturgie*, ed. Fernand Cabrol, Henri Leclerq et al., 15 vols (Paris: L. Letouzey, 1903-53), III (1914), 3045-131; Cyril E. Pocknee, *Cross and Crucifix in Christian Worship and Devotion* (London: A. R. Mowbray, 1962).

[18] Cf. Old English text, ch. 17 (lines 534-37); also Latin version (edited below), ch. 17 (lines 530-32).

self-sufficiency that might be perceived in the message of the legend, for Mary deeply appreciates that the eucharist, which can be ministered only by the priesthood, is central to Christian life, and she begs Zosimas to provide it for her so that she may die with its benefit. It is the celebration of the eucharist that she is rhapsodically alluding to in her reference in the Church of the Resurrection to the mysteries of God, when she says (as mentioned above), 'I was deemed worthy to see the life-giving cross, and saw the mysteries of God.' In a passage which also develops a theme of symbolic baptism,[19] Mary partakes of the eucharist at the church of St John the Baptist by the Jordan before crossing the river to begin her life in the desert, and at the end of her account of her life to Zosimas she asks him to meet her at the Jordan on the night of the Last Supper the following year, bringing with him the sacred elements of the sacrament. Having received the eucharist from him – on the very day that commemorates its institution – she utters the words of the Song of Simeon, 'Lord, lettest thou thy servant depart in peace' (Luke 2. 29), and, as Zosimas learns later, it is just after this that she dies. Thus key events in the narrative of the legend relate Mary to the eucharist, by participation in which she can be seen 'identifying herself as a disciple of Christ within the context of the church'.[20] As remarked by Kouli, in the many depictions of Mary in Byzantine art the saint is usually accompanied by Zosimas, from whom she is receiving his blessing or the eucharist.[21]

The popularity of St Mary of Egypt in Byzantine art attests to the influence of the Sophronian *Life*, as does the fact that, as well as having her own feast day, on 1 April (in the West it

---

[19] See below, Commentary, n. to lines 575-76 (p. 126).

[20] Walsh, 'Mother Mary of Egypt', p. 66.

[21] 'St Mary of Egypt', p. 68. On icons of St Mary of Egypt in Byzantine art, see Henry Maguire, *The Icons of their Bodies: Saints and their Images in Byzantium* (Princeton, NJ: Princeton University Press, 1996), pp. 28-31 and 73-74, with image at p. 32; Coon, *Sacred Fictions*, p. 90 (with image of Zosimas dispensing the eucharist to Mary); see also images of Mary in N. K. Moutsopoulos and G. Demetrokalles, *Géraki: Les églises du Bourgade*, Monuments d'agglomérations Byzantines 1 (Thessalonike: Kentron Vyzantinon Ereunon, 1981), pp. 67 and 232.

is usually 2 April but sometimes also 9 or 10 April), Mary came to be commemorated in the Greek Orthodox liturgy for Lent, in which she is celebrated on the fifth Sunday: Mary is the only woman celebrated in the liturgy of a Sunday in Lent.[22] It is also a mark of the appeal of the *Life* that over a hundred manuscripts of the Greek text are known; Kouli lists twenty-seven from the Greek National Library at Athens alone and another thirty-seven from the Bibliothèque Nationale in Paris, as well as referring to numerous manuscripts in other libraries.[23] And elsewhere within the area of the Eastern church there are versions of the St Mary of Egypt story deriving from the Sophronian original in Armenian, Ethiopic, Slavonic and Syriac.

ST MARY OF EGYPT IN THE LATIN WEST

Knowledge of St Mary of Egypt was brought to the West by Greek and Palestinian Christian settlers and travellers at an early date.[24] In the following centuries a number of Latin translations of the Sophronian *Life* were made, and we find Mary mentioned in the famous ninth-century martyrology of Usuard.[25] As well as the translation by Paul of Naples, there is a somewhat freer anonymous early translation (extant in manuscripts of the late ninth century and after),[26] which appears to have circulated widely, particularly in southern Europe (*BHL* 5417);[27] and part of the legend of St Mary of

---

[22] See Walsh, 'Mother Mary of Egypt', pp. 66-67. Not only do services commemorating Mary take place on the fifth Sunday in Lent, but her legend (in the Sophronian version) is also read on the following Thursday.

[23] 'St Mary of Egypt', p. 67, n. 12.

[24] Kunze refers to the evidence of frescos of the saint at Rome from the first half of the seventh century (*Studien*, p. 26).

[25] See *PL* 123, 897 (2 April); she is not in the martyrology of Hrabanus Maurus.

[26] Kunze (*Studien*, pp. 182-87) lists eleven manuscripts of the ninth and tenth centuries, as well as dozens of later manuscripts.

[27] Ed. Boninus Mombritius, *Sanctuarium seu Vitae Sanctorum*, 2nd ed., 2 vols (Paris: Apud Albertum Fontemoing, 1910 (original ed., Milan, 1480)), II, 134-43.

Egypt, based on the Sophronian version, was among the
translations of saints' lives made by Anastasius Bibliothec-
arius (ca. 810-ca. 880) (*BHL* 5416).[28] Other Latin versions
exist, some of them representing 'mixed' redactions, and
many questions of relationship and derivation remain to be
answered concerning the legend's Latin textual traditions.[29]
The thirteenth-century version by Vincent of Beauvais in his
great compilation *Speculum Historiale*, which in turn was the
source of Jacobus de Voragine's account of Mary later in the
same century in his popular *Legenda Aurea*, is based on the
anonymous version *BHL* 5417, though in some respects it
appears to be unlike all earlier versions.[30]

The version of Paul of Naples, a succinct and artful rendering of the Greek original, faithfully reflecting its themes and
emphases, was particularly popular. Well over a hundred
manuscripts of this text are known, of which fourteen are from
the ninth and tenth centuries.[31] These manuscripts are of very
wide provenance but relate especially to regions covering what
are now Germany, Belgium, Holland, northern France and
England. The tenth-century poem on Mary of Egypt written
by Flodoard of Reims (*BHL* 5418)[32] appears to be based on

[28] Ed. *PL* 129, 314-15 (the passage given here is that dealing with the
conversion of Mary at the church in Jerusalem).

[29] The seventeenth-century editors of the volume of *Acta Sanctorum* that
includes Mary of Egypt declined to provide a text of the *vita* based on Latin
manuscripts; instead, expressing dissatisfaction with extant Latin manuscripts, they produced their own Latin translation of the Greek: see *Acta
Sanctorum Aprilis, Tomus I*, ed. Godefridus Henschenius and Daniel Pape-
brochius, editio novissima, ed. Joannes Carnandet (Paris: Victor Palmé,
1866: original ed., Antwerp, 1674), pp. 77-84 (with discussion concerning
the translation, p. 76).

[30] Vincent of Beauvais, *Speculum Historiale*, 2 vols (Strassburg, 1473),
Book XVI, chs 65-73 (unpaginated); Jacobus de Voragine, *Legenda Aurea*,
ch. 56, ed. Th. Graesse, *Jacobi a Voragine Legenda Aurea, vulgo Historica
Lombardica dicta* (Dresden and Leipzig: Impensis Librariae Arnoldianae,
1846), 247-49; trans. William Granger Ryan, *Jacobus de Voragine: The
Golden Legend: Readings on the Saints*, 2 vols (Princeton, NJ: Princeton
University Press, 1993), I, 227-29. See Peter F. Dembrowski, ed., *La vie de
Sainte Marie l'Égyptienne: versions en ancien et en moyen français*,
Publications romanes et françaises 144 (Geneva: Droz, 1977), p. 15.

[31] See Kunze, *Studien*, pp. 174-80 (see further below, n. 74).

[32] Ed. *PL* 135, 541-48.

Paul's translation, as are other Latin redactions,[33] and many of the vernacular versions of the legend, including the Old English one edited here, go back to Paul, directly or indirectly.

The vernacular versions of the story of St Mary, which include texts in English (Old and Middle), German, Dutch, Norse, Irish, Welsh, French (including Anglo-Norman), Italian, Spanish and Portuguese,[34] indicate the extent of the legend's popularity. The earliest of the vernacular versions, the Old English translation based on Paul, is preserved in a manuscript of the very early eleventh century (as well as in two other fragmentary copies which date from only slightly later) and the translation itself probably originates from the tenth century.

It is likely that knowledge of St Mary of Egypt would have been brought to England by the Greek archbishop of Canterbury Theodore of Tarsus (602-90), but documentary evidence of interest in her in Anglo-Saxon England comes from considerably later in the period. Her feast day (given as 9 or 10 April) is recorded in a number of Anglo-Saxon calendars of the late-ninth and tenth centuries.[35] Direct evidence of Anglo-Saxon acquaintance with her *Life*, in the version of Paul of Naples (*BHL* 5415), is confined to the tenth and eleventh centuries. It is notable that Mary does not figure in the ninth-century *Old English Martyrology*.

A mid-tenth-century manuscript containing *BHL* 5415 (London, British Library, Cotton Claudius A. i), though

---

[33] See Kunze, *Studien*, p. 181.

[34] For bibliographical details, see Dembrowski, *La vie de Sainte Marie l'Égyptienne*, pp. 9-10; Poppe and Ross, *The Legend of Mary of Egypt*; Hermann Knust, *Geschichte der Legenden der h. Katharina von Alexandrien und der h. Maria Aegyptiaca* (Halle: Max Niemeyer, 1890), pp. 206-28.

[35] See *English Calendars before A. D. 1100*, ed. Francis Wormald, Henry Bradshaw Society 72 (London: Harrison, 1933), pp. 5, 19 and 47. As pointed out by Simon Lavery, there is a reference in a fifteenth-century record of relics held at Westminster Abbey to parts of Mary's skull from the collection of Queen Emma (d. 1052), but there is no early evidence for this (see Lavery's essay, 'The Story of Mary the Egyptian in Medieval England', in *The Legend of Mary of Egypt in Insular Hagiography*, ed. Poppe and Ross, pp. 113-48, at p. 115).

written on the Continent, appears to have been in England,[36] and *BHL* 5415 also occurred in a compendious collection of saints' lives, the 'Cotton-Corpus Legendary', a version of which was current in late Anglo-Saxon England. The Cotton-Corpus Legendary, or rather the original form of the collection referred to by that name,[37] had been assembled on the Continent in the ninth century and must have been in England by the late tenth century, if not earlier, for it served as Ælfric's main source for his saints' lives. It is also clear that the Old English translator of the *Life of St Mary of Egypt* was working from a Latin text similar to that found in two surviving copies of the Cotton-Corpus Legendary.[38]

The popularity of the legend of St Mary of Egypt in later centuries of the Middle Ages, including in England, is evident from the many translations of it that were made (as mentioned above) and from the number of manuscripts of the Latin texts and of summaries deriving from them (the best-known being that in the *Legenda Aurea*) that survive. Mary is also referred to by writers of sermons and other edifying literature.[39] The interesting post-medieval afterlife of her legend is briefly outlined by Jane Stevenson, who brings the story down to

---

[36] The manuscript contains glosses in Old English, as discussed by N. R. Ker, *Catalogue of Manuscripts Containing Anglo-Saxon*, reprinted with 'Supplement' (Oxford: Clarendon Press, 1990), pp. 176-77.

[37] The legendary is called after the manuscripts of its earliest surviving copy (mid-eleventh century), London, British Library Cotton Nero E. i, Parts I and II, and Cambridge, Corpus Christi College 9 (one copy in three volumes); though it was compiled on the Continent, the surviving copies of the legendary are English. On the Cotton-Corpus Legendary, see Patrick H. Zettel, 'Ælfric's Hagiographic Sources and the Legendary Preserved in B.L. MS Cotton Nero E. i + CCCC MS 9 and Other Manuscripts' (D.Phil. dissertation, Oxford University, 1979); see also Zettel's article, 'Saints' Lives in Old English: Latin Manuscripts and Vernacular Accounts: Ælfric', *Peritia* 1 (1982), 17-37; and Peter Jackson and Michael Lapidge, 'The Contents of the Cotton-Corpus Legendary', in *Holy Men and Holy Women: Old English Prose Saints' Lives and Their Contexts*, ed. Paul E. Szarmach (Albany, NY: State University of New York Press, 1996), pp. 131-46.

[38] See further, below, pp. 30-35 (the Cotton-Corpus copies are, of course, later than the Old English version).

[39] See Benedicta Ward, 'The Image of the Prostitute in the Middle Ages', *Monastic Studies* 16 (1985), 39-49, at pp. 41-44.

recent times, referring to twentieth-century works centring on Mary, including two novels, a poem and two operas.[40]

THE OLD ENGLISH VERSION AND ITS MANUSCRIPTS

The text of the anonymous Old English *Life of St Mary of Egypt* occurs in the very early eleventh-century manuscript London, British Library, Cotton Julius E. vii (ff. 122v-36r) (J), a manuscript celebrated as uniquely preserving Ælfric's *Lives of Saints* as a unified collection:[41] other manuscripts contain numbers of individual items from *Lives of Saints*, but do not treat it as a specific collection. The *Life of St Mary of Egypt* is one of four saints' lives in Cotton Julius E. vii not written by Ælfric (see below, p. 19).

There are also substantial fragments of the Old English *Life of St Mary of Egypt* in two other witnesses, British Library, Cotton Otho B. x (in correct order, ff. 26, 56; 16, 17; 15) (O), and Gloucester, Cathedral Library 35 (ff. 4-6) (G), the 'Gloucester Fragments'.[42] The former of these has been dated to the first half of the eleventh century, the latter to the mid-eleventh century. Cotton Otho B. x and Gloucester 35 each preserves three disconnected passages of the *Life*, amounting altogether to considerably less than half of the complete text, and some of the text in Cotton Otho and Gloucester is illegible. The dozen or so closing words of the

---

[40] 'The Holy Sinner', pp. 19-20.

[41] The collection is ed. and trans. Walter W. Skeat, *Ælfric's Lives of Saints*, EETS, OS 76, 82, 94 and 114 (London: Oxford University Press, 1881-1900; rpt as 2 vols, 1966), in which an older foliation, two behind that followed in the present edition, is observed. Skeat does not include in his edition the final items of the manuscript, which are not hagiographical in nature. According to its own table of contents, Cotton Julius E. vii originally ended with 'De interrogationibus Sigewulfi presbyteri', 'De falsis diis' and 'De xii abusiuis', but only the first and part of the second of these survive, the text of 'De falsis diis' breaking off abruptly at the end of the last remaining quire. These do not appear in Skeat.

[42] To avoid possible ambiguity, I use 'J', 'G' and 'O' only to refer specifically to texts of the *Life of St Mary of Egypt* rather than as abbreviations for the manuscripts as a whole.

Life (lines 958-60) survive from all three manuscripts,[43] but apart from these words only one other short passage is available for comparison in each of the witnesses (in the present edition, lines 554-72).

As described by Humphrey Wanley in 1705,[44] in its original state Cotton Otho B. x was a volume mostly of saints' lives, the majority being (unattributed) items by Ælfric from *Lives of Saints*, though as well as thirteen lives by Ælfric there were four anonymous lives (those of Euphrosyne, Christopher, Mary of Egypt and the Seven Sleepers), along with homiletic and other religious material. In 1731 this manuscript was severely damaged by fire and much of it was lost. A number of leaves were recovered, however, subsequently to be mounted on paper in a disordered sequence. Five leaves of the text of the *Life of St Mary of Egypt* remain, amounting to something under a quarter of the text as preserved in Cotton Julius E. vii, though due to the scorching of the fire one of these leaves (f. 26) is illegible in a number of places and another (f. 56) is almost completely illegible, at least to the naked eye.[45] There are a few contemporary or near-contemporary interlinear corrections in the surviving folios.

According to Wanley's description of Cotton Otho B. x, the text of the *Life of St Mary of Egypt*, which appears to have been complete in this manuscript, occupied ff. 76v-95v. Wanley supplied a transcription of the opening and closing words of each item in Cotton Otho. His transcription of the beginning of the *Life of St Mary of Egypt* reads, 'Ðas

---

[43] These are preserved in Cotton Julius and Gloucester and in the transcription of the beginning and end of the *Life* in Cotton Otho made by Humphrey Wanley (as discussed in the following paragraphs).

[44] Humphrey Wanley, *Antiquiæ Literaturæ Septentrionalis Liber Alter: Librorum Vett. Septentrionalium . . . Catalogus Historico-Criticus* (Oxford, 1705), pp. 190-93.

[45] An electronic edition of MS Cotton Otho B. x is currently being prepared by Kevin Kiernan, using ultraviolet imaging. Some of Kiernan's results are made use of by Linda Miller Cantara, 'St Mary of Egypt in BL Cotton Otho B. X: New Textual Evidence for an Old English Saint's Life' (MA dissertation, University of Kentucky, 2001), which may be consulted online at 'http://lib.uky.edu/ETD/ukyengl2001t00018/htlm/cantara.htm'.

herigendlicestra gehwyrfednesse ægþer ge dæda ge þeawa. 7
þa micclan hreowsunga. 7 swa ellenlic gewin þære arwyrþan
Egiptiscan Marian' (i.e. with only very minor disagreements
with J: see lines 1-3 of the edited text, below); his
transcription of the ending reads, 'Wuldor si urum drihtne
hælendum Criste. se lyfað 7 rixað on ealra worulda woruld.
Amen' (again closely similar to J, though with some
differences: see lines 958-60 of the edited text).[46]

Gloucester 35 consists of fragments from bindings, now
kept in a portfolio.[47] The first of the three leaves of the *Life
of St Mary of Egypt* is damaged, with many readings lost.[48]
The remaining two leaves were pastedowns, and present no
significant problems of legibility.[49] Over a fifth of the text of
the *Life* is preserved in Gloucester 35, including a substantial
passage missing from J (lines 303-52). There are sporadic
contemporary or near-contemporary interlinear and marginal
corrections.[50]

The text in Cotton Julius E. vii is complete, except for two
lacunas, a substantial one at lines 303-52 (about half of the
missing material can be supplied from G, but there is no Old
English equivalent to some 144 words of the Latin source) and

---

[46] Wanley, *Antiquiæ Literaturæ Liber Alter*, p. 191. On Cotton Otho B. x,
see further Ker, *Catalogue*, item 177 (pp. 224-29).

[47] These have been transcribed and translated by John Earle, *Gloucester
Fragments: Legends of St Swiðhun and Sancta Maria Ægyptiaca* (London:
Longman, Green, Longman and Roberts, 1861), pp. 102-13.

[48] The leaf had been cut vertically into two strips of similar size. These are
now pasted together again but with rectangular-shaped sections lost at the
top of one of the strips (the right-hand one on the recto side) and at the
bottom of the other, amounting to the loss of four half-lines at the top of the
page and one at the bottom; the strip missing a half-line at the bottom also
has four largish holes; and words are also indistinct at the beginning and end
of lines, where they are covered by pasting-strips.

[49] The *Life of St Mary of Egypt* ends on the second line of f. 6v. The rest of
this page is devoted to a separate (incomplete) text (transcribed by Earle,
Gloucester Fragments, p. 112), part of ch. 4 of the Old English Rule of St
Benedict (corresponding to Arnold Schröer, ed., *Die angelsächsischen
Prosabearbeitungen der Benedictinerregel*, Bibliothek der angelsächsischen
Prosa 2 (Kassel: Georg H. Wigand, 1888), p. 16, line 15 to p.18, line 4).

[50] On this manuscript, see Ker, *Catalogue*, item 117 (pp. 154-55). A
photozincographic facsimile of f. 6r is provided by Earle, *Gloucester
Fragments* (facing p. 97).

a short passage at lines 934-36 (which can be supplied from
O). It is also notable that a passage in J (not represented in G
or O) has been copied twice (lines 792-805), with significant
variation between the two versions of it (the second iteration
of this passage is referred to below as B). Of the thirty-one
surviving quires of Cotton Julius E. vii (the end of the
manuscript is imperfect), the *Life of St Mary of Egypt*
occupies the last two leaves of quire 16 (ff. 117-24), all of
quire 17 (ff. 125-32) and all of quire 18 (ff. 133-36) except for
the last page and a half, which are blank (ff. 136rv). The next
item starts at the beginning of quire 19. Apart from the page
and a half at the end of quire 18, there is no blank space
between items in this manuscript. Quire 18 is also distinctive
in having only four leaves, whereas all the other quires in
Cotton Julius have eight leaves, with the exception of quire 1,
an added bifolium, containing preliminary material.[51]

As noted above, Cotton Julius E. vii is the unique
manuscript of Ælfric's large hagiographical collection, *Lives
of Saints*. Ælfric must have first issued *Lives of Saints* before
about 998, the date of the death of ealdorman Æthelweard, to
whom he addresses his Old English preface to the collection.
Cotton Julius was copied not long after this, probably before
1020[52] and perhaps within Ælfric's own lifetime (d. ca.
1010). In key respects the manuscript appears to reflect
Ælfric's original intentions faithfully, presenting itself very

---

[51] On Cotton Julius E. vii, see Ker, *Catalogue*, item 162 (pp. 206-10); see
also D. G. Scragg, 'The Corpus of Anonymous Lives and Their Manuscript
Context, in *Holy Men and Holy Women*, ed. Szarmach, pp. 209-30, at pp.
217-18; and Joyce Hill, 'The Dissemination of Ælfric's *Lives of Saints*: A
Preliminary Survey', in *Holy Men and Holy Women*, ed. Szarmach, pp.
235-59, at pp. 236-42.
[52] An inscription on f. 3 indicates that Cotton Julius E. vii was in the
monastery of Bury St Edmunds (founded 1020, having been a house of
secular canons beforehand) in the thirteenth century. It may have been
copied there, but it is thought more likely that it was written in a southern
scriptorium and brought to Bury when the monastery opened: see G. I.
Needham, 'Additions and Alterations in Cotton MS Julius E VII', *Review of
English Studies*, New Series 9 (1958), 160-64; J. C. Pope, *Homilies of
Ælfric: A Supplementary Collection*, 2 vols, EETS, OS 259 and 260
(London: Oxford University Press, 1967-8), I, 85.

much as a unified literary production: it includes self-conscious prefaces by Ælfric, one in Latin and one in Old English, in which he sets out his principles and intentions; the collection itself is highly coherent, making available in English a selection of the lives of saints honoured by monks in special services (Ælfric's previous collections, his two series of *Catholic Homilies*, had included lives of saints celebrated by the faithful on feast days),[53] and presenting them in proper order according to the date of their feast day in the ecclesiastical calendar; the manuscript includes a table of contents, numbering the items of the collection from I to XXXVIIII (though there is no number XVIII).

On the other hand, there are some apparent curiosities concerning Cotton Julius, which indicate that the manuscript is not an exact representation of the book of saints' lives conceived by Ælfric. Perhaps the most striking of these curiosities concern the *Life of St Mary of Egypt* and its relationship to the collection, but there are further problematic features of Cotton Julius as well. It is notable, for example, that not all of Ælfric's writings in the manuscript are in fact saints' lives. Conflicting with his prefatory account of the subject matter of the collection, Cotton Julius also incorporates moral, biblical and other religious material by Ælfric.[54] More remarkable is the fact that not all the items in

---

[53] See *Ælfric's Catholic Homilies: The First Series. Text*, ed. Peter Clemoes, EETS, SS 17 (Oxford: Oxford University Press, 1997) and *Ælfric's Catholic Homilies: The Second Series. Text*, ed. Malcolm Godden, EETS, SS 5 (London: Oxford University Press, 1979). On saints celebrated by the faithful on feast days and saints honoured by monks, see Ælfric's Latin Preface to *Lives of Saints* (ed. and trans. Skeat, I, 2-5), lines 6-7 and 8-9, respectively.

[54] See n. 41 above; also, as Jonathan Wilcox points out, items I, XII, XIII and XVII are homilies for specific occasions, XVI is a homily for any occasion, and XVIII and XXV are biblical paraphrases (*Ælfric's Prefaces*, Durham Medieval Texts 9 (Durham: Durham Medieval Texts, 1994), p. 45). Despite their non-hagiographical nature, it is probable that it was Ælfric himself who was responsible for associating these items with the rest of the collection: see Hill, 'The Dissemination of Ælfric's *Lives of Saints*', p. 237. Clemoes sees these items as having been deemed suitable by Ælfric for inclusion because of their non-liturgical nature (P. A. M. Clemoes, 'The Chronology of Ælfric's Works', in *The Anglo-Saxons: Studies in Some*

the collection are *by* Ælfric. In his Old English preface Ælfric
makes an anxious plea that his work should be copied faithfully,[55] but embedded among Ælfric's own writings in Cotton
Julius E. vii are the *non-*Ælfrician lives not only of Mary of
Egypt but also of the Seven Sleepers, Eustace and Euphrosyne.[56] Two of these four, the *Seven Sleepers* and *Eustace*,
have been incorporated seamlessly into the overall structure of
the collection, but *Euphrosyne* and *Mary of Egypt* interrupt the
proper chronological order of the set, since their position in
Cotton Julius does not reflect the date of their feast day: the
life of St Euphrosyne,[57] whose feast day of 11 February is
recorded in the manuscript, follows immediately after that of
St Edmund (20 November), while the life of St Mary of
Egypt, whose feast day is not given in the manuscript but was
known to be 9 (or 2 or 10) April, immediately follows that of
the Seven Sleepers (27 July). *Mary of Egypt*, indeed, does not
even appear in the manuscript's table of contents.[58]

The omission of the *Life of St Mary of Egypt* from the
table of contents indicates that the decision to include it in
Cotton Julius E. vii was taken at a late stage in the process of
putting the manuscript together, after the table of contents had

---

Aspects of Their History and Culture Presented to Bruce Dickins, ed. Peter
Clemoes (London: Bowes and Bowes, 1959), 212-47, at pp. 221-22).
[55] Ælfric ends his Old English Preface,
> Ic bidde nu on godes naman gif hwa þas boc awritan wille .
> þæt he hi wel gerihte be þære bysne . and þær namare betwux
> ne sette þonne we awendon.   (lines 74-76)
[I pray now in God's name, if any man desire to transcribe this book,
he correct it well according to the copy; and set down therein no more
than we have translated. (trans. Skeat, I, 7)]
On Ælfric's anxieties about copyists, see Wilcox, *Ælfric's Prefaces*, pp. 45
and 70-71. Wilcox refers to Ælfric's 'unsuccessful' attempt 'to claim
authoritative fixed status for his works' (p. 71).
[56] See Clemoes, 'The Chronology of Ælfric's Works', p. 219. On the
stylistic and linguistic features of these lives, see my article, 'Contrasting
Features in the non-Ælfrician Lives in the Old English *Lives of Saints*',
Anglia 104 (1986), 316-48.
[57] This saint's name is mistakenly given as 'eufrosia' in the table of
contents, and as 'euphrasia' in the title of the life.
[58] To fit in with the manuscripts numbering in its table of contents, Skeat
designates the *Life of St Mary of Egypt* as item XXIIIB, the previous item
(the *Seven Sleepers*) having the number XXIII in the table of contents.

already been drawn up. This conclusion is borne out by the fact that special scribal arrangements were employed to allow for inclusion of the *Life*. Most of the manuscript was copied by a single scribe. Near the end of quire 14, however, and coinciding with the beginning of item XXIII, the *Legend of the Seven Sleepers* (f. 107v), there is a change from this main scribe to what Ker refers to as 'a less good but nearly contemporary hand'.[59] This second scribe copied from f. 107v to the end of f. 116v, thus covering most of the *Legend of the Seven Sleepers*. At f. 117r (the beginning of quire 16) the handwriting changes again, with what appears to be a third scribe (but may also be the first scribe writing in a compressed style) copying the rest of the *Legend* and all of the *Life of St Mary of Egypt*, and then leaving a page and a half blank at the end of quire 18. After this, the first scribe resumes in his or her normal (uncompressed) style at f. 137r (the beginning of quire 19) and copies to the end of the manuscript.[60]

As Clemoes explains,[61] the main scribe, having completed item XXII before the end of quire 14, seems to have gone straight on to start another item, XXIV, at the beginning of a new quire. Meanwhile, the copying of XXIII was begun by a second scribe and continued by a third (or by the first scribe writing in a style more compressed than usual), who went on to copy the *Life of St Mary of Egypt* after XXIII, and when these two items had been completed a page and a half were left over and remained blank at the end the short quire 18, which itself had been specially tailored to accommodate the *Life*. It is not known why the late decision should have been taken to include another item in Cotton Julius after the *Legend of the Seven Sleepers*. The fact that the ending of the latter is missing (the text breaks off abruptly in the middle of a speech)

---

[59] *Catalogue*, p. 210.
[60] Ker suggests that ff. 117-36 is not be the work of a third scribe. He writes that this stint 'may be in the main hand, but the writing is more compressed than elsewhere' (*Catalogue*, p. 210). Clemoes points out, however, that there is no need for compression in the handwriting, since there is no shortage of space at this point ('The Chronology of Ælfric's Works', p. 219, n. 2).
[61] 'The Chronology of Ælfric's Works', p. 219, n. 2.

may have prompted some editorial improvisation, though it is far from clear exactly how such an – apparently unexpected – editorial situation might have arisen.

As to why, a decision to add another item having been taken, the *Life of St Mary of Egypt* in particular should have been selected for insertion in the manuscript, the likelihood is that this was a text that was conveniently to hand and was deemed suitable by an 'editor', probably the person who had already deemed the *Legend of the Seven Sleepers* a suitable addition to the set.[62] It is even possible that the *Life of St Mary of Egypt* might have been copied into Cotton Julius directly from the same source manuscript as were the *Legend of the Seven Sleepers* and the other two non-Ælfrician items in the compilation, though the exemplars of these other three texts share a particular linguistic feature not found in the *Life*.[63] However the *Life of St Mary of Egypt* came to be included in Cotton Julius, it would hardly have been deemed suitable by Ælfric himself. Its inclusion reflects the willingness of the compilers of the manuscript pragmatically to adapt and appropriate inherited material to their own purposes, despite Ælfric's evident desire that the integrity of his hagiographical collection should be maintained.

Codicologically, then, as also, indeed, linguistically and stylistically (see below, pp. 35-43 and 43-50), the *Life of St Mary of Egypt* stands out from the other items in Cotton Julius. It is only, however, when we examine the content of the piece and the message it presented to its late Anglo-Saxon readers that the full extent of the singularity of this *Life* in its 'Ælfrician' manuscript context becomes apparent. The *Life of*

---

[62] Clemoes considers it to be very likely that both the *Life of St Mary of Egypt* and the *Legend of the Seven Sleepers* 'became associated with the set for the first time in J' ('The Chronology of Ælfric's Works', pp. 219-20); Clemoes draws attention to two binding fragments, Cambridge, Queens' College (Horne) 75, which indicate that at least one copy of *Lives of Saints* lacked these two items; see also Hill, 'The Dissemination', p. 245.

[63] See Roland Torkar, 'Zu den Vorlagen der ae. Handschrift Cotton Julius E. VII', *NM* 72 (1971), 711-15. Torkar points out that the *Life* contrasts with the other three items in lacking spellings of the possessive pronouns *minre*, *minra*, *þinre* and *þinra* without *n*.

St Mary of Egypt is a document which gives expression to a high ideal of monasticism and to a powerful image of female sanctity. Neither of these, however, is in tune with the character of the writings of Ælfric. Ælfric's writings are generally regarded as reflecting the dominant ideology of the late Anglo-Saxon church, as developed under the influence of the leaders of the 'Benedictine reform', particularly that of Bishop Æthelwold at Winchester.[64] St Mary of Egypt is an edifying model of spirituality and authority, but she does not present the kind of image of the female saint cultivated by Ælfric. She is not a virgin, is not said to be nobly born, and she is uneducated. And the more one looks at the highly contemplative quality of the religious life which the *Life of St Mary of Egypt* promotes, the less inclined one is to associate it with an Ælfrician outlook. I would suggest that Ælfric and people who shared his ideological perspective would have found aspects of the St Mary text unhelpful to their own aims and emphases.[65]

The inclusion of the *Life of St Mary of Egypt* in Cotton Julius points to a more eclectic tradition of transmission of vernacular Christian writing than that associated with Ælfric himself. This eclectic tradition is also reflected in the

---

[64] For an overview of the Benedictine reform and the late Anglo-Saxon church, see P. A. Stafford, 'Church and Society in the Age of Ælfric', in *The Old English Homily and its Backgrounds*, ed. Paul E. Szarmach and Bernard F. Huppé (Albany, NY: State University of New York Press, 1978), pp. 11-42. Ælfric's role as a driver of reform, whose ideas are by no means universally adopted, is stressed by Joyce Hill, 'Reform and Resistance: Preaching Styles in Late Anglo-Saxon England', in *De l'Homélie au Sermon: Histoire de la Prédication médiévale. Actes du Colloque internationale de Louvain-la-neuve (9-11 juillet 1992)*, ed. Jacqueline Hamesse and Xavier Hermand (Louvain-la-Neuve: Université Catholique de Louvain, Publications de l'Institut d'Études Médiévales, 1993), pp. 15-46; see also Hill's essay, 'The Benedictine Reform and Beyond', in *A Companion to Anglo-Saxon Literature*, ed. Phillip Pulsiano and Elaine Treharne (Oxford: Blackwell, 2001), pp. 151-69.

[65] See further my essay 'St Mary of Egypt and Ælfric: Unlikely Bedfellows in Cotton Julius E. vii?', in *The Legend of Mary of Egypt in Insular Hagiography*, ed. Poppe and Ross, pp. 99-112. The present paragraph and the remainder of the section reproduce with minor revisions material from this essay (pp. 102 and 110-12).

appearance of the *Life of St Mary of Egypt* in Cotton Otho B. x, which included both Ælfrician and non-Ælfrician saints' lives. The 'Gloucester Fragments' text of the *Life of St Mary of Egypt* also appeared along with material by Ælfric (his *Life of St Swithun*).

If the transmission of the *Life of St Mary of Egypt* took place outside Ælfric's immediate circle, the work itself certainly originated in an environment unaffected by his influence. We have no precise evidence concerning the date of the Old English translation, but, as we have seen, direct evidence for knowledge of the Latin *Vita* of St Mary of Egypt in Anglo-Saxon England dates from only the middle of the tenth century, and there is nothing in the Old English version which suggests a date of composition much earlier than this. The *Life of St Mary of Egypt* was undoubtedly translated in the later Anglo-Saxon period, most probably in the tenth century. It was in circulation long enough before its inclusion in Cotton Julius for significant corruption to have been introduced into the Old English text, but exactly *how* long it was in circulation we cannot tell. The likeliest conclusion we can come to is that the translation is either the work of a contemporary of Ælfric's or derives from a slightly earlier period. Whether it was written in the period of Ælfric or not, however, it is highly evident that in its approach and execution the *Life of St Mary of Egypt* is conspicuously lacking in Ælfrician features. As explained in a later section of this Introduction, the evidence of vocabulary in the *Life* suggests, indeed, that its original composition was of Anglian rather than West Saxon provenance.

The *Life of St Mary of Egypt* may be seen, therefore, as representing a tradition of non-Ælfrician hagiography in later Anglo-Saxon England. Other such traditions existed also, and are represented even in Cotton Julius itself. Going further, we might speculate that the *Life of St Mary of Egypt* was the product of an Anglian hagiographical tradition, to which the prose *Life of St Guthlac* might also have belonged. Jane Roberts sees the *Life of St Guthlac* as a non-West Saxon translation from the late ninth or early tenth century.[66] If this dating is correct, the *Life of St Guthlac* is possibly of an earlier generation than the *Life of St Mary of Egypt*. The Guthlac translation, however, agrees with the Mary of Egypt one in its theme of turning from the world and in the reverence it shows for the eremitical life.

Whatever the particular origin of the piece, the evidence of the extant manuscripts of the *Life of St Mary of Egypt* (all three written in Late West Saxon) suggests that interest in the *Life* was maintained to the end of the Anglo-Saxon period, despite the unsympathetic attitude that Ælfric and other 'Winchester' reformers might have had towards such a text. The *Life of St Mary of Egypt* would have been seen by an informed Anglo-Saxon reader as presenting a radically alternative spiritual ideal to that associated with what is regarded as the mainstream Winchester tradition, as represented in its most developed form in the writings of Ælfric.[67] This being the case, it is particularly ironic that the *Life* should have ended up included in a manuscript of Ælfric's *Lives of Saints*, and so relatively soon after the original issue of the collection. This inclusion reflects something of the variety of hagiographical material in circulation in late Anglo-Saxon England (material which scholarly preoccupation with Ælfric has perhaps tended to

---

[66] See Jane Roberts, 'The Old English Prose Translation of Felix's *Vita Sancti Guthlaci*', in *Studies in Earlier Old English Prose*, ed. Paul E. Szarmach (Albany, NY: State University of New York Press, 1986), pp. 363-79 (at p. 369). The Old English prose text is ed. Paul Gonser, *Das angelsächsische Prosa-Leben des heiligen Guthlac*, Anglistische Forschungen 27 (Heidelberg: Carl Winter, 1909).

[67] In my essay 'Mary of Egypt and Ælfric', I point out, with regard to gender, that Ælfric's writings reveal a discomfort at the idea of female Christian authority, as portrayed in the *Life* (p. 107), and, with regard to monasticism, I contrast the eremitical ideals of the *Life* with the coenobitic model favoured by Ælfric (pp. 104-7); on the latter topic, see further Mary Clayton, 'Hermits and the Contemplative Life in Anglo-Saxon England', in *Holy Men and Holy Women*, ed. Szarmach, pp. 147-75; on Ælfric's treatment of issues of gender, see Clare A. Lees, *Tradition and Belief: Religious Writing in Late Anglo-Saxon England*, Medieval Cultures 19 (Minneapolis and London: University of Minnesota Press, 1999), pp. 133-53.

overlook).[68] It also suggests that although as a teacher Ælfric was greatly respected by his contemporaries and successors, the extent of the influence of his full message was a good deal more limited than he would have liked. Even someone as interested in Ælfric as the Cotton Julius compiler evidently was appears to have been unconcerned at the dilution of Ælfric's message which the quite calculated addition of the *Life of St Mary of Egypt* to *Lives of Saints* involved.

THE OLD ENGLISH TEXTS: ISSUES OF TRANSMISSION AND RELATIONSHIP

Though earlier than G and O, J did not serve as an exemplar for either of these other copies of the *Life of St Mary of Egypt*, nor is there close affinity between the text preserved in J and those of G or O. It is notable that in places where G and O disagree significantly with J, their readings much more often, though not invariably, correspond better to the Latin source than do those of J. Both G and O preserve passages missing in J: lines 303-52 are in G but not J, and lines 934-36 are in O but not in J. And both these other copies have 'good' readings where J is evidently corrupt: to give a few examples, J has the meaningless *gerynysse* (line 411), where O's *gerecednysse* corresponds to the Latin *narrationis*, 'narration' (line 424 of the Latin text printed in the Appendix, below); J has *swingle*, 'whip' (line 414), where O's *spinle* corresponds to the Latin *fusum*, 'spindle' (line 427); J has *syllendan*, 'giving' (line 432), where O's *nellendan* corresponds to the Latin *nolentes*, 'unwilling' (line 443); J has *lichaman*, 'body' (line 446), where O's *gelicum* corresponds to the Latin *similibus*, 'like' (line 456); J has *ascimod*, 'shone' (line 501), where G's *ascunod* corresponds to the Latin *abominari*, 'detest' (line 502); J has *me*, 'me' (line 544), where G's *ne*

---

[68] Scragg ends his survey of anonymous saints' lives by commenting that Ælfric's lives 'in no sense filled a total vacuum. . . [T]he genre was already well established in England' ('The Corpus of Anonymous Lives', p. 225).

corresponds to the Latin *non*, 'not' (line 540). Such correspondences between G and O and the Latin are a feature of the surviving texts of the *Life*. They suggest that the two later witnesses reflect the original form of the Old English translation more faithfully than does J.

By comparison with G and O, it is clear that J, though substantially complete, presents a text with many deficiencies and imperfections, undoubtedly the result of an eventful textual prehistory. G and O themselves, however, also depart from the hypothetical Old English original, as the following examples indicate: at line 39, O lacks the noun *onhyringe*, 'imitation', which in J corresponds directly to the *imitationem* of the Latin source (line 52); at line 287, J's *dropum*, 'drops', exactly reflects the Latin *guttis* (line 289), unlike G's *dropung*, 'dripping, dropping' (which also lacks the required inflexional ending); at lines 453-54, the Latin *sanctae exaltationis . . . pretiosae crucis*, 'the holy exaltation of the precious cross' (lines 461-62), is closely reflected in J's *þære halgan deorwurðan rode upahefennysse*, 'the exaltation of the holy precious cross', whereas O's *þære halgan rode deorwurðan upahafenes* changes the referent of *deorwurðan* from *rode* to *upahafenes* (both Old English versions also have *halgan* going with *rode*, though in the Latin *sanctae* qualifies not *crucis* but *exaltationis*); at line 515, J's *minne lichaman*, 'my body', unlike G's *me*, 'me', is a close translation of the Latin *meam carnem*, 'my flesh' (line 513); at line 523, G omits J's *þrystlæcende*, 'daring', the equivalent of Latin *praesumens* (line 520); and at line 532, J's reading *þone ingang þæs siðfætes gegearwode*, 'prepared the entrance of the pathway', doesn't quite translate *ingrediendi viam prepararet*, 'prepared the way for my entry' (lines 527-28), but is closer than G's *þone ingang gerymde*, 'opened up the entrance'. These are instances in which J (which is otherwise often unreliable) rather than G or O can be seen as providing the truer image of the text of the Old English original.

The points mentioned in the above paragraphs suggest that the textual history of the Old English *Life* was far from straightforward. This history is now largely irrecoverable, of course, but one thing that the points mentioned above demonstrate clearly is that neither G nor O belongs to the same strand of transmission of the *Life* as that represented by J. Because there are less than eighteen lines in common *between* G and O (lines 557-72 and 958-60, the latter passage being supplied for O from Wanley's transcription), it is not possible to draw firm conclusions about the interrelationship of their texts of the *Life*. However, even within the small amount of text they have in common there are ten instances of interesting agreement between G and O, against J (nine in lines 557-72 and one in lines 958-60), which suggest that G and O are more closely related to each other than either of them is to J.

In the overlapping passages the following significant agreements between G and O should be noted: (i) at line 559, G and O both have the adjective *halgan*, 'holy', which is not in J; the fact that this word is not paralleled in texts of the source (see Latin version, lines 550-51) may suggest that it represents an addition made at some stage within the Old English textual tradition, an addition not reflected in J; (ii) at line 562, J reads *ne forlæt þu me*, 'do not you forsake me', translating the Latin *noli me derelinquere* (line 552-53), whereas both G and O have *ne forlæt me nu*, 'do not forsake me now'; again, the change seems to have occurred within the Old English textual tradition; (iii) at line 563, both G and O omit J's *þa*, 'then'; (iv) at line 564, both G and O have the verb *for*, 'went', corresponding to *egressa*, 'having gone out' (Latin, line 554), while J mistakenly has the adverb *forð*, 'forth'; (v) at line 566, G and O have *ða*, which here appears to be the demonstrative pronoun meaning 'those' (reflecting *hos*, 'these', Latin, line 557), while J has *ðær*, 'there', and a different construction, further removed from the Latin; (vi) at line 569, the J reading *rihtlicost gelædde*, 'led most directly', in contrast to G's *rihtost wære*, 'was most direct', and O's *rihtor wære*, 'was more direct', corresponds to *ducit*, 'leads' (Latin, line 560); (vii) at line 569, G and O have the verb *wiste*, 'knew, found out' (reflecting *cognoscens*, 'learning',

Latin, line 560), where J has mistakenly omitted a verb (*ongæt*, 'perceived', has been inserted by a later hand); (viii) at line 571, G has *togewriðende* and O *towriðende*, 'binding together, adding' (= *adnectens*, Latin, line 563), where J has the incorrect grammatical form *towriðenne*); (ix) at lines 559-60, G and O contrast grammatically with J, having *eft clypode*, 'called out again', where J reads *and eft clypigende*, 'and calling out again'; (x) at line 959-60, G and O read *on ealra worulda woruld*, 'throughout all ages', while J omits *ealra*.

In these passages not only do both our fragmentary texts, G and O, appear generally closer to the Latin than J, but they also agree with *each other* with remarkable consistency. Even in the two instances cited above where J reflects the Latin better, G and O are in step together, having the distinctive readings *halgan* (line 559) and *rihtost/rihtor wære* (line 569).

There are six minor disagreements between G and O in the overlapping passages, in three of which J agrees with O (JO here preserving what look like the original readings) and in the other three J agrees with G. J agrees with O against G in the following instances: (i) at line 559, where J and O portray Mary as 'gazing at the likeness of the mother of God' (*Godes cennestran anlicnysse hawigende*), translating *ad Dei genitricis ymaginem prospiciens* (Latin, line 550-51), G omits the word *anlicnysse*, and has the sense 'gazing at the mother of God'; (ii) at line 571, J and O have the reading *siðfæt*, 'journey', corresponding directly to *iter* (Latin, line 561), while G, in what looks like a local scribal error, has the otherwise unattested word *siðfæc*; (iii) at line 960, G has the phrase *a butan ende*, 'ever without end', which is lacking in J and O and is not paralleled in the Latin (see line 901-2). J agrees with G against O in the following instances: (i) at line 566, both J and G have *genoh*, 'enough', which is lacking in O; at line 569, O reads *ic þider*, 'I thither', where J and G omit the adverb; (iii) at line 959, *a*, 'ever', appears in J and G (though not in quite the same place) but not in O.

J itself was gone over by contemporary or near-contemporary readers who made minor revisions and alterations to the text, thereby remedying a small proportion of its deficiencies and imperfections. Correction of the text of the *Life of St Mary of Egypt* is less widespread than is the case with other items in the manuscript,[69] but particularly notable in the *Life* are the sporadic interventions distinguished by the presence of a comma-like *caret* sign written below the line and by a script which looks like that of the main scribe of the manuscript. Changes highlighted in this way are not confined to the *Life of St Mary of Egypt* but occur evenly distributed throughout the whole manuscript. Discussing the corrections accompanied by the comma-like sign, G. I. Needham comments (with reference to the manuscript as a whole), 'Almost all the corrections marked in this way repair short, straightforward omissions, often of only single letters, and have all the appearance of being the result of collation with an exemplar.'[70] There are seventeen occurrences of the comma-like sign in the *Life*,[71] in all of which the alterations are very minor. At line 13, for example, *nyðrung* is changed to *genyðrung*, at line 102 *gecwedenem* is changed to *gecwedenum*, at line 274 *geswic* is changed to *geswinc*, and at line 806 *byrhnysse* is changed to *byrhtnysse*. Lexical additions are confined to the insertion of *et salus mea* in the psalm quotation at line 150, the change of *for* to *oferfor* at line 185, the insertion of *hale* at line 589, and that of *findan* at line 598. In four of its occurrences, the comma-like sign is followed by a dot.[72] There are also corrections indicated by a dot below the line without the accompanying *caret* sign, as at line 66 (*westten* corrected to *westen*) and at line 128 (*rine* corrected to *ryne*). It should also be noted that there are a great number of obvious errors in J which have not been highlighted by correctors, for example *þeawas* instead of *þeowes* at line 17, *nydþeafe* for *nydþearfe* at line 129, *geore* for *georne* at line 478, and *georðe* for *seo eorðe* at line 915.

---

[69] See Needham, 'Additions and Alterations'.
[70] 'Additions and Alterations', p. 161, n. 1.
[71] See lines 13, 102, 109, 128, 150, 185, 186, 227, 274, 472, 589, 598, 631, 806, 839, 860, 951.
[72] See lines 102, 186, 472 and 598.

SOURCE

As mentioned earlier in the Introduction, the source of the Old English *Life of St Mary of Egypt* is Paul of Naples's Latin version, *Vita Sanctae Mariae Egyptiacae* (*BHL* 5415), itself a translation of the Greek life traditionally attributed to Sophronius of Jerusalem (*BHG* 1042). For the most part, the Old English version appears to follow this source closely, certainly eschewing the interventionist approach of Ælfric, for example, who boldly abbreviates, restructures and refines his hagiographical sources for his own purposes.

Comparison of the Old English with Latin texts leads to the conclusion that the particular form of *BHL* 5415 used by the Anglo-Saxon translator must have been in key respects similar to those found in copies of the 'Cotton-Corpus Legendary' (C-C). C-C survives only in manuscripts of the second half of the eleventh century and later, but, as mentioned above (see p. 13), an earlier form of it was in use in England at least by the late tenth century. There are two surviving manuscripts of this legendary containing the *Vita Sanctae Mariae Egyptiacae*: British Library, Cotton Nero E. i, Part I (ff. 179r-184v) (N), and Salisbury, Cathedral 221 (ff. 195v-204v) (S). N was copied at Worcester in the third quarter of the eleventh century, perhaps ca. 1060, S at Salisbury towards the end of the eleventh century. The source of the Old English would also have been similar, though to a lesser degree than with respect to C-C, to the text of *BHL* 5415 in Cotton Claudius A. i (C), a tenth-century manuscript which appears to have been in England in the Anglo-Saxon period, though written on the Continent.

The immediate source of the Old English version would have had features not reflected in either C-C or C. It is clear, however, that C-C and C, and particularly the former, represent that immediate source better than other texts of *BHL* 5415. They certainly correspond to the Old English more closely than does the standard printed edition of Paul's work, which is still that of Rosweyde (R), first published in 1615,

and reprinted by Migne in 1849 in *Patrologia Latina*.[73] The
Latin text given in the present volume is based on N, collated
with the other C-C witness, S, and with C, which presents a
version similar, but far from identical, to that of the C-C
variants. The following discussion is based on comparison of
the C-C and C texts of the *Vita* with those in the ninth- and
tenth-century manuscripts listed by Kunze, which are the
earliest known witnesses.[74] R does not provide a good text of
the *Vita* and lacks significant distinctive features reflected in
the Old English (but see n. 85, below), and so it not satisfactory for our present purposes.

The Old English translation has a number of features in
common with C-C and C, which I have not found in other
versions of the *Vita*. Thus, (i) at line 238, the Old English
lacks an equivalent to *Sustine me infirmum et indignum*,
'Wait for me, a weak and unworthy one', a clause that is
omitted in C-C/C (line 242) but found in the other
manuscripts listed by Kunze;[75] (ii) *þæt an*, 'only' (line 336),

---

[73] See above, n. 4. About two-thirds of the 'mixed text' edited by Aloysius
Lipomanus, *Vitae Sanctorum Priscorum Patrum*, 6 vols (Venice, 1553), II,
384v-391v, follows *BHL* 5415, the remainder mostly corresponding to the
version *BHL* 5417, printed by Mombritius (see above, n. 27); the version
edited by F. Laurentius Surius, *De Probatis Sanctorum Historiis, partim ex
tomis Aloysii Lipomani*, 6 vols (Cologne, 1571), II, 598-609, (rejecting the
version printed previously by Lipomanus) in large part follows *BHL* 5415
but departs from it in the central account of Mary's conversion and life in the
desert, which corresponds to *BHL* 5417.
[74] See Kunze, *Studien*, p. 174. The MSS are the ninth-century Bern,
Bürgerbibliothek 705 (ff. 1r-43r), St. Gallen, Stiftsbibliothek 577 (pp. 269-
97), and Vatican, Biblioteca Apostolica, Palat. lat. 582 (ff. 141v-153r); the
ninth/tenth-century Vatican, Reg. Suec. lat. 586 (ff. 11r-29v); and the tenth-
century Vatican, Palat. lat. 846 (ff. 47r-55v), Paris, Bibliothèque Nationale,
lat. 2873A (ff. 96r-105v) (contains only lines 278-823), Paris, Bibliothèque
Mazarine 1707 (ff. 1r-37r), Munich, Bayerische Staatsbibliothek, Clm
19162 (ff. 219r-242r), Munich, Clm 4618 (ff. 185v-203r), Karlsruhe,
Badische Landesbibliothek, Aug. 91 (ff. 5r-15v) (bottom lines of each folio
affected by fire damage), Dresden, Sächsische Landesbibliothek, A 62 (80v-
87v) (the text of the *Vita* shows much abbreviation and rewording, and is
also illegible in many places due to water damage from World War II),
Bamberg, Staatsbibliothek, Patr. 108 (Q VI 15) (51r) (beginning only), Bern,
168 (ff. 2v-15r), and Vatican, Reg. Suec. lat. 490 (ff. 40r-52v).
[75] Cf. Greek μεῖνόν με τὸν ἀσθενῆ καὶ ἀνάξιον, 'wait for me, the weak
and unworthy one' (*PG* 87.3, 3705B).

corresponds to C-C/C *tantum* (Latin, line 331) rather than to the 'regular' *autem*, 'however';[76] (iii) at line 632 of the Latin, C-C and C have *uox*, 'voice', instead of the original reading *lux*, 'light', as preserved in the other manuscripts:[77] the distinctive C-C/C reading corresponds to the Old English *stemn*, 'voice' (line 650).

Significantly, there are also agreements between the Old English and C-C, as against *all* the other witnesses under consideration, including C. Thus, (i) at line 473, *ongean stode*, 'stood against', reflects the distinctive C-C reading *est obuia*, 'is against' (Latin, line 481), rather than the curious C reading *minitasset*, 'had threatened', or other Latin variations;[78] (ii) at line 533, *gefylled*, 'filled', corresponds uniquely to C-C *repleta* (Latin, line 529), rather than to C *inuenta*, 'found', or to the 'regular' reading *reperta*, 'found'.[79]

I have not identified unique correspondences between the Old English and C. There are many textual peculiarities in C, but these are not reflected in the Old English. Thus, (i) at line 25 of the Old English, the phrase *On his lifes þeawum*, 'in the conduct of his life', directly translates *uitae moribus* (Latin, line 33), as found in C-C and other witnesses, where C has the different reading *uirtute et uitae moribus*, 'in the virtue and conduct of his life'; (ii) at line 155 of the Old English, *mets-ode*, 'provided (food)', translates *annonabat* (Latin, line 164), as found in C-C and other witnesses, rather than C *onerabat*, 'loaded'; (iii) at line 187, *þæs regoles mærsunge*, 'celebration of the rule', reflects *canonem quidem celebrabat*, 'indeed celebrated the rule' (Latin, lines 197-98), as found in C-C and other witnesses, rather than C's formulation *iuxta canonem*, 'according to the rule'; (iv) at line 237, *hihte*, 'hope',

---

[76] Cf. Greek μόνον, 'only' (*PG* 87.3, 3708D). Karlsruhe, Aug. 91 has neither word; Paris, Bibliothèque Nationale, lat. 2873A has *uere*, altered to *uero*.

[77] Cf. Greek φῶς, 'light' (*PG* 87.3, 3717B).

[78] The Greek has τεταγμένης, 'arrayed, set in order' (*PG* 87.3, 3713B), different from both C-C and C (there is much disagreement among Latin texts at this point).

[79] Cf. Greek γεγένημαι, 'I came to be', 'I found myself' (*PG* 87.3, 3713D).

translates *spem* (Latin, line 242), as found in C-C and other witnesses, not C *spiritum*, 'spirit'; (v) at lines 368-69, *is nu witodlice sceortlice to areccenne*, 'is now indeed brief to tell', translates *nunc breue est dicere* (Latin, line 388-89), as found in C-C and other witnesses, not C *nunc longum est dicere*, 'now is long to tell'; (vi) at line 389, *sumne*, 'a certain one', translates *aliquem*, 'someone' (Latin, line 405), as found in C-C and other witnesses, rather than C *aliquem iuuenem*, 'a certain young man'; (vii) at line 486, *belucen*, 'closed', reflects *obserrabat* (*sic*), 'barred' (Latin, line 491), as found in C-C and other witnesses, not C's inappropriate *obseruabat*, 'watched'; (viii) at lines 931-32, *þæt weorc þinre þenunge*, 'the task of your duty', translates *opus officii* (Latin, lines 871-72), as found in C-C and other witnesses, not C *officium funeris*, 'service of funeral'; (ix) at line 950, *rehte*, 'related', translates *retulit* (Latin, line 891), as found in C-C and other witnesses, not C *recurrit et*, 'returned and'.

The C readings mentioned in the previous paragraph represent distinctive textual features not reflected in the Old English version. It is notable that all of the C-C readings mentioned above go directly back to the Greek and are the regular Latin readings.[80] C also omits a number of sentences and phrases which must have been in the version of the Latin text that served as the immediate source of the Old English version, since they are duly translated: lines 54-5, *forð heonon underfonde þa toweardan mede on þære ecan eadignysse*, 'receiving hereafter their coming reward in eternal blessedness', corresponding to *hinc preparate futurae bonitatis accipientes*, 'receiving here . . . of the goodness prepared for them in the future' (Latin, lines 65-66); lines 414-15, *þe ic seldon gewunode on handa to hæbbenne*, 'that I was seldom accustomed to have in my hands', though the Old English departs here from C-C *hunc enim sic post tempus conueniebat me tenere*, 'for it

---

[80] For (i), see Greek, col. 3697C; for (ii), see Greek, col. 3704A; for (iii), see Greek, col. 3704C; for (iv), see Greek 3705B; for (v), see Greek, col. 3709D; for (vi), see Greek col. 3712A; for (vii), see Greek, col. 3713B; for (viii), see Greek, col. 3725A; for (ix), see Greek, col. 3725A.

suited me to carry this about after a time' (Latin, lines 428-29) (but there is nothing at all related to this in C); lines 570-72, *symle þa axunga þære æscan towriðende* ..., 'adding always enquiry to enquiry ...', translating *Interrogationi autem interrogationem adnectens* ..., 'Adding then enquiry to enquiry ...' (Latin, line 563) (an entire sentence omitted in C); lines 706-7, *Gebletsod sy God, se þe þa mænigfealdan wundru ana wyrceað*, 'Blessed be God, who alone brings about wonders of many kinds', translating *Benedictus Deus qui facit mirabilia magna solus*, 'Blessed is God, who alone performs great wonders' (Latin, line 676); the Latin continues here, *gloriosa et uehementer stupenda, quibus non est numerus*, 'glorious things and exceedingly amazing, of which there is no number' (lines 676-77), which is not translated into Old English (again an entire sentence omitted in C). All of this material omitted from C is present in the C-C copies and in other texts of *BHL* 5415.

There are also places where the Old English version avoids C-C peculiarities. The following examples are notable: (i) at line 64 of the Old English, the reading *þe ic sylf nyte*, 'which I myself do not know', translates *quod ignorem*, 'which I do not know' (cf. Latin, line 74), the original reading,[81] as found most Latin texts (including C), where C-C reads *quo dignior sim*, 'in which I might be more worthy'; (ii) at line 121, *geedniwodon*, 'renewed', translates *innouantes*, 'renewing' (cf. Latin, line 135), the original reading,[82] as found in most Latin texts (including C), where C-C reads *inuocantes*, 'calling'; (iii) at lines 620-24, the sentence beginning *Ic gewilnode þæs wines* ..., 'I desired the wine', reflects the normal word-order of the Latin (lines 603-7),[83] rather than that found in C-C, in which the elements of the sentence appear in a different sequence (C has the normal order); (iv) at line 752, the phrase *God wuldrigende*, 'glorifying God',

---

[81] Cf. Greek version, ὅπερ οὐκ οἶδα, 'which I do not know' (col. 3700C).

[82] Cf. Greek, νεουργοῦντας, 'renewing' (col. 3701C).

[83] The Latin sentence (in both variants) mentions that Mary used to drink wine to the point of drunkenness, a detail that does not appear in the Greek version, as represented in *PG* 87.3 (cf. col. 3717A),

translates *Dans gloriam Deo*, 'giving glory to God' (Latin, line 715), the original reading,[84] as found in most Latin texts (including C), rather than C-C *Dans gloriam*, 'giving glory' (with *Deo* omitted); (v) at line 763, *rynes*, 'course', translates *cursus* (cf. Latin, line 726), as found in most Latin texts (including C), where C-C has the idiosyncratic *Rursus*, 'again'. The Old English reading *gleawesta*, 'most skilful' (line 874), follows the 'regular', and original,[85] Latin *scitissimus*, where both C-C and C have *citissimus*, 'swiftest' (Latin, line 816).

Such discrepancies do not disprove that the Old English translator worked from an earlier form of the Cotton-Corpus Legendary, but they clearly indicate that, if he or she did, such a version would have been at least somewhat different from that represented in the two existing (later) copies, N and S. What is striking about the evidence of the Old English version is that where it contrasts with existing copies of C-C, or indeed with C, it generally preserves what must have been original readings.[86] While we cannot be sure that the source of the Old English translation formed part of an early version of C-C, it is reasonable to say that the translation is based on a good early text of *BHL* 5415, similar to (but in some respects 'better' than) that of existing copies of C-C.

LANGUAGE

In the vast majority of its key features, the language of the *Life of St Mary of Egypt* is typical of Late West Saxon, the carefully regularized form of written Old English that was

---

[84] Cf. Greek, δοὺς τῷ θεῷ δόξαν, 'giving glory to God' (col. 3720C).

[85] Cf. Greek ἐμπειρότατος, 'most skilful' (col. 3724A). Curiously, in this instance R agrees with C-C/C.

[86] There is even an instance in which the Old English agrees with the text printed by Lipomanus (see above, n. 73) against C-C/C and our other Latin manuscripts but evidently reflecting the original reading: at line 672, *forneah*, 'almost', translates *paene* (Lipomanus, f. 389v), which does not appear in the other versions (cf. Latin, line 650) but must derive from the Greek σχεδόν, 'almost' (*PG* 87.3, 3717C).

adopted as standard in the later tenth century and cultivated throughout England until the end of the Anglo-Saxon period and beyond.[87] With some minor inconsistencies between the three texts, spelling and distinctions in word form in the *Life* for the most part conform to Late West Saxon practice. Interestingly, however, there is one area, that of vocabulary, in which significant contrasts with normal West Saxon usage are apparent (to be discussed below).[88]

The three texts of the *Life* exhibit a certain amount of linguistic variation, with J and G being generally more 'correct' than O, but in each there is a high degree of internal consistency in the treatment of phonological and morphological elements. In the light of the many scribal deficiencies we have already observed in J, the linguistic regularity of this copy is particularly notable. And that regularity becomes all the more notable when the text of the *Life of St Mary of Egypt* in Cotton Julius E. vii is compared with that of the immediately preceding item in the manuscript, the *Legend of the Seven Sleepers*. Linguistically, the latter is generally less consistent than the *Life*, despite the fact that the same 'compressed' hand is evident in both texts, our scribe having been entrusted with the task of copying from about half-way through the *Legend of the Seven Sleepers* to the end of the *Life of St Mary of Egypt*.[89] A likely explanation for this discernible shift in linguistic practice is that the differences in word forms go back to the scribe's exemplar(s).

Though generally the text of J conforms closely to the Late West Saxon standard, a number of occasional departures from regular practice are evident. Many of these should be taken as symptomatic of the breakdown of phonological distinctions,

[87] For an excellent account of the features of Late West Saxon, see Richard M. Hogg, 'Phonology and Morphology', in *The Cambridge History of the English Language: Volume I, The Beginnings to 1066*, ed. Richard M. Hogg (Cambridge: Cambridge University Press, 1992), pp. 67-167.

[88] For discussion of aspects of syntax, see below, pp. 41 and 43-50.

[89] For discussion of linguistic forms in the *Legend*, see Hugh Magennis, *The Anonymous Old English Legend of the Seven Sleepers*, Durham Medieval Texts 7 (Durham: Durham Medieval Texts, 1994), pp. 13-18.

particularly in inflexion, in the spoken language at the time when the text was being produced. Among the non-standard features of J are the following:

(i) confusion in verb inflexions ending in *n*. This is very infrequent in J, but the following forms occur: *begytanan* (line 152), *oncnawan* (line 498), *ophrinon* (G *æthrinen*) (line 522) and *becuman* (line 758), past participles; *gewenden* (line 253) and *gangen* (line 462), infinitives; *arisan* (line 303) and *hreowan* (line 427), preterite indicative plurals; *willan* (O *willen*) (line 394) and *nellan* (= O) (line 398), present subjunctive plurals (other subjunctive plurals in J are in -*on*, except for *hæbben* (line 399) and *belucen* (line 486)). O has *coman* (J *comon*) (line 37) and *reowan* (J *hreowan*) (line 427), preterite indicative plurals; *underþeodan* (J *underðeoddon*) (line 39), preterite subjunctive plural (O also has *gewriðen* (J *gewriðon*) (line 38), preterite subjunctive plural); and *gehealdan* (J *gehealden*) (line 435), past participle; G has *ongyten* (line 323), infinitive; and *awurpon* (J *aworpen*) (line 501), past participle (note also the G subjunctive plural form *befæsten* (J *befæston*) (line 937)).

(ii) occasional inconsistency in weak verb endings. J is extremely regular in its weak verb forms, being particularly careful to keep to endings in *od(-)* for the preterite of Class II verbs. The following exceptional forms occur: *næmnede* (line 262), *gedrefedon* (line 611) and *afremdad* (line 798); O has *gegaderade* (J *gesamnode*) (line 416), *apolade* (J *aðolode*) (line 436) and *gemænsumede* (J *gemænsumode*) (line 579). Also with regard to Class II verbs, J is invariable in having the -*g*-spelling in the present participle and inflected infinitive, while G and O have forms both with and without the *g*, e.g., O *drohtniende* (J *drohtnigende*) (line 58), *notigende* (= J) (line 603); G *bletsianne* (J *bletsigenne*) (line 281), *þeowigende* (= J) (line 284) (the *Legend of the Seven Sleepers* also has some forms without the *g*).

(iii) irregular suffixes in nouns and adjectives. As with verbs, nominal and adjectival inflexions are also extremely regular in

J. Aberrant forms are *witon* (a.pl.) (line 105) for *witan*, *lufu* (a.s.) (line 363; O *lufan*), *lufu* (d.s.) (line 117) as well as *lufe* (line 371; O *lufan*), *bletsungan* (a.s.) (line 238) as well as *bletsunga* (lines 146 and 276), *wynlustas* (g.s.) (line 403; O *wynlustes*), and *geðances* (a.pl.) (lines 637 and 643). Abstract feminine nouns of the '*in* declension'[90] normally end in *u* or *o* in oblique cases, but *hæle* (g.) (line 682) also occurs. Note also the nominative singulars *tunga* (line 428) and *eara* (line 429) (also *godcunda* (line 464), n.s.n.), where O has the 'normal' forms *tunge* and *eare*.[91]

The declension of *wæter* is inconsistent in J. Oblique singular forms normally have 'parasite *e*',[92] but the following plural forms occur, some of which have the *e* and some of which do not: accusative *wæteru* (lines 803 and 805), *wætru* (lines 803B and 809) and *wættru* (line 796B); dative *wæterum* (line 815) and *wættrum* (line 814). Elsewhere neuter nominative and accusative plurals are normally in -*e*, including *wintre* (line 617).

There are instances in J of confusion between -*re* and -*ra* in the ending of adjectives and nouns: note *nanre nytena* (g.pl.) (line 224), *þæra dura* (g.s.) (line 470), *þære ... wildeora* (g.pl.) (lines 617-18), *geare* (g.pl.) (line 655), *þære hlafa* (g.pl.) (line 663), *ealra þæra nihte* (g.s.) (line 805), *ealre* (g.pl.) (line 923; G *ealra*).[93] This confusion also occurs a number of times in the *Legend of the Seven Sleepers*.

J is also remarkable for the absence of substitution of -*on* and -*an* for -*um* in the datives of nouns and adjectives. This feature, which is widely found in late Old English texts, including the *Legend of the Seven Sleepers* and the G and O copies of the *Life*, is entirely lacking in the J text. Examples in O and G are *wintran* (O, line 372) for *wintrum*, *minon þingon* (O and G, line 557) for *minum þingum*, and *menniscan* (O,

---

[90] See A. Campbell, *Old English Grammar* (Oxford: Clarendon Press, 1959), § 588.7.
[91] For abbreviations used in this and following paragraphs, see p. 210.
[92] See Campbell, *Old English Grammar*, § 574 (3).
[93] Note also G *þære welera* (g.pl.) (line 322).

line 561) for *menniscum*.

(iv) possible non-West Saxon inflections. The only instances which stand out as not conforming to a Late West Saxon paradigm are the forms *seo* (line 545; G *sy*), *syo* (line 787) and *sih* (line 433; O *si*), occurrences of the first/third person singular of the present subjunctive of the verb 'to be' (which usually appears as *sy* in J). The form *sih* might be explained as a scribal slip (the following word begins with the similar looking *tih*), but the other two forms may be due to non-West Saxon influence: *syo* = *sio*, a form found in Kentish and also a possible Mercian form (though not recorded), while *seo* is found in Kentish and Mercian.[94]

With regard to non-inflectional aspects of the language of J, the most interesting orthographical-phonological feature is arguably the frequent appearance of *æ* for *e*. Forms such as *cwæðende* (line 361) (as well as the normal *cweðende*, line 493 etc.), *wæg* (line 553; cf. *weg*, line 569), *twægen* (line 600; cf. *twegen*, line 151) and *ðægnas* (line 742) appear to reflect Mercian practice,[95] and *æ* for *e* is also found, for example, in *geræcednyssa* (line 15; cf. *gerecednyssum*, line 21), *gesæt* (past participle) (line 75; cf. *geset*, line 123), *gebæd* (line 298; cf. *gebede*, line 82) and *blætsigende* (line 754; cf. *bletsigende*, line 949). The reversal of *æ* for *e* is seen in *ahrefnode* (line 610; O *aræfnde*). This use of *æ* for *e* appears only rarely in O and G (and in instances where J has *e*): O has *mæniscon* (line 561; J *menniscum*) and *pæningas* (O, line 565; J *penegas*); G has *unwæmme* (line 499; J *unwemmed*). With reference to the J instances of *æ* for *e* cited above, compare *cweþende* (O, line 361), *weg* (G, line 553; cf. also O, line 569), *twegen* (O, line 600), *gerecednesse* (O, line 15), *gebed* (G, line 298).

Other orthographical-phonological features in J, such as the occasional introduction of 'unhistorical' initial *h* in words beginning with *l* and *r*,[96] and the consistent use of *wur-* for

---

[94] See Campbell, *Old English Grammar*, § 768 (*d*).

[95] See Campbell, *Old English Grammar*, § 328.

[96] 'Unhistorical' *h* is seen in *hreowan* (line 427; O *reowan*), *ahrefnode* (line

earlier *weor-* (O has both *weor-* and *wur-*, G only *wur-*) are also interesting, but these are very well attested in other Late West Saxon texts.[97]

A notable non-West Saxon form in G (the corresponding part of J is lacking) is the undiphthongized *get*, 'yet' (line 328).[98] In O, the forms *self* (lines 33 and 609; J *sylf*) and *sellanne* (line 397; J *syllanne*) are found, which lack the normal Late West Saxon development of *sel-* to *syl-*,[99] and, also in O, the absence of a 'glide' between *sc* and a back vowel in *scamað* (line 365; J *sceamað*) and *scortlice* (line 368; J *sceortlice*) is in line with Mercian practice.[100]

Thus there are sporadic features in all three of our texts which might be taken as non-Late West Saxon, and perhaps specifically Mercian, in character. Since there is no pattern of agreement in the instances in which these features occur in our texts, however, we cannot be sure at what stage they came to be introduced. They may well represent traces of Mercian or other non-West Saxon influence in the original composition of the *Life of St Mary of Egypt*, but they might possibly have arisen in transmission, or they may be due to a combination of both of these possibilities. It is salutory to note that, in Cotton Julius E. vii, *æ* for *e* occurs not only in the *Life of St Mary of Egypt* but also in the *Legend of the Seven Sleepers*, which is not regarded as a possible non-West Saxon text.[101]

610; O *aræfnde*), *hrepsunge* (line 782), *hleorende* (line 896) and *hleorde* (lines 907 and 958; G, line 958, *leorde*); examples of the reverse of this feature are *opran* (for *ophran*) (line 854; cf. *oðrinan* corrected to *ophrinan*, line 860) and *rægeles* (line 945; G *hrægles*) (cf. *hræglunge*, line 661). O has examples both of loss of *h* (*rapor*, line 369; J *hraðor*) and of unhistorical *h* (*onhæled*, line 376; J *onæled*), though these examples do not coincide with those in J. On this topic, see D. G. Scragg, 'Initial *h* in Old English', *Anglia* 88 (1970), 165-96.

[97] On *wur-* forms in West Saxon, see Campbell, *Old English Grammar*, §§ 320-21. Examples in J are *arwurðan* (line 3), *gewurðe* (line 20; O *geweorðe*) and *swuran* (line 218).

[98] See Campbell, *Old English Grammar*, § 187.

[99] See Campbell, *Old English Grammar*, §§ 325-26.

[100] See Campbell, *Old English Grammar*, § 183.

[101] See the *Legend of the Seven Sleepers* (ed. Magennis), lines 477 (*swæfne*), 660 (*spræcende*), 695 (*geinsæglod*, *insæglan* and *twægen*) etc.

If phonological evidence that the *Life* might be of non-West Saxon origin is inconsistent and uncertain, the lexical evidence is a good deal more persuasive, and there also is a notable syntactical feature of the work which may indicate Anglian provenance, the use of absolute participial constructions in the nominative or accusative: it has been pointed out that such constructions are not idiomatic in West Saxon but are confined to texts of Anglian origin or to texts with an Anglian element.[102] With regard to vocabulary, it is notable that in key respects the *Life of St Mary of Egypt* contrasts with the other items in Cotton Julius E. vii. There are some points of lexical similarity, of uncertain significance, between the *Life of St Mary of Egypt* and two of the other three non-Ælfrician pieces in the manuscript, the *Life of St Eustace and his Companions* and the *Life of St Euphrosyne*, but the overall pattern is one of contrast, with the *Life of St Mary of Egypt* standing out as distinctive.[103]

A feature of the standardization of Late West Saxon as a literary language was the emergence in the later tenth century of a specifically 'Winchester' tradition of vocabulary. As first pointed out by Helmut Gneuss[104] and explained in detail by Walter Hofstetter,[105] this Winchester tradition, in choosing between certain Old English synonyms, shows consistent preference for one set of words and avoids another set

---

[102] See E. von Schaubert, *Vorkommen, gebietsmässige Verbreitung und Herkunft altenglischer absoluter Partizipialkonstruktionen in Nominativ und Akkusativ* (Paderborn: Ferdinand Schöningh, 1954), pp. 130-58 and 158-65. See further below, pp. 49-50.

[103] See further my article 'Contrasting Features', esp. pp. 334-35.

[104] Helmut Gneuss, 'The Origin of Standard Old English and Æthelwold's School at Winchester', *ASE* 1 (1972), 63-83; see also Mechthild Gretsch, 'Æthelwold's Translation of the "Regula Sancti Benedicti"', *ASE* 3 (1974), 149-51.

[105] Walter Hofstetter, *Winchester und der spätaltenglische Sprachgebrauch: Untersuchungen zur geographischen und zeitlichen Verbreitung altenglischer Synonyme*, Münchener Universitäts-Schriften, Philosophische Fakultät, Texte und Untersuchungen zur Englischen Philologie 14 (Munich: Wilhelm Fink, 1987); Hofstetter summarizes the results of his research in his article, 'Winchester and the Standardization of Old English Vocabulary', *ASE* 17 (1988), 139-61.

altogether. In the conditions cultivated at Winchester by
bishop Æthelwold a distinctive usage in vocabulary emerged,
and this was adhered to by Old English writers closely
associated with Winchester in the period of the late Anglo-
Saxon monastic reform.

Hofstetter identifies thirteen groups of synonyms as indicators of Winchester usage. When he applies these indicators to
Ælfric's writings he finds almost total consistency with
Winchester practice: in over 98% of cases in the thirteen
groups, Ælfric chooses 'Winchester' words rather than 'non-
Winchester' ones. The *Life of St Mary of Egypt*, on the other
hand, has no Winchester words at all. For example, where
Ælfric uses *gedyrstlæcan* for 'to dare', the *Life* has *(ge)þryst-
læcan*, which Ælfric and other 'Winchester' writers never use;
where Ælfric has *gearcian* for 'to prepare', the *Life* has the
non-Winchester *gegearwian* and related words; where Ælfric
has *gelaþung* for 'congregation', the *Life* has *gesamnung*.[106]
This consistent pattern of disagreement sets the *Life* firmly
apart from Ælfric and suggests that it originated, temporally
and/or culturally, outside the sphere of Winchester influence
on the lexical aspect of literary language.[107]

Not only does the *Life of St Mary of Egypt* lack distinctive
Winchester words, it also contains a sufficiently strong
Anglian element in its vocabulary to indicate the probability
that the work is Anglian in origin. Such is the conclusion of
Franz Wenisch in his definitive study of specifically Anglian
vocabulary.[108] Wenisch refers to a number of words in the

---

[106] See Hofstetter, *Winchester und der spätaltenglische Sprachgebrauch*,
esp. pp. 38 and 241.

[107] By way of comparison, it is relevant to cite Hofstetter's percentage
figures for Winchester lexical usage in the other non-Ælfrician lives in
Cotton Julius E. vii: *Legend of the Seven Sleepers*, 61.54%; *Life of St
Eustace*, 42.68%; *Life of St Euphrosyne*, 28.57% (*Winchester und der Spätaltenglische Sprachgebrauch*, pp. 154-55, 227 and 228).

[108] Franz Wenisch, *Spezifisch anglisches Wortgut in den nordhumbrischen
Interlinearglossierungen des Lukasevangeliums*, Anglistische Forschungen
132 (Heidelberg: Carl Winter, 1979); see also the seminal work by Richard
Jordan, *Eigentümlichkeiten des anglischen Wortschatzes: Eine wortgeo-
graphische Untersuchung mit etymologischen Anmerkungen*, Anglistische
Forschungen 17 (Heidelberg: Carl Winter, 1906).

Life which should be regarded as 'specifically Anglian' – *bewerian*, in the sense 'to forbid' (lines 464, 475, 527 and 531), *foregangan*, 'to go before' (line 453), *hwilchwugu*, 'some' (line 357), *leoran*, 'to depart' (lines 896, 907 and 958), *nænig*, 'no' (lines 14, 785 and 924), *ofgifan*, 'to give over to' (line 894), *in*, 'in, on' (lines 577, 830, 832 and 947), *ymbsellan*, 'to enclose' (line 343, supplied from G) – and he mentions other words 'favoured' in Anglian texts: *aræfnian*, 'to endure' (line 610), *bebeodan*, in the sense 'to entrust, commit' (line 513), *sworettan*, 'to breathe hard, sigh' (line 287; G *sprecan*), and *sworettung*, 'sighing, sigh' (lines 247, 762 and 918).[109] Also notable is *bearn* (line 514), 'child', which was widely replaced by *cild* in Late West Saxon.[110] This list represents a significant element of Anglian vocabulary and justifies the view that the *Life* is 'probably of Anglian origin'.[111]

What looks like evidence of assimilation to standard Late West Saxon practice is seen in the O and G readings *on* (O, line 577, and G, line 947; J *in* on both occasions) and the G reading *nan* (line 924; J *nænig*). A similar kind of assimilation may be evident in O's use of *andwyrdan* for 'to answer' (lines 594 and 600; J *andswarode*), Ælfric's normal choice,[112] as well as having *andswarian* (line 608; = J).

STYLE AND REGISTER IN THE OLD ENGLISH *LIFE*

The Old English *Life of St Mary of Egypt* is a lightly

---

[109] *Spezifisch anglisches Wortgut*, pp. 257-58.
[110] See Jordan, *Eigentümlichkeiten*, pp. 96-97.
[111] Wenisch, *Spezifisch anglisches Wortgut*, p. 327; further convincing lexical detail indicating Anglian origin is provided by von Schaubert, *Vorkommen, gebietsmässige Verbreitung und Herkunft*, pp. 141-49.
[112] See Karl Jost, 'Unechte Ælfrictexte', *Anglia* 51 (1927), 81-103 and 177-219 (at p. 184). Note, however, that Ælfric also uses *andswarian*, though rarely; see further Malcolm Godden, 'Ælfric's Changing Vocabulary', *English Studies* 61 (1980), 206-23, in which Godden goes on to point out that Anglian forms occur even in Ælfric's writings, and wisely urges caution in the application of word-studies to anonymous literary texts (pp. 222-23).

abbreviated translation of its Latin source, generally following that source closely, in some places indeed rendering the Latin in a word-for-word manner, though more usually introducing an element of paraphrase. It is a version that clearly sets out to convey not only the factual detail of its inherited narrative but also the urgency and heightened emotional tone with which that narrative is expressed, particularly in the highly personal utterances of the two central characters. The translator has worked hard to achieve a register appropriate to the spiritually inspiring subject matter of the story and reflective of its dignity and seriousness. The result is a notably formal kind of Old English narrative prose, mainly paratactic in structure but self-consciously Latinate in its phrasing and in some of its larger syntactical structures, and in particular imitating grammatical characteristics of the Latin *Vita*. Parataxis is itself a feature of the *Vita*, but its use is extended in the Old English, in which *and* clauses and clauses introduced by adverbial *þa* appear ubiquitously in passages of narrative.[113] The Latinate quality of the translation is particularly evident in the unusually frequent resort to participial constructions, including 'absolute' phrases (free-standing *noun/pronoun* + *participle* phrases, in Old English usually in the dative case). Also suggestive of Latin practice is the insistent use of the sentence adverbs *soðlice* (31 times in J) and *witodlice* (40 times in J),[114] corresponding to *autem/enim*.

The writing is also characterized by a striking fondness for rhetorical ornamentation, seen especially in the cultivation of balanced phrasing and word pairing and in the use of alliteration. Compared to the lucid fluency of Ælfric's writing in his saints' lives and elsewhere, the style of the *Life of St Mary*

---

[113] On parataxis, see Bruce Mitchell, *Old English Syntax*, 2 vols (Oxford: Clarendon Press, 1985), §§ 1683-8. Examples of parataxis being introduced in the Old English are *On his lifes þeawum he wæs swiþe gefrætewod* (line 25) for *uitae moribus et uerbo ornatus* (Latin, lines 33-34), *Ðas wisan he ealle on him hæbbende wæs, and* (line 40) for *Haec itaque in se omnia habens* (Latin, line 53), and *and fram þysum weorcum* (line 133) for *propter quod* (Latin, line 145).
[114] Note line 408: J *soðlice*, O *witodlice*; line 954: J *soðlice*, G *witodlice*.

of Egypt may appear somewhat laboured and unidiomatic, but this style is a deliberately fashioned one and should not be viewed as being the result of lack of imagination on the part of a writer too closely tied to his or her source.[115] It is a distinctive and highly literary style, which seeks to exploit the resources of the high-status language of Latin in a vernacular context.[116]

Word doubling is a pervasive feature of the style of the *Life* and occurs with respect to finite and non-finite verb forms, nouns and adjectives. A few examples are *gehyrde and geaxode* (lines 19-20) (Latin *audiui*, line 13), *getyd and gelæred* (line 27) (Latin, *instructus et . . . educatus*, line 35), *to his bysne and to his larum* (line 38) (Latin, *eius exemplis atque doctrinis*, line 51), *mæge ongytan and oncnawan* (line 73) (Latin *cognoscas*, line 83) and *gedafenlic ne pæslic* (line 495) (Latin *condecens nec oportunum*, lines 497-98). As in these examples, the doubling in the Old English version often reflects the same feature in the Latin, but its use is considerably extended. Something like half of the doublets in the Old English are not paralleled in the Latin. At lines 546-47 the phrase *synfulra and forworhtra hreowsunge and dædbote* doubles both elements of the corresponding Latin *peccatorum paenitentiam* (lines 541-42).

In some cases the word doubling is accompanied by alliteration, as in *gehealt and gehæleð* (lines 91-92) (Latin *sanat*, line 102), *to biddenne and to bletsigenne* (lines 280-81) (Latin *benedicere et orare*, lines 284-85), and *to gefyllenne and to*

---

[115] In an earlier analysis of the style of the *Life* I referred to its 'pedestrian' character and commented unfavourably on the quality of its execution ('Contrasting Features', pp. 332 and 336) but did not go on to suggest a conscious rationale behind this style. For useful brief comments on the style of the Old English *Life*, see also Andy Orchard, 'Hot Lust in a Cold Climate: Comparison and Contrast in the Old Norse Versions of the Life of Mary of Egypt', in *The Legend of Mary of Egypt in Insular Hagiography*, ed. Poppe and Ross, pp. 175-204, at pp. 188-91.

[116] For stylistic contrasts between the *Life* and the other hagiographical items in *Lives of Saints*, see my 'Contrasting Features'; the *Life* also contrasts with the Anglian *Life of St Guthlac*, mentioned above (pp. 23-24), which does not cultivate a Latinate style: on the latter, see Gonser, *Das angelsächsische Prosa-Leben des heiligen Guthlac*, pp. 52-94.

gefremmane (line 549) (Latin *implere*, line 543). Alliteration
is not a feature of the Latin *Vita*, and its 'artful' use in our
text, as in other later Old English prose, may be seen as
reflecting the influence of vernacular traditions on prose
rhetoric.[117] Alliteration appears not only in doublets in the
Old English *Life* but is cultivated much more widely.
Examples are *þam wyrtum þe on þam westene weoxon* (lines
160-61), *sæde sawende* (line 177), *to gewitan on his wordum*
(lines 327-28), and the more elaborate *þone unalyfedan bryne
minra leahtra þe ic hæfde on þære lufe þæs geligeres* (lines
370-71). Repetition of the same opening syllable in
consecutive or closely adjacent words is seen in (for example)
forlætað forwurðan (lines 440-41), *beswicende besmat* (line
451) and *astigan . . . astrehte* (line 646).

A passage that exemplifies sustained use of sound-
repetition and word doubling, both in combination and
separately, is Mary's fervent speech at lines 674-85:

> Þus ic wæs lange on mænigfealdum and mislicum nydþearf-
> nyssum and on unmætum costnungum winnende and wraxlig-
> ende, and me þa siþþan oþ þeosne andweardan dæg and mine
> earman sawle and minne lichaman þæt godcundlice mægen
> geheold, mid me sylfre symle smeagende of hu micclum yfelum
> heo me alysde. Soðlice ic eom afeded of þam genihtsumestan
> wistmettum minre fylle, þæt is mid þam hihte minre hæle, and ic
> eom oferwrigen mid þam oferbrædelse Godes wordes, se ðe
> ealle þincg befehð and befædmað. Ne leofað na se man soðlice
> be hlafe anum ac of æghwilcum worde þe forðgæð of Godes
> muþe.

In this passage (in which word order is also used to rhetorical
effect) the word doubling of the opening sentence is empha-
sized by the *m*, *n* and *w* alliteration, and there are further
alliterating phrases in *mid me sylfre symle smeagende* (the *s*
sound also being picked up in the following *alysde* and
Soðlice); *afeded . . . fylle*; *mid þam hihte minre hæle*; *ic eom
oferwrigen mid þam oferbrædelse Godes wordes* (which as

---

[117] On the 'artful' and ornamental, as opposed to the strictly structural, use
of alliteration in Old English prose, see Andy Orchard, 'Artful Alliteration in
Anglo-Saxon Song and Story', *Anglia* 113 (1995), 429-63, at pp. 458-63.

well as vowel and *w* alliteration has repetition of *ofer-*); *befehð and befædmað*; and *leofað . . . soðlice be hlafe*. The doublets *mænigfealdum and mislicum* and *nydþearfnyssum and . . . costnungum* correspond to doublets in the Latin, *multis et diuersis* (line 651) and *necessitatibus et temptationibus* (lines 651-52), but *winnende and wraxligende* and *befehð and befædmað* each translate a single word, *eluctans* (line 652) and *continet* (line 657).

Latinate syntactical structuring is already apparent in the first sentence of the prologue to the Old English *Life* (lines 1-6), which has the highly unusual element order *complement + subject*, and in which the elaborately extended complement delays resolution of the sentence to the last few words:

> Ðas herigendlicestan gehwyrfednysse ægþer ge dæda ge þeawa and þa micclan hreowsunga and swa ellenlic gewinn þære arwurðan Egyptiscan Marian, hu heo hyre lifes tida on þam westene gefylde, of Grecisc geþeode on læden gewende Paulus se arwurða diacon sancte Neapolis þære cyrcan.

The structure of the sentence, including its developed parallelism and the appositional *hu* clause embedded in its object, has been taken directly from the Latin (see apparatus criticus to Latin text, below, p. 140). Instead of recasting the material in a more 'natural' Old English order, the translator has chosen to imitate the rhetorical sweep of the Latin, thereby producing an arresting, highly-wrought Old English sentence. Even the word order of the closing phrase of the Latin, *sanctae Neapolis ecclesie*, is reproduced in the unidiomatic-looking *sancte Neapolis þære cyrcan*.

The second sentence of the prologue similarly takes its lead from the structure of its Latin equivalent, but heightens the parallelism of the three phrases in the sequence *æfter þæra eagena forlætnysse and eft æfter þæra wulderfæstan onlihtnysse and æfter þam forðgewitendum frecednyssum* (lines 8-10) by insistently repeating the *æfter* each time (in the Latin, lines 2-4, *post* appears only twice, two of the phrases being linked by *et*, without *post*) and by having abstract nouns in *-nyss* in all three phrases (the corresponding Latin words are *amissionem, inluminationem* and the more concrete *pericula*). The presence of light alliteration (on *l* and *f*) in these phrases also contributes to the rhetorical patterning.

As mentioned above, sentence structure throughout the *Life* is marked by the frequent occurrence of Latinate participial constructions. Participial constructions become particularly common in the narrative itself but are already evident in the opening sentences of the prologue. Thus in the second sentence we find a participial usage that occurs a number of times in the *Life*, in which the present or past participle (in this instance the present) is used in an 'attributive' manner: *æfter þam forðgewitendum frecednyssum* (line 10), literally 'after the passing-forth dangers', i.e. 'after the dangers had passed'. This particular attributive use of the participle is a construction modelled on Latin practice (though, with reference to the example cited, the past participle rather than the present is required in Latin; thus *Vita*, line 4, *post illa transacta pericula*, the source of *þam forðgewitendum frecednyssum*). Not all occurrences of the construction in the Old English are taken directly from the source. A few lines later, for example, *þone onfangenan talent* (line 17), 'the having-been-received talent', corresponds to *talentum accipiens* (Latin, lines 9-10), 'receiving the talent', but is not a literal translation.[118]

In narrative contexts, use of participles is a staple element of Old English literary prose. In the *Life of St Mary of Egypt*, however, it is cultivated with a particularly mannered insistence, appearing much more widely than in other texts. There are places where sentences are made up of whole series of participles, notably in the following example, which has six present participles, as well as three coordinately-linked finite verbs and two subordinate clauses (the sentence continues with further subordinate material):

---

[118] Other examples are *æfter þam onfangenum gebede* (line 82) (Latin *accepta oratione*, line 95), *þa begytanan gestreon* (line 152) (Latin *ea quae intus erant reposita*, line 162), and *mid forðagotenum tearum* (line 941) (Latin *multipliciter effusa prece*, line 882).

Ða witodlice Zosimus mid þære gewunelican æ þæs mynstres
Iordane þæt wæter oferfor, lytles hwega for þæs lichaman
nedbehæfednyssum mid him hæbbende, and on þæs regoles
mærsunge geond þæt westen for, and on þære tide þæs gereordes
and þæs gecyndes nydþearfnysse brucende, on niht on eorþan
sittende and hwon restende, and slep swa hwær swa hine seo
æfenrepsung gemette, and eft on ærne mergen forgangende, swa
he wæs unablinnendlice on fore geseted, and begangende . . .
(lines 184-92)

In such sequences the mood of the Old English verbs often,
though not always, agrees with that of verbs in the Latin.[119]

Perhaps the most notable feature of participial usage in the
Life is the frequent occurrence of absolute phrases. These
appear most commonly in the dative and as direct translations
of ablative absolutes in the Latin, e.g. *Ðas and þysum gelicum
him þencendum* (line 68) (cf. Latin, line 78, *Haec et his similia eo cogitante*), *Ðysum þus gecwedenum wordum fram þam
abbode* (line 102) (cf. Latin, line 113, *Haec dicente abbate*),
Ðysum þus gefylledum (line 147) (cf. Latin, line 157, *Haec*
[sic] *ita se habentibus*).

There are also at least three absolute phrases in the nominative or acccusative.[120] At lines 716-17 *þas þincg ealle þus*

---

[119] In the quoted passage the Old English agrees with the Latin (lines 195-
203) to a limited extent in the mood of its verbs, having *oferfor* for *trans-
meauit*, *hæbbende* for *deportans* and *restende* for *quiescens*, but note the
following changes: *for* for *pertransiens* and *slep* for *somnum . . . gustans*
(Old English finite verb for Latin present participle); *brucende* for *soluebat*,
sittende for *Sedebat*, and *forgangende . . . and begangende* for *properare
incipiebat* (Old English present participle for Latin finite verb). An example
of exact correlation with the Latin is lines 326-27, *byfiende and þa eorþan
behealdende, and nan þing eallinga sprecende* (cf. Latin, lines 323-24,
tremens, terram conspiciens, et nihil ullomodo loquens).
[120] As discussed by Else von Schaubert, *Vorkommen, gebietsmässige Verbreitung und Herkunft*, pp. 53 and 62-63. Von Schaubert argues (pp. 60 and
61) for two other nominative absolutes, *ic heardlice mine breost cnyssende*
(lines 638-39) (translating a Latin finite clause, *Quando . . . uiriliter pectus
meum tundebam*, lines 618-20) and *Zosimus þa witodlice gehyrende* (line
686) (translating the Latin appositive *Audiens autem Zosimas*, line 661), but
these are doubtful cases, which should probably be taken as phrases in
apposition, with a tautologous pronoun in the former (see Mitchell, *Old
English Syntax*, § 3838) and a redundant *and* following the latter.

oncnawenne (which could be either nominative or accusative) corresponds to an ablative absolute in the Latin (lines 685-86, *his omnibus acceptis*); at line 794 *þus he mid tearum biddende* (nominative) corresponds to a dangling participial phrase in the Latin (line 747, *Haec orans cum lacrimis*); and at lines 809-10 *Zosimus wundrigende and teoligende his cneowa to bigenne hire ongeanweardes* (nominative) corresponds to a nominative absolute in the Latin (line 762, *Zosimas autem stupens et genuflectere nitens*).

As mentioned above (p. 41), these nominative/accusative absolutes have been taken as evidence of an Anglian provenance for the *Life*. In the context of our discussion of style and register, they contribute to the elevation and formality that characterize the writing in this Old English work. There is little suggestion of colloquial language, and though there are many passionate utterances in the *Life*, the translator is at pains to maintain a dignified tone and a sense of reverence for the *halgan gerecednyssa* ['holy story'] which his or her version transmits to its vernacular audience. Appropriation of aspects of Latin sentence structure and of Latin stylistic traits is central to the Old English writer's approach. The resulting somewhat mannered style may appear strained in places, but is nonetheless a notable achievement by a thoughtful Old English writer, working in an environment as yet unaffected by the influence of Late West Saxon literary traditions.

SELECT BIBLIOGRAPHY

Editions and Translations of the Old English Version:

Donovan, Leslie A., trans., *Women Saints' Lives in Old English Prose* (Cambridge: D. S. Brewer, 1999), pp. 97-120

Earle, John, ed. and trans., *Gloucester Fragments: Legends of St Swiðhun and Sancta Maria Ægyptiaca* (London: Longman, Green, Longman and Roberts, 1861), pp. 102-13

Skeat, Walter W., ed. and trans., *Ælfric's Lives of Saints*, EETS, OS 76, 82, 94 and 114 (London: Oxford University Press, 1881-1900; rpt as 2 vols, 1966), II, 2-53

Other Editions and Translations:

Dembrowski, Peter F., ed., *La vie de Sainte Marie l'Égyptienne: versions en ancien et en moyen français*, Publications romanes et françaises 144 (Geneva: Droz, 1977)

D'Evelyn, Charlotte, and Anna J. Mill, ed., *The South English Legendary*, EETS, OS 235, 236 and 244 (London: Oxford University Press, 1956, 1956, 1959), I, 136-48

Kouli, Maria, trans., 'Life of St Mary of Egypt', in *Holy Women of Byzantium: Ten Saints' Lives in English Translation*, ed. Alice-Mary Talbot (Washington, DC: Dumbarton Oaks Research Library and Collection, 1996), pp. 65-93

Kunze, Konrad, ed., *Die Legende der heiligen Maria Aegyptiaca. Ein Beispiel hagiographischer Überlieferung in 16 unveröffentlichten deutschen, niederländischen und lateinischen Fassungen*, Texte des späten Mittelalters und der frühen Neuzeit 28 (Berlin: Erich Schmidt, 1978)

Migne, J.-P., ed., *Vita Mariæ Ægyptiacæ*, PG 87.3, 3697-726

Mombritius, Boninus, ed., *Sanctuarium seu Vitae Sanctorum*,

2nd ed., 2 vols (Paris: Apud Albertum Fontemoing, 1910 (original ed., Milan, 1480)), II, 134-43

Rosweydus (Rosweyde), Heribertus, ed., *Vitae Patrum* (Antwerp, 1615), 381-92; rpt *PL* 73, 671-90

Ryan, William Granger, trans., *Jacobus de Voragine: The Golden Legend: Readings on the Saints*, 2 vols (Princeton, NJ: Princeton University Press, 1993), I, 227-29

Ward, Benedicta, trans., *Harlots of the Desert: A Study of Repentance in Early Monastic Sources* (London and Oxford: Mowbray, 1987), pp. 35-56

The Life of St Mary of Egypt and its Background:

Coon, Lynda L., *Sacred Fictions: Holy Women and Hagiography in Late Antiquity* (Philadelphia, PA: University of Pennsylvania Press, 1997)

Delmas, F., 'Remarques sur la vie de Sainte Marie l'Égyptienne', *Échos d'Orient* 4 (1900-1), 35-42

Knust, Hermann, *Geschichte der Legenden der h. Katharina von Alexandrien und der h. Maria Aegyptiaca* (Halle: Max Niemeyer, 1890)

Kunze, Konrad, *Studien zur Legende der heiligen Maria Aegyptiaca im deutschen Sprachgebiet*, Philologische Studien und Quellen 49 (Berlin: Erich Schmidt, 1969)

Stevenson, Jane, 'The Holy Sinner: The Life of Mary of Egypt', in *The Legend of Mary of Egypt in Medieval Insular Hagiography*, ed. Erich Poppe and Bianca Ross (Blackrock, Co. Dublin: Four Courts Press, 1996), pp. 19-50

Walsh, Efthalia Makris, 'The Ascetic Mother Mary of Egypt', *Greek Orthodox Theological Review* 34 (1989), 59-69

The Old English Version:

Chase, Colin, 'Source Study as a Trick with Mirrors: Annihilation of Meaning in the Old English "Mary of Egypt"', in *Sources of Anglo-Saxon Culture*, ed. Paul E. Szarmach, Studies in Medieval Culture 20 (Kalamazoo, MI: Medieval Institute Publications, Western Michigan

University, 1986), pp. 23-33

Karras, Ruth Mazo, 'Holy Harlots: Prostitute Saints in Medieval England', *Journal of the History of Sexuality* 1 (1990), 3-32 (see esp. pp. 6-12)

Magennis, Hugh, 'On the Sources of the non-Ælfrician Lives in the Old English *Lives of Saints*, with Reference to the Cotton-Corpus Legendary', *Notes and Queries*, New Series 32 (1985), 292-99

---, 'Contrasting Features in the non-Ælfrician Lives in the Old English *Lives of Saints*', *Anglia* 104 (1986), 316-48

---, 'St Mary of Egypt and Ælfric: Unlikely Bedfellows in Cotton Julius E. vii?', in *The Legend of Mary of Egypt in Insular Hagiography*, ed. Poppe and Ross, pp. 99-112

Orchard, Andy, 'Hot Lust in a Cold Climate: Comparison and Contrast in the Old Norse Versions of the Life of Mary of Egypt', in *The Legend of Mary of Egypt in Insular Hagiography*, ed. Poppe and Ross, pp. 175-204 (see esp. pp. 188-91)

Scheil, Andrew, 'Bodies and Boundaries in the Old English *Life of St Mary of Egypt*', *Neophilologus* 84 (2000), 137-56

Saints' Lives in Anglo-Saxon England:

Conner, Patrick W., 'Religious Poetry', in *A Companion to Anglo-Saxon Literature*, ed. Phillip Pulsiano and Elaine Treharne (Oxford: Blackwell, 2001), pp. 251-67 (see esp. pp. 258-63)

Earl, James W., 'Typology and Iconographic Style in Early Medieval Hagiography', *Studies in the Literary Imagination* 8 (1975), 15-46

Hill, Joyce, 'The Dissemination of Ælfric's *Lives of Saints*: A Preliminary Survey', in *Holy Men and Holy Women: Old English Prose Saints' Lives and Their Contexts*, ed. Paul E. Szarmach (Albany, NY: State University of New York Press, 1996), pp. 235-59

Hill, Thomas D., '*Imago Dei*: Genre, Symbolism, and Anglo-Saxon Hagiography', in *Holy Men and Holy Women*, ed. Szarmach, pp. 35-50

Lapidge, Michael, 'The Saintly Life in Anglo-Saxon England', in *The Cambridge Companion to Old English Literature*, ed. Malcolm Godden and Michael Lapidge (Cambridge: Cambridge University Press, 1991), pp. 241-63

Lapidge, Michael, and Michael Winterbottom, ed. and trans., *Wulfstan of Winchester: The Life of St Æthelwold* (Oxford: Clarendon Press, 1991), pp. ci-cxii

Magennis, Hugh, 'Conversion in Old English Saints' Lives', in *Essays in Anglo-Saxon and Related Themes in Memory of Lynne Grundy*, ed. Jane Roberts and Janet Nelson, King's College London Medieval Studies 17 (London: King's College London Centre for Late Antique and Medieval Studies, 2000), pp. 287-310.

Rollason, David, *Saints and Relics in Anglo-Saxon England* (Oxford: Blackwell, 1989)

Scragg, D. G., 'The Corpus of Anonymous Lives and Their Manuscript Context', in *Holy Men and Holy Women*, ed. Szarmach, pp. 209-30

Whatley, E. G., 'Late Old English Hagiography, ca. 950-1150', in *Hagiographies: Histoire internationale de la littérature hagiographique latine et vernaculaire en Occident des origines à 1550*, II, ed. Guy Philippart, Corpus Christianorum: Hagiographies 2 (Turnhout: Brepols, 1996), pp. 429-99

Woolf, Rosemary, 'Saints' Lives', in *Continuations and Beginnings; Studies in Old English Literature*, ed. E. G. Stanley (London: Thomas Nelson and Sons, 1966), pp. 37-66

TEXT AND TRANSLATION

EDITORIAL PROCEDURE

The following text of the Old English *Life of St Mary of Egypt* is based on that in London, British Library MS Cotton Julius E. vii (ff. 122v-136r) (J). All departures from J are indicated in the textual apparatus, which presents a full account of the manuscript text and scribal alterations to it. In places where J is deficient, readings from the fragmentary copies of the *Life* in Gloucester, Cathedral Library MS 35 (ff. 4-6) (G), and British Library, Cotton Otho B. x (in correct order, ff. 26, 56; 16, 17; 15) (O) are accepted, where available, but no attempt has been made to use these to provide a critical edition of the work as originally produced by the Old English writer. G and O together preserve less than half of the total text.

A passage in J (lines 792-805) has been copied twice; in the textual apparatus the second iteration is referred to as B.

Numbers in round brackets indicate chapter divisions (following those of the Latin version). | (with accompanying marginal annotation) indicates manuscript foliation; * identifies material discussed in the Commentary (below, pp. 122-29). Italics are used for material in Latin and also for two passages, lacking in J, which are supplied from G and O respectively (lines 303-52 and 934-36). Spaced points indicate omission. These are enclosed in square brackets where there is no scribal evidence that the text is deficient. Abbreviations are silently expanded. Capitalization and punctuation follow modern convention, as does word division (for manuscript practice in these matters, see Skeat's edition). Manuscript accents are not reproduced (for these, see again Skeat's edition).

A collation with the surviving texts of G and O is provided at the end of the text (see below, pp. 130-37). In this, manuscript variation in the use of capitals and accents and in the use of *þ* and *ð* is not systematically recorded.

DE TRANSITU MARIAE
AEGYPTIACE

Ðas herigendlicestan gehwyrfednysse ægþer ge dæda ge
þeawa and þa micclan hreowsunga and swa ellenlic
f.123r gewinn þære arwurðan | Egyptiscan Marian, hu heo hyre
lifes tida on þam westene gefylde, of Grecisc geþeode on
5   læden gewende Paulus se arwurða diacon* sancte Neapolis þære cyrcan.

    Witodlice hit is geræd þæt Raphahel se heahengel
wære to Tobie sprecende æfter þæra eagena forlætnysse
and eft æfter þæra wulderfæstan onlihtnysse and æfter
10   þam forðgewitendum frecednyssum þe he of genered
wæs, and þus cwæð: 'Soðlice hit is swiðe derigendlic þæt
man cynnes* digle geopenige, and eft þære sawle is
micel genyðrung þæt mon þa wuldorfæstan Godes weorc
bediglige.'* For þam þingum ic nænige þinga ne
15   forsuwige þa halgan geræcednyssa. Se me gecydde þæt ic
on gefealle on þone genyðredan cwyde þæs slawan
þeowes, se þone onfangenan talent fram his hlaforde
butan geweaxnysse ahydde on eorðan.* Ac ne sy me nan
man to ungeleafful be þam þingum writende þe ic ge-
20   hyrde and geaxode on þissa wisan, ne gewurðe hit þæt ic

---

*Title] fourth line up from bottom of f. 122v, in large red capitals,
followed by punctus elevatus.*
1 Ðas herigendlicestan gehwyrfednys] *in large capitals, taking up full
line, with decorated red initial Ð extending down over the two following lines (to bottom of page), decoration extending into the left and
bottom margins;* gehwyrfednysse *ends on next line.*
7 Witodlice] *large decorated red capital 'wynn', mostly in margin,
with decoration extending upwards and downwards over seven lines.*
13 genyðrung] ge *inserted above line, with comma-like correction sign
below.*
17 þeowes] *O; J* þeawas.

THE PASSING
OF MARY OF EGYPT

Paul the worthy deacon of the church at holy Naples translated from the Greek language into Latin the most praiseworthy conversion, both in deeds and in morals, and the great repentance and very brave struggle of the worthy Mary of Egypt, how she completed the days of her life in the desert.

Truly it is read that Raphael the archangel spoke to Tobit after the loss of his eyes and again after their glorious re-enlightenment and after the passing of the dangers from which he was preserved, and he said this: 'In truth it is very injurious that one should reveal secrets of one's kin, and yet it is a great disgrace to the soul that one should keep secret the glorious works of God.'

Because of such things, on no account will I conceal this holy story in silence. He has made clear to me that I may fall headlong into the ignominious sentence of the lazy servant who hid in the ground without increase the talent which he had received from his lord. But let no one be too disbelieving of me as I write concerning the things I heard and found out about in this matter; and far be it from me that I should engage in falsification in the details of the holy narrative or that I

on þam halgum gerecednyssum wæge oþþe ic þa spræce
forsuwige.

ITEM RATIO DE EADEM

(1) Sum wer wæs on anum mynstre on Palestina ðære
25   mægþe. On his lifes þeawum he wæs swiþe gefrætewod.
Se wæs fram cildhade on munuclicum þeawum healice
getyd and gelæred. Se wæs gehaten Zosimus. Ðes
witodlice, swa ic ær cwæð, on anum Palestina mynstre
fram frymþe drohtnode, and he wæs on forhæfednysse
30   weorcum se afandedesta geworden on eallum þam
munuclicum regolum. And he ealle þæs regoles bebodu
and fulfremednysse þæs munuclican þeowtscypes
untallice geheold, and he eac swilce wisan him þær sylf
toeacan geihte, forþan þe he gewilnode his flæsc þam
35   gaste underþeodan. Swa soðlice he wæs fulfremod on
f.123v eallum munuclicum | þeawum, þæt wel oft munecas of
feorrum stowum and of mynstrum to him comon, þæt hi
to his bysne and to his larum hi gewriðon and to þære
onhyringe his forhæfednysse hi underðeoddon.
40   (2) Ðas wisan he ealle on him hæbbende wæs, and he
næfre fram þam smeagungum haligra gewrita his mod
awende. And ealle þa godnyssa þe he bebreac he wæs
gastbrucende, and an weorc he hæfde unforswigod and
næfre geteorod, þæt wæs sealmsang, mærsung, and
45   haligra gewrita smeagung. Wel oft eac swilce, þæs ðe hi
rehton,* þæt he wære gefremed wyrðe beon þære godcundan onlihtnysse þurh æteowednysse fram Gode

---

22 forsuwige] *followed by punctus elevatus, then rest of line empty,
and next line empty.*
23 ITEM RATIO DE EADEM] *centred, in large red capitals, and
followed by punctus elevatus.*
24 Sum . . . ðære] *MS line written in capitals, with initial S as large
red decorated capital, partly in margin, extending into empty line
above and into the next two lines below.*
42 awende] *O* awænde; *J* awenda.
47 æteowednysse] *O* ætywednysse; *J* æteowednyss.

should conceal the telling of it in silence.

FURTHER ACCOUNT OF SAME

(1) There was a man in a monastery in the region of Palestine. He was very much adorned with regard to the conduct of his life. From childhood he had been instructed and trained in monastic customs in a profound manner. He was called Zosimus.

This man, thus, as I have already said, lived his life from the beginning in a monastery in Palestine, and in works of abstinence he became the most accomplished in all the rules of the monastery. Blamelessly he kept all the requirements of the rule and the perfection of the monastic service, and he also added for himself there similar practices as well, since he wished to subject his flesh to the spirit. Indeed, so much was he perfected in all monastic customs that very often monks came to him from distant places and monasteries, in order that they might attach themselves to his example and his teachings and subject themselves to emulation of his abstinence.

(2) He devoted himself entirely to these practices, and he never diverted his mind from meditations upon Holy Scriptures. And all the benefits that he enjoyed he would use in a spiritual manner; and he had one task unconcealed by silence and never tired of – that was the singing of psalms, exaltation, and the study of Holy Scriptures. Very often also too, as they recounted, he was made worthy of divine enlightenment through revelation from God of the holy vision –

þære gastlican gesihþe, swa þæt nan wundor is ne eac
ungelyfedlic þincg, be ðæm þe Dryhten sylf cwæð,
50 'Eadige beoð þa clænheortan, forðan þe hi God geseoð.'*
Swa miccle ma þa sceawiað þa opennysse þære godcundan onlihtnysse þe heora lichaman symle geclænsiað
mid syfrum þeawum and mid þurhwæccendlican mode,
forð heonon underfonde þa toweardan mede on þære
55 ecan eadignysse. Witodlice, swa he sylf sæde Zosimus,
þæt he sylf wære* fram þam modorlicum beorðrum* on
þæt mynster befæst, and oþ þæt þreo and fiftigðe gear he
wæs þær on þam regole drohtnigende. And æfter þysum
he wæs gecnyssed fram sumum geþancum swa swa he
60 wære on eallum þingum fulfremed and he nanre maran
lare ne bysene ne beþorfte on his mode. And he wæs þus
sprecende: 'Hwæðer ænig munuc on eorðan sy þæt me
mage aht niwes getæcan oððe me on ænigum þingum gefultumian þæs þe ic sylf nyte oððe þæt ic on þam
65 munuclicum weorcum sylf ne gefylde, oþþe hweðer ænig
þæra sy þe westen lufiað þe me on his dædum beforan
sy.'
Ðas and þysum gelicum him þencendum,* him ætstod
sum engel* and him to cwæð, 'Eala þu Zosimus, swiðe
70 licwyrðlice þu gefyldest. Swaþeahhwæðere nis nan man
f.124r þe hine fulfremedne æteowe. | Miccle mare is þæt
gewinn þæt þe toweard is þonne þæt forðgewitene, þeah
þu hit nyte. Ac þæt þu mæge ongytan and oncnawan hu
miccle synd oþre hælo wegas, far ut of þinum earde and
75 cum to þam mynstre þæt neah Iordane is gesæt.'
(3) He þa sona witodlice of þam mynstre for þe he
fram his cildhade on drohtnode, and to Iordane becom
ealra wætera þam halgestan. He eode þa innon þam
mynstre þe him se engel bebead. Þa ongan he ærest
80 sprecan to þam munece þe þæs mynstres geat bewiste,

---

48 is] *O; not in J.*
54 underfonde] *O; J* to under.
61 ne *(first)*] *O; not in J.*
66 westen] westten, *with dot below second* t.

which is no marvel nor moreover an unbelievable matter: concerning this the Lord himself said, 'Blessed are the pure in heart, for they shall see God.' So much the more shall those people behold the manifestation of divine enlightenment who constantly purify their bodies with abstinent behaviour and vigilant mind, who will receive hereafter their coming reward in eternal blessedness.

As Zosimus himself said, then, he was entrusted by himself into that monastery from the time his mother gave birth to him, and until his fifty-third year he remained there living by the rule. And after this he was oppressed by certain thoughts to the effect that he might be perfect in all things and might need no further teaching or example in his mind. And he would speak thus: 'Can it be that there is any monk on earth who can teach me anything new or help me in any matters that I myself do not know or that I myself have not perfected in monastic works, or is there anyone among those who love the desert who is superior to me in his actions?'

As he pondered these things and others like them, there stood by him an angel, and it said to him, 'O Zosimus, you have succeeded in a most praiseworthy manner. However, there is no person who may show himself perfect. Much greater is the struggle that lies ahead of you than that which has passed, though you do not know it. But in order that you may be able to perceive and understand how great are other paths to salvation, go out from your land and come to the monastery which is situated near the Jordan.'

(3) Then, indeed, he went at once away from the monastery in which he had dwelt from his childhood, and he came to the Jordan, the holiest of all rivers. He then went inside the monastery to which the angel had directed him. Then he began to speak first to the monk in charge of the gate

and he hine þam abbude gecydde and him to gelædde.

Ða æfter þam onfangenum gebede, swa hit mid munecum þeaw is, he him to cwæð, 'Hwænne come þu hider, broðor, oþþe for hwilcum þingum geðeoddest þu
85 þe to swa eadmodum munecum?'

Zosimus him andwyrde, 'Nis me nan neod, fæder, þe to secgenne hwanon ic come, ac ic for lare intingan eow her gesohte, forþon ic her fela gastlicra þeawa on eow geaxode, and þa synd beforan gesegnesse Gode lic-
90 wurðe.'

Se abbod him to cwæð, 'God, se þe ana gehealt and gehæleð swa fela mettrumnyssa, he þe and us on his godcundum bebodum gestrangige and us gerecce þa weorc to begangenne þe him licige. Ne mæg ænig mann
95 oþerne getimbrian buton he hine sylfne gelomlice behealde and he mid sylfrum andgyte þæt beo sylf wyrcende, God to gewitan hæbbende. Ac swaþeahhwæð-ere, forþan þe þu cwæde þæt þe Cristes soðe lufu hyder us gelædde eadmodne munuc us to gesecenne, ac* wuna
100 her mid us, gif þu forðy come, and us ealle se Goda Hyrde ætgædere fede mid þære gife þæs Halgan Gastes.'

Ðysum þus gecwedenum wordum fram þam abbode, Zosimus his cneowa gebigde and, onfangenum gebede, on þam mynstre wunode, (4) þær he geseah witodlice
105 ealle witon on þeawum and on dædum scinende and on
f.124v gaste weallende and Drihtne þeo|wigende. Þær wæs unblinnendlic staþolfæstnys Godes herunge æghwylcne dæg and eac nihtes. And þær næfre unnytte spræce næron ne geþanc goldes and seolfres oþþe oþra gestreona, ne
110 furðon se nama mid him næs oncnawen, ac þæt an wæs swiðost fram heom eallum geefst, þæt heora ælc wære on lichaman dead and on gaste libbende.

---

88 gastlicra] gastlica. and] *followed by* beforan, *faintly underlined.*
102 gecwedenum] gecwedenem, *with* v *written above fourth* e *and a dot below, preceded by comma-like mark.*
109 goldes] *in the space after this is inserted* oðð *above the line, with comma-like sign below.*

of the monastery, who announced him to the abbot and led him to him.

After he [Zosimus] had received his blessing, as it is customary among monks, he [the abbot] said to him, 'When did you come here, brother, or for what reasons have you associated yourself with such humble monks?'

Zosimus answered him, 'There is no need, father, for me to tell you where I have come from, but I have sought you out here for reasons of learning, because I have heard about many spiritual practices among you here, and they are beyond expression pleasing to God.'

The abbot said to him, 'May God, who alone cares about and heals so many weaknesses, strengthen you and us in his divine precepts and direct us to attend to the works that are pleasing to him. No man can uplift another unless he constantly pays attention to himself and with sober understanding works towards that same thing himself, with God as his guide. Nonetheless, since you have said that true love of Christ has led you here to us, to seek us out as a humble monk, remain here with us then, if you have come for that reason, and may the Good Shepherd feed us all together with the grace of the Holy Spirit.'

These words having been spoken by the abbot, Zosimus bent his knees and, after receiving his blessing, he remained in the monastery, (4) where he truly beheld all the elders shining in their behaviour and deeds, enthusiastic in spirit and serving the Lord. Every day and also at night there was unceasing steadfastness there in the praising of God. And there were never any idle conversations there, nor was there thought of gold and silver or of other riches – of which the very names were unknown to them; but the one goal that they hastened to most was that each of them should be dead in body and living in spirit.

Mid þam soðlice hi hæfdon ungeteorodne mete,* þæt
wæron þa godcundan gespræcu; heora lichaman witod-
115 lice mid þam nydþearfnyssum anum feddon, þæt wæs
mid hlafe and mid wætere, to þam þæt hi þe scearpran on
þære soðan Godes lufu hi æteowdon. (5) Þas weorc
Zosimus behealdende hine sylfne geornlice to fulfremednysse aþenede gemang þam emnwyrhtum, þe
120 þone godcundan neorxnewang butan ablinnendnysse
geedniwodon.

Þa æfter þysum genealæhte seo tid þæs halgan
Lenctenfæstnenes þe eallum Cristenum mannum geset is
to mærsigenne, and hi sylfe to clænsunga for wurðunga
125 þære godcundan þrowunga and his æristes. Ðæt geat
soðlice þæs mynstres næfre geopenod wæs ac symle hit
wæs belocen, and hi swa butan æghwilcre gedrefednysse
heora ryne gefyldon, ne hit næfre næs to geopenigenne
buton wenunga hwilc munuc for hwilcere nydþearfe ut
130 fore. Seo stow wæs swa westen and swa digle þæt næs na
þæt an þæt heo wæs ungewunelic ac eac swilce uncuð
þam landleodum him sylfum. On þas wisan wæs se regol
fram ealdum tidum gehealden, and fram þysum weorcum
is to gelyfanne þæt God Zosimus on þæt mynster ge-
135 lædde.

(6) Nu ic wille æfter þysum areccan hu þæs mynstres
gesetnysse* healdende wæs. On þam drihtenlican dæge
þære forman fæstenwucan, þe we nemniað Halgan Dæg,
þær wæron gewunelice gedone þa godcundan gerynu,
140 and þonne gemænsumedon heo þæs libbendan and þæs
f.125r unbesmitenan licha|man ures Drihtnes Hælendes Cristes,
and þonne æfter þam ætgædere, hwon gereordende,
syþþan wæron ealle on þæt gebædhus gegaderode, and

---

113 mete] *not in J.*
119 aþenede] aþened.
128 ryne] rine, *with* y *written above* i, *and dot below.* gefyldon]
fyldon, *with* ge *written above preceding space, and comma-like sign
below.*
129 nydþearfe] nydþeafe.

At the same time, they had food which never fails, that is, the divine discourses; their bodies, in truth, they fed with the bare necessities alone, that is, with bread and water, with the intention that they should show themselves the keener in the true love of God.

(5) When Zosimus beheld these practices, he eagerly applied himself to perfection among his co-workers, who renewed divine paradise without ceasing.

Then after this the season of the Lenten fast drew near, which is established for all Christians to celebrate and for them to purify themselves in honour of the divine passion and resurrection. In truth the gate of the monastery was never opened but was always shut up, and thus they fulfilled their routine without any disturbance; nor was it ever to be opened unless perchance some monk went out for some necessary purpose. The locality was so desolate and so hidden that not only was it uninhabited but it was also even unknown to the people of the country themselves. In this way the rule was kept from ancient times, and from these practices it is to be believed that God led Zosimus to that monastery.

(6) Now I will relate next how a tradition of the monastery was kept. On the Lord's day of the first week of the fast, which we call Holy Day, the divine sacramental rites were performed in the usual way, and then they participated in the communion of the living and undefiled body of our Lord Jesus Christ, and after that, having taken a little to eat, they were then all gathered together in the oratory, and on bended knees

mid gebigedum cneowum and eadmodum gebede heora
145 ælc operne grette and heora abbudes eadmodlice
bletsunga bædon, þæt hi on þam godcundan gewinne þe
fæstlicor gestrangode wæron. Ðysum þus gefylledum,
þæs mynstres geatu wæron geopenode, and hi þonne
þisne sealmsang sungon togædere: '*Dominus illuminatio*
150 *mea et salus mea; quem timebo?*'* And swa ætgædere ut
foron. Ænne oððe twegen on þam mynstre hi forleton,
næs na to þam þæt hi þa begytanan gestreon heoldon –
næs þær swilces nan þincg – ac þæt hi þæt gebedhus
butan þam godcundan symbelnyssum ne forleton. And
155 heora æghwilc hine sylfne metsode swa swa he mihte
oþþe wolde: sum him mid bær þæs lichaman geniht-
sumnysse, sum þæra palmtreowa æppla, sum beana mid
wætere ofgotene, sum nan þincg buton þone lichaman
ænne and þone gegyrlan, ac hi wæron gefedde mid [. . .]*
160 þæs gecyndes neadþearfnysse abæde, þæt wæs mid þam
wyrtum þe on þam westene weoxon; and hine þær æghwylc sylfne on forhæfednysse band swa him sylfum
geþuhte, swa þæt heora nan nyste oþres wisan oþþe
dæda.
165   Ðonne hi hæfdon Iordane þa ea oferfaren, þonne
asyndrede hine æghwilcne* feor fram oþrum, and heora
nan hine eft to his geferum ne geþeodde, ac gif heora
hwilc operne feorran geseah wið his weard, he sona of
þam siðfæte beah and on oþre healfe wende, and mid him
170 sylfum leofode and wunode on singalum gebedum and
fæstenum. On þas wisan witodlice þæt fæsten gefyllende,
hi eft to þam mynstre cyrdon, ær ðan drihtenlican æristes
dæge, þæt wæs on þam symbeldæge þe we Palmdæg
gewunelice nemnað. Æghwilc on his agenum ingehyde
175 mid him sylfum habbende wæs his agenes geswinces

---

148 þonne] þone.
150 *et salus mea*] *written above the line in the space after (first) 'mea',*
with comma-like sign below.
152 hi] he.
173 symbeldæge] symbel *separated from* dæge *by a space due to*
erasure of six or seven letters.

and with humble prayer each of them greeted the other and humbly asked for the blessing of their abbot, so that they might be the more firmly strengthened for the divine struggle. When these things had been completed, the gates of the monastery were opened, and they then sang this psalm together: *'Dominus illuminatio mea et salus mea; quem timebo?'* And so they went out together. They left one or two behind in the monastery, not at all for the purpose of guarding the valuables they had acquired – there was nothing of such a kind there – but so that they would not leave the oratory without the divine solemnities. And each one of them provided food for himself according as he could or wished to: one took with him a sufficient supply for the body, another fruits from the palm-trees, another beans soaked in water, another nothing except only his body and clothing; but they were nourished [when] the necessity of nature required, that is, with the plants that grew in the desert; and each one bound himself to abstinence there as seemed good to himself, in such a way that none of them knew the conduct or deeds of another.

When they had crossed over the river Jordan, then each one separated himself far from the others, and none of them joined up with his companions again, but if anyone of them saw another in the distance coming towards him, he immediately turned away from the path of his journey and went in another direction, and lived and remained by himself in continuous prayers and fasts. Having fulfilled the fast in this manner, then, they returned again to the monastery before the Lord's day of the resurrection, that is, on the feast-day that we traditionally call Palm-day. Each one kept in his own

f.125v gewit|nysse, hwæt he wyrcende wæs and hwilcra
geswinca sæde sawende, and heora nan oþerne ne axode
on hwilce wisan he þæs geswinces gewin gefylde.

(7) Ðis wæs witodlice þæs mynstres regol, and þus
180 fulfremodlice wæs gehealden æghwilc, swa ic ær cwæð,
þæt hine sylfne on þæt westen to Gode geðeodde, and
mid him sylfum wunnon þæt hi mannum ne licodon
buton Gode sylfum.

Ða witodlice Zosimus mid þære gewunelican æ þæs
185 mynstres Iordane þæt wæter oferfor, lytles hwega for þæs
lichaman nedbehæfednyssum mid him hæbbende, and on
þæs regoles mærsunge geond þæt westen for, and on
þære tide þæs gereordes and þæs gecyndes nydþearfnysse
brucende, on niht on eorþan sittende and hwon restende,
190 and slep swa hwær swa hine seo æfenrepsung gemette,
and eft on ærnemergen forgangende, swa he wæs
unablinnendlice on fore geseted, and begangende, forðan
þe he gewilnode, swa swa he eft sæde, þæt he sumne
fæder on þam westene funde, þe hine on sumum þingum
195 getimbrede þæs þe he sylf ær ne cuðe; and swa six and
twentig daga þæt færeld þurhteah, swilce he to sumum
menn mid gewisse fore.

Ða þa seo tid middæges to becom, þa oðstod to
sumere hwile hine fram þam siðfæte ahæbbende and
200 eastweardes wendende, and hine gewunelice gebæd,
forþan þe he gewunode on þam gesettum tidum þæs
dæges þone ryne his siðfætes gefæstnian and standende
singan and mid gebigedum cneowum gebiddan.

Ða he soðlice sang and mid þære geornfullan be-
205 healdnysse up locode and þone heofon beheold, þa
geseah he him on þa swiðran healfe þær he on gebedum
stod swa swa he [. . .]* on mennisce gelicnysse on
lichaman hine æteowan, and þa wæs he ærest swiþe
afyrht, forþan þe he wende þæt hit wære sumes gastes

---

185 oferfor] for, *with* ofer *written above, and comma-like sign below.*
186 nedbehæfednyssum] nedbehæfednysse, *with* v̈ *written above final*
e, *and dot preceded by comma-like mark below.*

conscience within himself the witness of his own toil, as to what he had been occupied with and of what labours he had sowed the seeds; and none of them asked another in what manner he had fulfilled the struggle of his toil.

(7) This was, then, the rule of the monastery, and so perfectly did each one conduct himself, as I have already said, that he united himself with God in the desert, and they strove in themselves to please not men but God himself.

Then, following the traditional law of the monastery, Zosimus crossed over the river Jordan, bringing with him some little for the body's necessities, and he made his way through the desert in observance of the rule, taking the necessities at meal-time and according to the requirements of nature, and at night sitting on the ground and resting a little; and he would sleep wherever nightfall found him, and in the early morning [he would be] proceeding on his way again, in accordance with the course on which he was unceasingly set, and travelling on – because he desired, as he himself said afterwards, to come across some father in the desert, who might edify him in certain matters which he himself was not aware of before. And so for twenty-six days he continued on that journey, as though he were purposefully travelling to some particular person.

When it came to the hour of midday, he stopped for some length of time, breaking off his journey and turning to the east, and he prayed in the usual manner, for he was accustomed at the set times of the day to fix the course of his journey and to stand and sing and to pray on his bended knees.

Now, while he sang and with keen regard looked up and gazed at the sky, he noticed then to his right, as he stood at his prayers, as though he [. . .] appearing in human physical form, and he was at first greatly frightened, because he thought that

210 scinhyw þæt he þær geseah; ac sona swaþeahhwæþere
mid Cristes rode tacne getrymmede hine and him þone
f.126r ege fram awearp. | Ða eac witodlice se ende his gebedes
wæs gefylled, he þa his eagan bewende and þær soðlice
man geseah westweardes on þæt westen efstan, and
215 witodlice þæt wæs wifman þæt þær gesewen wæs. Swiðe
sweartes lichaman heo wæs for þære sunnan hæto, and þa
loccas hire heafdes wæron swa hwite swa wull and þa na
siddran þonne oþ þone swuran.

(8) Ða wisan Zosimus georne behealdende wæs and
220 for þære gewilnedan swetnysse þære wuldorfæstan
gesihðe he fægen gefremed ofstlice arn on þa healfe þe
he efstan geseah þæt him þær æteowde. Ne geseah he
witodlice on eallum þam dagum ær nane mennisclice
gesihðe ne nanre nytena oþþe fugela oððe wildeora hiw,
225 and he forðy arn geornlice and gewilnode to oncnawenne
hwæt þæt wildeora wære þe him æteowde.

Sona swa hi Zosimus geseah, þa witodlice, his ealdan
ylde ofergetiligende and þæt geswinc his syðfætes ne
understandende, mid hrædestan ryne þenigende arn,
230 forþam þe he gewilnode hine geðeodan þam þe ðær fleah.
He witodlice hire wæs ehtende, and heo wæs fleonde; ða
wæs Zosimus ryna hwæðra sticmælum near gefremed.
Ða þa he swa neah wæs þæt heo mihte his stemne
gehyran, þa ongan he forð sendan þyllice stemne mid
235 hluddre clypunga wepende and þus cwæð: 'Hwi flihst þu
me forealdodne syngigan, þu Godes þeowen? Geanbida
min,* for þam hihte þæs edleanes ðe þu swa micclum
geswunce. Stand and syle me þines gebedes bletsungan
þurh þone God þe him nænne fram ne awyrpð.'
240 Ðas word soðlice Zosimus mid tearum geypte. Þa
becom heo yrnende to sumere stowe, on þære wæs
getacnod swilce fordruwod burna. Þa ða hi witodlice
þyder becomon, þa sceat heo inn on þone burnan and eft
upp on oþre healfe. Zosimus þa soðlice clypigende and

---

227 hi] he, *with hi written above, and comma-like sign below.*

it might be a phantom of some spirit that he saw there; but immediately, however, he strengthened himself with the sign of the cross of Christ and threw off his fear from him. And when the end of his prayer had been completed, he then turned his eyes and really saw there a human being hastening westwards in the desert, and it was actually a woman that appeared there. She was extremely black in her body because of the sun's heat, and the hair of her head was as white as wool and no longer than down to her neck.

(8) Zosimus kept gazing intently at these details, and because of the longed-for loveliness of that glorious sight, filled with joy he ran speedily in the direction in which he had seen hastening that which had appeared to him there. Truly, in all the days before he had not seen the sight of any human being or the appearance of any animals or birds or wild beasts, and therefore he ran eagerly and desired to learn what kind of wild beast that might be which appeared to him.

As soon as Zosimus saw her, overcoming his old age and taking no notice of the difficulty of his path, he ran exerting himself with a very rapid onward course, because he desired to unite himself with that which fled there. He kept pursuing her and she kept fleeing; then as each of them kept on their courses little by little Zosimus got to be closer. When he was near enough that she could hear his voice, he began then to send forth the following speech in a loud cry, weeping and speaking thus: 'Why, you handmaid of God, do you flee from me, a sinner worn out with old age? Wait for me, for the sake of the hope of the reward for which you have striven so much. Stop and give me the blessing of your prayer, in the name of the God who casts no one away from him.'

Zosimus uttered these words amidst his tears. Then she came running to a particular spot in which was marked out, as it were, a dried-up stream. When they got there, she darted into the stream and up onto the other side again. Zosimus stood then on the other side of the stream which was apparent

245 nahwider forðgangende stod þa on oþre healfe þæs
f.126v burnan þe þær gesewen wæs, and toge|ihte þa tearas þam
tearum, and gemænigfealdode þa sworetunga þam
siccetungum, swa þæt þær nan þincg gehyred næs buton
seo geomerung þæs heofes.

250   (9) Ða witodlice se lichama þe ðær fleah ðyllice
stemne forð sende and þus cwæð: 'Ðu abbod Zosimus,
miltsa me for Gode, ic þe bidde, forþon ic ne mæg me þe
geswutelian and ongeanweardes þe gewenden, forþon ic
eom wifhades mann and eallunga lichamlicum wæfelsum
255 bereafod, swa swa þu sylf gesihst, and þa sceame mines
lichaman hæbbende unoferwrigene. Ac gif þu wille me
earmre forworhtre þine halwendan gebedu to forlætan,
awyrp me þonne hyder þinne scyccels þe þu mid
bewæfed eart, þæt ic mæge þa wiflican tyddernysse
260 oferwreon and to ðe gecyrran and þinra gebeda onfon.'
     Ða gegrap Zosimus swiðlic ege and fyrhtu witodlice,
forþan þe he gehyrde þæt heo be his naman næmnede
hine, þone ðe heo næfre ær ne geseah ne næfre
foresecgan ne gehyrde, buton þæt he swutellice ongeat
265 þæt heo mid þære godcundan foresceawunge onliht wæs.
He þa fæstlice swa dyde swa heo bebead, hine þam
scyccelse ongyrede þe he mid bewæfed wæs, on
bæclincg gewend, hire to wearp. Heo þa þæs onfeng and
hire lichaman oferwreah, and gegyrede hire be þam dæle
270 þe heo mæst mihte and mæst neod wæs to beheligenne.
Heo þa to Zosimam wende and him to cwæð, 'Hwi wæs
þe, la abbod Zosimus, swa micel neod me synful wif to
geseonne, oððe hwæs wilnast þu fram me to hæbbenne
oþþe to witenne, þæt þu ne slawedest swa micel geswinc
275 to gefremmanne for minum þingum?'
     He þa sona on þa eorðan hine astrehte and hire blet-

---

245 forðgangende] *suggested by Skeat; J has* furð clypigende, *with*
clypigende *wrongly repeated from the previous phrase; there are two
dots over the* y *of* clypigende, *instead of the normal single dot, the
extra dot evidently signifying expunction.*
274 geswinc] geswic, *with* n *written above, and comma-like sign
below.*

there, calling out and getting no further on in any direction; and he added tears to tears and multiplied his groans with sighs, so that nothing was heard there except the lamentation of his grief.

(9) Then, indeed, the figure which was fleeing sent forth the following speech and said this: 'Abbot Zosimus, have pity on me for God's sake, I beg you, because I cannot show myself and turn towards you, for I am a person of the female sex and am completely bereft of bodily clothing, as you yourself see, and I have the shame of my body uncovered. But if you wish to grant me, a wretched sinner, your salutary blessings, then throw here to me your cloak which you are wearing, so that I can cover up my womanly frailty and turn to you and receive your prayers.'

Then an intense dread and fear seized Zosimus, because he heard that she called him by his name, whom she had never seen previously or heard tell of before – except that he perceived clearly that she had been enlightened with divine foreknowledge. Unhesitatingly he did as she instructed, took off the cloak he was wearing [and], with his back turned, threw it to her. She grabbed hold of it then and put it over her body, and covered herself up in the parts she was most able to and which there was most need to conceal. She then turned to Zosimus and said to him, 'Why, O abbot Zosimus, was there so great a need for you to see me, a sinful woman, or what do you wish to have from me or to learn, to the extent that you did not slacken in exercising so much toil on my account?'

He then immediately prostrated himself on the ground and

sunga bæd. Heo ongean hi astrehte and his bletsunga
bæd.

(10) Ða æfter manega tida fæce cwæð þæt wif to
280 Zosime, 'Ðe gedafenað, abbud Zosimus, to biddenne and
f.127r to bletsigenne, forþan þu eart underwreðed mid þære |
sacerdlican lare,* and þu eart tellende Cristes gerynu mid
þam gyfum þæra godcundlican,* æt his þam halgan
weofode manegum gearum þeowigende.'

285   Ðas word witodlice gebrohton on Zosime micelne ege
and fyrhtu, and he wæs byfigende and he wæs geondgoten mid þæs swates dropum.* Ða ongan he sworettan
swa swa eallunga gewæced, on þam oreðe belocen, and
þus cwæð: 'Eala, ðu gastlice modor, geswutela nu hwæt
290 þu sie of þære gesihþe, forþam þu eart soðlice Godes
þinen. Geþinga me nu, of þam geongran* dæle for
þyssere worulde dead gefremed. On þam geswutelað on
þe seo godcunde lufu* ealra swiðost, þæt þu me be
naman næmdest, þone þu næfre ær ne gesawe. Ac for-
295 þam þe seo gyfu ne bið oncnawen of þære medemnysse
ac gewuna is hi to getacnigenne of þære sawla dædum,
bletsa þu me for Drihtne, ic þe bidde, and syle me þæt
unbereafigendlice gebæd þinre fulfremednysse.'

Ða ongan heo hire onemnþrowigan þæs ealdan witan
300 staðolfæstnysse, and cwæð, 'God sy gebletsod, se ðe is
sawla hælu tiligende.'

Ða forgeaf heo Zosime, andswarigende, 'Amen.'

Ða arisan hi butu of þære eorþan. *Ða ongan eft þæt
wif sprecan to þam ealdan and ðus cwæð: 'Eala man, for*

---

277 hi] *G; J* hine.
292 dead] *G; J* deað.
296 is hi] *G; J* he is.
299 heo] *G; J* he.
302 Amen] *in capitals, followed by punctus elevatus.*
303 of þære eorþan] *substantial lacuna in J at this point, though no
scribal indication of omission: MS reads* of þære eorþan . þa ðincg þe
be me synd *(see line 353 below). Subsequent material in italics is
supplied from G, which itself also fails at line 352.* eft] *conjectural
reading.*
304 *man] most of word lacking.*

asked for her blessing. She in turn prostrated herself and asked for his blessing.

(10) Then after a period of many hours the woman said to Zosimus, 'It befits you, abbot Zosimus, to pray and to bless, because you are sustained by the special knowledge of the priesthood, and you fathom the sacramental rites of Christ with the gifts of godly things, serving for many years at his holy altar.'

These words really brought great dread and fear upon Zosimus, and he kept trembling and was suffused with drops of sweat. Then he began to sigh, as though completely overcome with weakness and gasping for breath, and he spoke as follows: 'O spiritual mother, reveal now what you are in your appearance, for you are truly God's handmaid. Intercede for me now, you who have been made dead to this world with regard to the concerns of youth. In this above all divine love is manifest in you, that you called me by my name, whom you had never before seen. But since grace is not recognized on grounds of rank but is accustomed to indicate itself by the works of the soul, you bless me, for the Lord's sake, I beg you, and grant me the inalienable blessing of your perfection.'

Then she began to take pity on the old man's persistence and said, 'Blessed be God, who works for the salvation of souls.'

Then she gave Zosimus [her blessing] and he answered 'Amen'.

Then they both arose from the ground. Thereupon the woman began to speak to the old man again, saying this: 'O

305 *hwylcre wisan come þu to me synfulre? Swaþeah-*
hwæðere, forþam þe þe seo gyfu þæs Haligan Gastes to
þam gerihte þæt ðu hwylce þenunga minon lytlan
lichaman to gehyðnysse gegearwige, sege me hu nu to-
dæge on middanearde Cristes folc sy gereht and hu ða
310 *caseres, oððe hu is nu gelæswod seo heord Cristes*
rihtgeleaffullan gesamnunga.'

Zosimus hire andswarode, 'Eala þu halige modor,
þinum halgum gebedum God hæfð forgyfen staðolfæste
sibbe. . . . muneces, and for Drihtne . . . middanearde and
315 *for me synfullum, þæt me ne wurðe ge. . . geswinc þises*
siðfætes and se weg swa myccles west. . .'

. . . '. . . , abbot Zosimus, for me and for eallum
gebiddan, forðam þe . . .ade, swa swa ic ær cwæþ . . . and
for þam þe we habbað þæt gebod h . . . willan ic do.'
320 *And þus cweðende, hi to þam . . . upahafenum eagum*
on þa heahnysse and aþenedum earmum, ongan gebiddan
mid þære welera styrungum on stilnesse, swa þæt ðær
næs eallinga nan stemne gehyred þæs þe man ongyten
mihte. Þæs gebedes eac swylce Zosimus nan þing
325 *ongytan ne mihte. He stod witodlice, swa swa he sylf*
sæde, byfiende and þa eorþan behealdende, and nan þing

---

305 *come]* partly illegible, as are synfulre *and* swaþeahhwæðere.
306-7 *Haligan Gastes to þam gerihte]* very indistinct.
310 *Cristes]* partly illegible.
312 *halige modor]* indistinct.
314 *. . .]* half of MS line lacking. Drihtne *. . .] f. 4r* ends with drihtne;
half of line lacking at beginning of f. 4v, including first part of
middaneard.
315 *and]* inserted above line. ge*. . .]* half of MS line lacking, with ge *of*
geswinc indistinct.
316-17 *west. . .]* half of MS line lacking.
318 *. . .ade]* some five words illegible, the last possibly sacerdhade.
. . .] some four words illegible.
319 *h. . .]* some ten words illegible, the first possibly hyrsumnysse.
320 *þam . . . upahafenum]* both words largely indistinct, and separated
by two illegible words.
322 *styrungum]* ty indistinct.
323 *þe]* indistinct.
326 *eorþan]* ending indistinct.

sir, for what reason have you come to me in my sinfulness? However, since the grace of the Holy Spirit has guided you for the purpose that you may do some service to the benefit of my little body, tell me how now today Christ's people are ruled in the world and how the emperors are, or how the flock of Christ's true-believing congregation are now looked after.'

Zosimus answered her, 'O holy mother, in accordance with your holy prayers, God has granted a firm peace. . . . of a monk, and for God's sake [pray] for the world and for me in my sinfulness, so that the toil of this journey and the path over so great a desert may not become [fruitless] to me.'

Then she said, '[It befits you,] abbot Zosimus, to pray for me and for all, since . . . , as I said before, . . . and since we have the requirement . . . will I shall do.'

And speaking thus, she . . . with eyes raised on high and outstretched arms, began to pray, moving her lips in silence, so that no voice at all could be heard there that one could perceive. Thus Zosimus could make out nothing of the prayer. As he himself said, he stood trembling and looking at the

*eallinga sprecende. He swor witodlice, God him to
gewitan on his wordum foresettende, þæt ða get þa þa
heo þus . . . on þære gebedes astandendnysse, he his hine*
330 *þa eagan lythwon fram ðære eorðan upahof þæt he
geseah hi upahefene swa swa mannes elne fram þære
eorðan and on þære lyfte hangiende gebiddan ongan. Ða
þa he þis geseah, þa wearð he gegripen mid mycelre
fyrhto and hine on eorðan astrehte and mid swate*
335 *ofergoten wearð and swiðlice gedrefed. Naht geþrystlæhte specan, butan wið him sylfum þæt an* . . .*

(11) *Ða þa he on þære eorðan læg astreht þa g. . .
hwon hit gast wære þæt ðær mid hwylcere hiwunga
gebæde hi. Heo ða þæt wif hi bewende and þone munuc*
340 *up arærde, þus cweðende: 'To hwy gedrefest þu abbot
þine geþohtas to geæswicianne on me swylce ic hwylc
gast syrwiende gebedu fremme? Ac wite þu man þæt ic
eom synful wif, swa þeahhwæðere utan ymbseald mid
þam halgan fulluhte, and ic nan gast ne eom ac æmerge*
345 *and axe and eall flæsc, and nan gastlice . . .'*

*. . . cwæþ, heo hire andwlitan gebletsode mid þære
halgan rode tacne, and hire eagan and weleras and eac
hire breost mid þære bletsunga heo getrymede, and þus
cwæð: 'God us alyse, abbot Zosimus, fram urum wiðer-*

---

327 *to*] *indistinct.*
328 *ða*] *inserted above line.*
329 . . .] *one or more words illegible.*
333 *geseah*] *partly indistinct.*
334 *astrehte*] *partly indistinct.*
335 *geþrystlæhte*] *last four letters indistinct.*
336 . . .] *three or more words illegible; Skeat suggests* drihten .
gemiltsa me .
337 *þa he on*] *largely illegible. g.* . .] *some eight words illegible.*
340 *fest þu*] *indistinct.*
343 *swa þeahhwæðere*] þeah *indistinct.*
344 *eom*] *indistinct.*
345-46 *gastlice . . . cwæþ*] lice *indistinct, followed by some five
illegible words, then* cwæþ, *which is also partly illegible.* heo]
illegible.
347 *weleras*] *beginning of word illegible.*
349 *cwæð*] *indistinct.*

ground and saying nothing at all. In fact, he swore, proposing God as witness of his words, that while she continued thus with her prayer, he raised his eyes a little from the ground to see her elevated just the height of a man's forearm above the ground, and she began to pray hanging in the air. When he saw this he was seized then with great fear, and he prostrated himself on the ground, and he was covered in sweat and very much agitated. He did not dare to speak, except that within himself he said only . . .

(11) As he lay stretched out on the ground, then . . . it could possibly be a spirit that was praying there in some sort of pretence. The woman turned then and raised up the monk, speaking as follows: 'Why, abbot, do you vex your thoughts to take offence with me, as though I were some spirit engaging in prayer deceitfully? But know, sir, that I am a sinful woman, although protected from without by holy baptism, and I am no spirit but dust and ashes and wholly flesh, and nothing spirit-like . . .'

. . . spoke, she blessed her face with the holy sign of the cross, and she fortified her eyes and lips and also her breast with that blessing, and said this: 'May God deliver us, abbot

350 *winnan and and fram his anbrincgellan, forðam þe his*
æfst is mycel ofer us.'
Ðas word se ealda hyrende hine adune astrehte . . .
(12) . . . ' . . . þa ðincg þe be me synd, sona þu flihst
fram me on þi gemete swilc man næddran fleo. Ac swa-
355 þeahhwæðere ic þe arecce, naht forhælende, and þe ærest
bidde þæt þu ne geteorige for me gebiddan, þæt ic geearnige and gemete on domes dæge hwilcehwugu mildheortnysse.'
Se ealda mid tearum ofergoten ongan biterlice wepan.
360 Þa ongan þæt wif cyðan and gereccan eall þa þincg þe be
hire gedone wæron, þus cwæðende: (13) 'Ic hæfde
broþor and eðel on Egyptum* and þær mid minum
magum wunode. Þa on þam twelftan geare minre ylde þa
f.127v ongan ic heora lufu forhycgan, | and to Alexandrian þære
365 byrig becom. Ac me sceamað nu to gereccenne hu ic on
þam fruman ærest minne fæmnhad besmat and hu ic unablinnendlice and unafyllendlice þam leahtrum þæra
synlusta læg underþeoded. Þis is nu witodlice sceortlice
to areccenne, ac ic nu swaþeah hraðor gecyðe þæt þu
370 mæge oncnawan þone unalyfedan bryne minra leahtra þe
ic hæfde on þære lufe þæs geligeres. Ac miltsa me,
abbud; eac on xvii wintrum ic openlice folca meniu
geondferde on þam bryne forligeres licgende. Ne forleas
ic na minne fæmnhad for æniges mannes gyfum oþþe ic
375 witodlice ahtes onfenge fram ænigum þe me aht gyfan
woldon, ac ic wæs swiðe onæled mid þære hatheortnysse
þæs synlustes, þæt ic gewilnode butan ceape þæt hi me
þe mænigfealdlicor to geurnon, to þy þæt ic þe eð mihte
gefyllan þa scyldfullan gewilnunga mines forligeres. Ne
380 þu ne wen na þæt ic aht underfenge for ænigum welan, ac
symle on wædlunga lyfde, forþon ic hæfde, swa ic ær
sæde, unafyllendlice gewilnunga, swa þæt ic me sylfe

---

350 anbrincgellan] inc *indistinct.*
352 se ealda hyrende] *partly indistinct.* astrehte] *only first two letters*
legible. Here G fragment breaks off, with latter half of f. 4v lacking.
367 leahtrum] *followed by* and (and *not in* O).

Zosimus, from our enemy and from his incitement, because his malice against us is great.'

When the old man heard these words he stretched himself downwards . . .

(12) . . . ' . . . the things concerning me, you will at once flee from me in the way one might flee from a serpent. But nonetheless I will tell you, and I will hide nothing; and first I beg you not to cease to pray for me, so that I may merit and find some degree of mercy on Judgement Day.'

The old man began to weep bitterly, suffused with tears. Then the woman began to relate and recount all the things that happened concerning her, speaking as follows: (13) 'I had a brother and my homeland in Egypt, and I lived there with my parents. In the twelfth year of my age I began then to spurn their love, and I went to the city of Alexandria. But it shames me now to recount how in the beginning I first defiled my maidenhood and how unceasingly and licentiously I lay en-slaved to the vices of desires for sin. This is now to be recounted briefly, but I reveal it nonetheless the more readily so that you may appreciate the illicit fire of the vices to which I was subject in my love of sexual depravity. But have pity on me, abbot; for all of seventeen years I roamed openly through the crowd of the population, lying in the fire of promiscuity. Nor did I lose my maidenhood at all in exchange for gifts from anyone or in fact that I might receive anything from any people who wished to give me anything, but I was very much on fire with the passion of desire for sin, so that I desired that they might rush to me the more numerously without payment, my purpose being to satisfy the more easily the disgraceful desires of my sexual depravity. Do not imagine at all that I undertook anything for any wealth, but I always lived in poverty, because I had, as I have said already, insatiable

unablinnendlice on þam adale þæs manfullan forligeres
besylede, and þæt me wæs to yrmðe.* And þæt ic me
385 tealde to life, þæt swa unablinnendlice þurhtuge þæs
gecyndes teonan.

'Þa ic þus leofode þa geseah ic on sumere tide micele
meniu Affricana and Egypta togædere yrnende swa swa
to sæ. Ða gemette ic færunga heora sumne, and þone
390 axode hwider he wende þæt seo mæniu efstan wolde. He
me andswarode and þus cwæð, þæt hi to Hierusalem
faran woldon for þære halgan rode wurðunga, þe man
æfter naht manegum dagum wurðian sceolde. Ða cwæð
ic to him, "Wenst þu hwæðer hi me underfon willan, gif
395 ic mid him faran wille?" Ða cwæð he, "Gif þu hæfst þæt
f.128r færeht, ne forwyrnþ þe heora ænig." Ða cwæð ic to him, |
"Broðor, soðlice næbbe ic nan færeht to syllanne, ac ic
wille faran and an þæra scypa astigan, and þeah hi nellan
hi me afedað, and ic me sylfe heom befæste, and hæbben
400 hi minne lichaman to gewealde for þam færehte, þæt hi
me þe hrædlicor underfon." Miltsa me, abbud, forðon ic
gewilnode mid him to farenne, þæt ic þe ma emwyrhtena
on þære þrowunge mines wynlustas hæfde. (14) Ic cwæð
ær to þe, "Ðu halga wer, miltsa me, þæt þu me ne genyde
405 to areccenne mine gescyndnysse." God wat þæt ic heora
forhtige, for þam þe ic wat þæt þas mine word ægðer
gewemmað ge þe ge þas lyfte.'

Zosimus soðlice þa eorðan mid tearum ofergeotende
hire to cwæð, 'Eala þu gastlice modor, sege for Gode, ic
410 þe bidde, and ne forlæt þu þa æfterfylgednysse swa
halwendre gerecednysse.'

And þus cwæð: 'Se geonglincg gehyrde sona þæt
bysmor minra worda and hlihhende me fram gewat. Ic þa
sona þa swingle* me fram awearp þe ic seldon gewunode
415 on handa to hæbbenne, and to þære sæ arn, þær þær ic hi
geseah gesamnode. Þa geseah ic tyn geonge men ætgædere standende be þam waruðe, genoh þæslice on

---

390 hwider] O; J hwæþer.
411 gerecednysse] O; J gerynysse.

desires, so that I unceasingly defiled myself in the mire of
wicked promiscuity; and that was my misery. And that I
counted as life, that I should unceasingly perpetrate wrongs
against nature.'

'While I lived thus, on a particular occasion I saw a large
crowd of Africans and Egyptians hurrying together as if to the
sea. I quickly fell in with one of them then and asked him
where he thought the crowd intended to hasten to. He
answered me and said this, that they intended to go to
Jerusalem for the honouring of the holy cross, which would be
celebrated after not many days. Then I said to him, "Do you
think they will be willing to take me, if I wish to go with
them?" He said, "If you have the fare-money, none of them
will stop you." Then I said to him, "Brother, in truth I have no
fare-money to give, but I intend to go and board one of the
ships, even though they don't wish to support me, and I will
give myself over to them, and instead of the fare-money they
may have my body in their power, so that they may receive
me the more readily." Pity me, abbot, because I desired to go
with them in order to have more fellow-workers in the passion
of my lusting for pleasure. (14) I said to you before, "Have
pity on me, you holy man, that you don't compel me to relate
my shamefulness." God knows that, because these words of
mine defile both you and the air itself, I am frightened of
them.'

Soaking the ground with his tears Zosimus then said to her,
'O spiritual mother, tell for God's sake, I beg you, and do not
leave off the continuation of so salutary a story.'

And she spoke thus: 'The young man straightaway heard
the shamefulness of my words and he went off laughing away
from me. At once then I threw from me the whip that I was
seldom accustomed to have in my hands, and ran towards the
sea, where I saw them gathered. Then I saw ten young men
standing together by the shore, good-looking enough in body

lichaman and on gebærum, and ful licwurðe me þuhte to
mines lichaman luste. Ic me þa unsceandlice swa swa ic
420 gewuna wæs tomiddes heora gemengde and him to
cwæð, "Nimað me on eower færeld mid eow. Ne beo ic
na eow unlicwyrðe." And ic hi þa ealle sona to þam
manfullum leahtrum and ceahhetungum bysmerlicum
astyrede mid manegum oþrum fullicum and fracodlicum
425 gespræcum.

'Hi þa witodlice mine unsceamlican gebæra geseonde
me on heora scip namon to him and forð hreowan. Eala,
Zosimus, hu mæg ic þe areccan, oþþe hwilc tunga mæg
hit asecgan, oþþe eara gehyran, þa mandæda þe on þam
430 scipfærelde wæron and on þam siðfæte gefremede, and
f.128v hu ic to syngi|genne genydde ægðer ge þa earman
willendan and þa earman syllendan?* Nis nan
asecgendlic oððe unasecgendlic fracodlicnysse hiwung
þæs ic ne sih tihtende and lærende, and fruma gefremed.
435 Beo la nu on þysum gehealden, forþan þe ic wundrige hu
seo sæ aðolode and adruge mine þa unrihtlican lustas,
oððe humeta seo eorðe hyre muð ne untynde and me swa
cwyce on helle ne besencte, þe swa manega sawla on
forspillednysse grin gelædde, ac þæs þe ic hopige þæt
440 God mine hreowsunga sohte, se ðe nænne ne forlætað
forwurðan ac ealle hale gedeð þe on hine gelyfað, forðon
soðlice he nele þæs synfullan deað ac langsumlice his
gehwyrfednysse bið.*

'We þa swa mid micclum ofste witodlice to Hierus-
445 alem foron, and swa mænige dagas swa ic ær þære rode
symbelnysse on þære ceastre wunode mid lichaman*
fullicum weorcum me gemængde, and eac wyrsum. Næs
ic na genihtsumigende on þam geongum ðe on þære sæ
mid me oððe on þam siðfæte hæmdon, ac ic eac swilce

---

419 unsceandlice] J sceandlice, un *having been erased; O* unsceandlice.
427 on heora] *written twice, with a line through the first occurrence.*
445 rode] O; *omitted in J.*
447 gemængde] O; J gemægde. eac wyrsum] O; J eac wyrcum, *faintly
underlined.*

and in demeanour, and admirable indeed, it seemed to me, for the pleasure of my body. Shamelessly then, as was my custom, I mingled amongst them and said to them, "Take me on your journey with you. I will not be unpleasing to you." And straightaway I excited them all then to wicked sins and shameful bouts of sniggering, with many other dirty and lewd expressions.

'When they saw my shameless behaviour, then, they took me with them on board their ship and sailed forth. O Zosimus, how can I recount to you, or what tongue can say it or what ear can hear the vile deeds that were enacted on that voyage and on that journey, and how I compelled to sin both the wretches who were willing and the wretches who gave to me. There is no form of obscenity, speakable or unspeakable, of a kind that I did not incite and teach, after becoming its instigator. O be assured of this now, for I marvel how the sea endured and put up with those wicked lusts of mine, or how it was that the earth did not open its mouth and plunge me into hell alive as I was, I who led so many souls into the trap of perdition – but I expect that it was because God looked for my repentance, he who lets no one perish but causes all to be safe who believe in him, for truly he wishes not the death of the sinner but patiently waits for his conversion.

'Thus with great speed then we travelled to Jerusalem, and for as many days as I stayed in the city before the feast of the cross, I engaged in impure bodily acts, and even worse. I wasn't content with the young men with whom I had had sex on the sea or on the journey, but I also polluted likewise in the

450 mænga ælðeodige and ceastergewarena on þa dæda
minra scylda gegaderigende and beswicende besmat.

(15) 'Ða þa seo symbelnyss becom þære halgan deorwurðan rode upahefennysse,* ic foregeode, þa geongan
swa swa ær on þæt grin forspillednysse teonde. Þa geseah
455 ic soðlice on ærnemergen hi ealle anmodlice to þære
cyrcan* yrnan. Þa ongan ic yrnan mid þam yrnendum,
and samod mid heom teolode toforan þam temple
becuman. Þa þa seo tid becom þa halgan rode to
wurþigenne, þa ongan ic nydwræclice gemang þam folce
460 wið þæs folces þringan, and swa mid micclum geswince
ic unsælige to þæs temples dura becom mid þam þe þær
ineodon. Þa ic sceolde in on þa dura gangen, þa
ongunnon hi butan ælcere lættinge ingangan; me witod-
f.129r lice þæt godcunda mægen | þæs ganges bewerede, and ic
465 sona wæs ut aþrungen fram eallum þam folce, oððe ic
ænlipigu on þam cafertune to læfe oþstod. Þa ongan ic
þencan þæt me þæt gelumpe for þære wiflican unmihte,
and ic me þa eft ongan mæncgan to oþrum, þæt ic wolde
on sume wisan inn geþringan, ac ic swanc on idel, mid
470 þam þe ic þone ðerscwold þæra dura gehran.

(16) 'And hi ealle þyder inn onfangene wæron butan
ælcere lettinga; þa wæs ic ana ut asceofen. Ac swilce me
hwilc strang meniu ongean stode* þæt me þone ingang
beluce, swa me seo færlice Godes wracu þa duru
475 bewerede, oððe ic eft standende on þæs temples cafertune
wæs. Þus ic þrywa oþþe feower siþum þrowode minne
willan to geseonne and eac to fremanne, and þa ða ic naht
ne gefremode þa ongan ic ofer þæt georne wenan, and
min lichama wæs swiðe geswenced for þam nyde þæs
480 geþringes. Ða gewat ic witodlice þanone, and me ana
gestod on sumum hwomme þæs cafertunes and on
minum mode geornlice þohte and smeade for hwilcum

---

451 gegaderigende] gegaderigendum; O gegadriende.
472 asceofen] asceafen, *with* o *written above second* a, *and dot
preceded by comma-like mark below.*
478 georne] geore.

works of my iniquities many foreigners and townspeople whom I had gathered together and seduced.

(15) 'When the feast of the exaltation of the holy precious cross arrived, I went about as before enticing the young men into the trap of perdition. Then in the early morning I saw them all running eagerly to the church. I began to run then with those who were running, and along with them I strove to get to the front of the temple. When the time came to venerate the holy cross, then in the midst of the people I began to push forcefully against the crowd, and so with great difficulty I, in my wretched state, got to the temple door with those who went in there. When I expected to enter the door, they began to go in without any impediment; truly, divine power hindered my passage, and I was immediately pushed away from all the people, until I alone stood in the courtyard by myself. Then I began to think that this had happened to me because of my womanly weakness, and I began again to mingle in with the others, so that in some way I would push in; but I laboured in vain when I touched the threshold of the door.

(16) 'And they were all received inside without any hinderance, while I alone was thrust out. But as if some strong host stood in front of me to bar entry for me, so God's vengeance suddenly blocked the door, until again I was left standing in the courtyard of the temple. Thus three or four times I attempted to see and also attain what I wished, and when I didn't succeed at all then I began earnestly to think it over, and my body was tired out with the force of the pushing. So then I went away from there, and I stood alone in a particular corner of the courtyard, and in my mind I earnestly pondered and considered for what reason it was that the sight of the life-

intingum me wære forwyrned þæs liffæstan treowes
ansyn. Þa onhran soðlice min mod and þa eagan minre
485 heortan hælo andgit, mid me sylfre þencende þæt me
þone ingang belucen þa unfeormeganda minra misdæda.
Ða ongan ic biterlice wepan and swiðe gedrefed mine
breost cnyssan and of inneweardre heortan heofende
forðbringan þa geomorlican siccetunga.
490   'Ða geseah ic of þære stowe þe ic on stod þære halgan
Godes cennestran anlicnysse* standende, and ic cwæð to
hire geornlice and unforbugendlice behealdende, and
cweðende, "Eala þu wuldorfæste hlæfdige, þe þone soðan
God æfter flæsces gebyrde acendest, geara ic wat þæt hit
495 nis na gedafenlic ne þæslic þæt ic þe swa grimlice
forworht eom þæt ic þine anlicnysse sceawige and
f.129v gebidde mid swa mænigfealdum besmitenum | gesihþum.
Þu wære symle fæmne oncnawan and þinne lichaman
hæbbende clæne and unwemmed; forþon witodlice genoh
500 rihtlic is me swa besmitenre fram þinre clænan un-
gewemmednysse beon ascunod and fram aworpen. Ac
swaþeahhwæðere, forþan ðe ic gehyrde þæt God wære
mann forðy gefremod, þe þu sylf acendest, to þon þæt he
þa synfullan to hreowsunga gecygede, gefultuma me nu
505 anegre ælces fylstes bedæled. Forlæt me and me þa leafe
forgif to geopenigenne þone ingang þinre þære halgan
cyrcan, þæt ic ne wurðe fremde geworden þære deor-
wurþan rode gesihðe, on þære gefæstnod wæs ealles
middaneardes Hælend, þone þu femne geeacnodost, eac
510 swilce fæmne acendest, se þe his agen blod ageat for
minre alysednysse. Ac hat nu, þu wuldorfæste hlæfdige,
me unmedemre for þære godcundan rode gretinge þa
duru beon untynede, and ic me þe bebeode and to
mundbyrdnysse geceose wið þin agen bearn, and inc bam
515 gehate þæt ic næfre ofer þis minne lichaman ne besmite

---

495 þe] *inserted above line by later hand.*
501 ascunod] *G; J* ascimod, *with* nod *written above* mod *by later hand.*
502 wære] *G; J* re *(at beginning of line), with* wæ *added later in left-hand margin by later hand.*

giving tree was being denied me. Then truly knowledge of salvation touched my mind and the eyes of my heart, when I reflected that the inexpiable circumstances of my misdeeds had closed the entrance against me. Then I began to weep bitterly and to beat my breast in great tribulation and, as I lamented from deep in my heart, to bring forth sorrowful sighs.

'Then from the place where I stood I noticed an image of the holy mother of God set up, and I earnestly spoke to her, beholding her unswervingly and saying, "O glorious lady, who bore the true God in bodily childbirth, I fully know that it is not proper or fitting that I who am so dire a sinner should look upon and pray to your image, with eyes in so many ways defiled. You were always known as a virgin who kept your body pure and unstained; for that reason it really is quite right for me, being so polluted, to be excluded and cast out from your pure spotlessness. But nevertheless, since I have heard that the God whom you yourself bore became man for this reason, to call sinners to repentance, aid me now, alone as I am, bereft of every help. Allow me and give me leave to open the entrance of your holy church, so that I may not be made a stranger to the sight of the precious cross, on which was fastened the Saviour of all the world, whom you conceived as a virgin and also likewise gave birth to as a virgin, he who shed his own blood for my redemption. But command now, O glorious lady, the door to be unfastened for me in my unworthiness to greet the divine cross, and I will commit myself to you and choose you as my advocate against your Son, and I promise both of you that never after this will I

þurh þæt grime bysmergleow þæs manfullan geligeres, ac
sona ic, halige fæmne, þines suna rode geseo, ic mid þam
wiðsace þissere worulde and hire dædum mid eallum
þingum þe on hyre synd, and syððan fare swa hwider swa
520 þu me to mundbyrdnysse geredst."

(17) 'Þus cwæðende, ic wearð þa gelæd* mid þære
hætu þæs geleafan and mid þam truwan ophrinon, and be
þære arfæstan Godes cennestran mildheortnysse þrystlæcende, ic me of þære ylcan stowe astyrede ðe ic þis
525 gebæd cwæð, and me eft to þam ingangendum gemengde. Syþþan næs nan þincg þe me utsceofe oþþe me
þæs temples dura bewerede, and ic þa ineode mid þam
ingangendum. Ða gegrap me witodlice stranglic fyrhto,
and ic wæs eall byfigende gedrefed þa ic me eft to þære
f.130r dura geðeodde þe me wæs ær ingang belocen, | swilc me
eall þæt mægen þe me ær þæs inganges duru bewerede
æfter þan þone ingang þæs siðfætes gegearwode. Swa ic
wæs gefylled* mid þam gastlicum gerynum innon þam
temple, and ic wæs gemedemod gebiddan þa gerynu þære
535 deorwurðan and þære geliffæstan rode. Ða ic þær geseah
þa halgan Godes gerynu, hu he symle geare is þa hreows-
igendan to underfonne, ða wearp ic me sylfe forð on þa
flor and þa halgan eorðan gecyste.

'Ða ic uteode, þa becom ic eft to þære stowe of þære
540 ic ær þære halgan cennestran anlicnysse geseah, and mine
cneowa gebigde beforan þam halgan andwlitan, þysum
wordum biddende: "Eala þu fremsumesta hlæfdig, þe me
þine arfæstan mildheortnysse æteowdest and mine þa
unwurðan bena þe fram ne awurpe, ic geseah þæt wuldor
545 þe we synfulle mid gewyrhtum ne geseoð. Seo wuldor
ælmihtigum Gode, se þe þurh þe onfehð þæra synfulra
and forworhtra hreowsunge and dædbote. Hwæt mæg ic
earm, forðoht, mare geðencan oððe areccan? Nu is seo
tid to gefyllenne and to gefremmane, swa ic ær cwæð

---

540 anlicnysse] G; not in J.
544 þe] G; J þu. ne] G; J me.
545 geseoð] G; J geseow.

defile my body in the terrible shameful lust of wicked promiscuity, but as soon as I see, holy virgin, the cross of your
Son, I will at that moment forsake this world and its works
along with everything that is in it, and afterwards I will go
wherever you guide me as my advocate."

(17) 'Saying this, I was led then with the heat of faith and
touched with belief, and becoming bold with the mercy of the
gracious mother of God, I stirred myself from the same place
where I had spoken this prayer and I joined myself again with
those who were going in. From now on there was nothing that
pushed me out or hindered me from the temple door, and I
entered with those who were going in. Then in truth a
powerful fear seized me, and I was trembling all over in
excitement when I again came to the door where entry had
previously been closed to me – it was just as if all the force
that previously had guarded the door against my entry,
afterwards prepared the entry for my path.

'So I was filled with the spiritual mysteries within the
temple, and I was deemed worthy to pay reverence to the
mysteries of the precious and life-giving cross. When I saw
there the holy mysteries of God, how he is always ready to
receive those who repent, then I threw myself forth on the
floor and kissed the holy ground.

'When I had gone out, I arrived back again at the place
from which I had previously seen the image of the holy
mother, and I bent my knees before the holy countenance,
asking with these words: "O most benign lady, who showed to
me your gracious mercy and did not cast my unworthy prayer
away from you, I have seen the glory which we sinful people
do not see by our deserts. Glory be to God Almighty, who
through you accepts the repentance and penitence of sinners
and wrong-doers. What more can I, who am wretched and
despaired of, think or tell? Now is the time to fulfil and
accomplish what I said with respect to your worthy surety.

550 þinre ðære licwurðan mundbyrdnysse. Gerece me nu on
þone wæg þe þin willa sy. Beo me nu hælo latteow
æteowod and soðfæstnysse ealdor, beforan me gangende
on þone wæg þe to dædbote læt."

'Ða ic þus cwæð, þa gehyrde ic feorran ane stefne
555 clypigende, "Gif þu Iordane þæt wæter oferfærst, þær þu
gefærst and gemetst gode reste."

'Ða ic þas stemne gehyrde and for minum þingum
ongeat beon geclypode, ic wepende spræc and to þære
halgan Godes cennestran anlicnysse hawigende and eft
560 clypigende, "Eala þu hlæfdige, ealles middaneardes
cwen, þurh ðe eallum menniscum cynne hælo to becom.
Ne forlæt þu me."

f.130v 'Ðus cwæðende, ic þa ut eode of þæs | temples
cafertune, and ofstlice for. Ða gemette ic sum man, and
565 me þry penegas sealde, mid þam ic me þry hlafas
gebohte, ða ic me hæfde genoh gehyððo to mines
siðfætes geblædfæstnysse. Ða axode ic þone þe ic þa
hlafas æt bohte, hwilc se wæg wære þe to Iordane þære
ea rihtlicost gelædde. Ða þa ic þone weg wiste, ic
570 wepende be þam siðfæte arn, (18) symle þa axunga þære
æscan towriðende, and gemang þam ðæs dæges siðfæt
wepende gefylde. Witodlice þæs dæges wæs underntid þa
ða ic gegyrnode þa halgan deorwurðan rode geseon, and
sunne hi þa to setle ahylde, and þære æfenrepsunga
575 genealæhte, ða ic becom to Sanctes Iohannes cyrcan þæs
Fulwihteres,* wið Iordanen gesette; and ic me þyder inn
eode and me þær gebæd, and sona in Iordane þa ea astah
and of þam halgan wætere mine handa and ansynu þwoh,
and me þær gemænsumode þam liffæstan and þam un-
580 besmitenum gerynum ures Drihtnes Hælendes Cristes on

---

559 halgan] *GO; not in J.*
564 for] *G* fór, *O* for; *J* forð.
566 ða] *G* þa, *O* Ða; *J* Ðær.
569 wiste] *GO; not in J, in which* ongæt *is inserted above the line in a later hand.*
571 towriðende] *O* towriþende; *G* togewriðende; *J* towriðenne.
574 hi] *O; J* heo.

Direct me now on the road according to your wish. Be now a guide to salvation appearing to me and a source of truthfulness, going before me on the road that leads to penitence."

'When I spoke thus, I heard then from afar a voice calling out, "If you cross over the river Jordan, there you will experience and obtain good repose."

'When I heard this utterance and realized that it had been called out on my account, I spoke weeping and gazing at the likeness of the holy mother of God, crying out again, "O lady, queen of all the world, through you salvation came to all the human race. Do not forsake me."

'Speaking thus, I went out from the courtyard of the temple and went hurriedly on my way. Then I met someone, and he gave me three pennies, with which I bought myself three loaves, which I took as subsistence for the blessing of my journey. Then I asked the person from whom I bought the loaves which was the road that led most directly to the river Jordan. When I found out the way, I ran weeping on my journey, (18) twisting always enquiry onto enquiry, and in this way, weeping, I completed the day's journey. Now, it was morning-time of the day when I strove to get to see the holy precious cross, and the sun was sinking to its setting and it was approaching nightfall by the time I arrived at the church of St John the Baptist, situated by the Jordan. And I went in there and prayed, and, immediately after, I descended into the Jordan and washed my hands and face with the holy water, and I partook in the life-giving and undefiled sacrament of our

þære ylcan cyrcan þæs halgan forryneles and fulluhteres
Iohannes, and þær geæt healfne dæl anes hlafes and þæs
wæteres ondranc, and me þær on niht reste, and on ærne-
morgen ofer þa ea for. Þa ongan ic eft biddan mine
585 lættewestran Sancta Marian, þæt heo me gerihte þyder
hire willa wære.

'Ðus ic becom on þis westen, and þanone oð ðisne
andweardan dæg ic feorrode, symle fleonde, minne God
anbidigende and gehihtende, se þe hale gedeð ealle fram
590 þissere worulde brogan þa ðe to him gecyrrað.'

Zosimus hire to cwæð, 'Eala min hlæfdige, hu
mænige gear synt nu þæt þu on þysum westene
eardodost?'

Þæt wif him andswarode, 'Hit is for seofon and
595 feowertigum wintrum, þæs þe me þincð, þæt ic of þære
halgan byrig ut for.'

f.131r   Zosimus hire to cwæð, 'And hwæt mihtest þu þe | to
æte findan, oþþe be hwilcum þingum feddest þu ðe oþ
þis?'

600 Heo him andswarode, 'Twægen healfa hlafas ic
brohte hider mid me, þa ic Iordanem oferfor. Naht
micclan fæce þa adruwodon hi swa swa stan and
aheardodon, and þæra ic breac notigende to sumere
hwile.'

605 Zosimus hire to cwæð, 'And mihtst þu swa manegra
tida lencgu oferfaran, þæt þu ne freode þone bryne þære
flæsclican gehwyrfednysse?'

Heo þa gedrefedu him andswarode, 'Nu þu me axast
þa ðincg þe ic swiðe þearle sylf befortige, gif me nu to
610 gemynde becumað ealle þa frecednysse þe ic ahrefnode

---

582 anes] *O; J* þæs.
585 Sancta Marian] *in capitals.*
589 God anbidigende] *O (indistinct); J* gód anbidigenne. hale] *written
above the line, above* þe *and* gedeð, *with comma-like sign below; also
in O.*
595 þæs] is þæs.
598 findan] *written above the line, above* æte *and* oþþe, *with dot
below, preceded by comma-like mark.*

Lord the Saviour Christ in that same church of the holy
Precursor and Baptist John; and there I ate half of one loaf and
drank some of the water, and I rested there for the night, and
early the next morning I went across the river. Then I began
again to ask my guide Saint Mary to direct me to where she
wished.

'So I came to this desert, and from then until this present
day I have kept apart, always fleeing away, waiting and
hoping for my God, who delivers from the danger of this
world all those who turn to him.'

Zosimus said to her, 'O my lady, how many years have
there been now, that you have lived in this desert?'

The woman answered him, 'It has been forty-seven years,
according to my reckoning, since I went out from the holy
city.'

Zosimus said to her, 'And what could you find for yourself
to eat, or with what things did you feed yourself until now?'

She answered him, 'I brought two and a half loaves here
with me when I crossed over the Jordan. After no length of
time they dried up just like stone, and became hard, and I
subsisted on those, making use of them for some time.'

Zosimus said to her, 'And were you able to pass the length
of so many seasons without thinking longingly of the burning
of the instinctive pull of the flesh?'

In a troubled state then, she answered him, 'Now you are
asking me about things of which I myself am exceedingly
afraid, if all the dangers that I endured and the unwise

and þæra unwislicra geþanca þe me oft gedrefedon, þæt
ic eft fram þam ylcan geþohtum sum geswinc þrowige.'
    Zosimus cwæð, 'Eala hlæfdige, ne forlæt þu nan
þincg þæt þu me ne gecyðe, ac geswutela ealle þa þincg
615 be endebyrdnysse.'
    (19) Ða cwæð heo, 'Abbud, gelyf me, seofontyne
wintre ic wan on þam gewilnunga þære manðwæra and
ungesceadwisra wildeora lustum.* Þonne me hingrigan
ongan, þonne wæron me þa flæscmettas on gewiln-
620 ungum. Ic gyrnde þara fixa þe on Egyptum wæron. Ic
gewilnode þæs wines on þam ic ær gelustfullode to
oferdruncennysse brucan, and nu hit is me eac swilce
swyðe on gewilnunga, forþon þe ic his ær ofer gemet
breac, þa ic on worulde wæs. Eac ic her wæs swiðe
625 geþrest for þyses westenes wæterwædlnysse, uneaðe þa
frecendlican nydþearfnysse adreogende. Me wæs swilce
swiðlic lust þæra sceandlicra sceopleoða me gedrefdon,
þonne hi me on mode gebrohton þa deoflican leoþ to
singanne þe ic ær on worulde geleornode. Ac ic þonne
630 mid þam wepende, mine breost mid minum handum
cnyssende, and me sylfe myngode mines foregehates and
þære mundbyrdnysse þe ic ær fore geceas, and swa geond
f.131v þis weste hreafigende* | þurh min geðoht, becom toforan
þære godan and þære halgan Godes cennestran anlic-
635 nysse, þe me ær on hyre truwan underfeng. And ic
beforan hyre wepende bæd, þæt heo me fram aflymde þa
fulan geðances þe mine earman sawla swencton. Ðonne
ic soðlice oferflowendlice sorgigende weop, and ic
heardlice mine breost cnyssende þonne geseah leoht
640 gehwanon me ymbutan scinende, and me þonne sona
sum staþolfæstlic smyltnyss to becom.
    'Ara me nu, abbud. Hu mæg ic ðe gecyðan mine
geþances, ða ic me ondræde* eft genydan to þam geligre,
þæt swyðlice fyr minne ungesæligan lichaman innan ne

---

617 manðwæra] fullra written above ðwæra in a later hand.
631 me] written above the line and comma-like sign below.
639 geseah] geseah ic

thoughts that often oppressed me come into my mind, namely that I may again experience some tribulation from those same thoughts.'

Zosimus said, 'O lady, do not leave out anything that you may not reveal to me, but divulge everything in its proper order.'

(19) Then she said, 'Abbot, believe me, for seventeen years I struggled against the lusts of appetites of the placid and irrational wild animals. When I began to feel hungry, then my desires were for meats. I longed for the fish that I used to have in Egypt. I desired the wine in which formerly I loved to indulge to the point of drunkenness, and now likewise it is still very much in my desires, because formerly I indulged in it to excess, when I was in the world. I was also very thirsty here because of the desert's lack of water, and was hardly able to bear the terrible need. Likewise I had an excessive desire for lewd songs [that] troubled me, when they brought it into my mind to sing the devil's songs which I had learned formerly in the world. But when this happened I would weep and beat my breast with my hands, and I would remind myself of my vow and of the surety I had previously chosen; and so eagerly I would come in my thoughts before the image of the good and the holy mother of God, who had previously received me in covenant with her. And weeping in front of her I would ask that she would drive away from me the foul thoughts that afflicted my wretched soul. Then indeed I wept in my over-whelming grief, and as I beat my breast hard I saw then a light shining everywhere about me, and at once a secure peace came upon me then.

'Pardon me now, abbot. How can I reveal my thoughts to you, which I feared might drive me again to sexual depravity, causing an intense fire to burn up my unhappy body from

645   forbernde? And me eallunga þræscende to þære hæmetes
        [. . .]* þonne geseah þyllice geþohtas on astigan, þonne
        astrehte ic me sylfe on eorðan and þa wangas mid tearum
        ofergeat, forðon þe ic to soðan gehihte me ætstandan þa
        ðe ic [. . .]* me sylfe ær of þære eorðan, ær me seo swete
650   stemn* gewunelice oferlihte and me ða gedrefedan
        geðohtas fram aflymde. Symle ic witodlice minre heortan
        eagan to þære minre borhhanda on nydþearfnysse up
        ahof, and hi biddende þæt heo me gefultumode on þysum
        westene to rihtre dædbote, þa þe þone ealdor æghwilcre
655   clænnysse acende. And þus ic seofontyne geare rynum on
        mænigfealdum frecednyssum, swa swa ic ær cwæð,
        winnende wæs on eallum þingum oþ þisne andweardan
        dæg, and me on fultume wæs and mine wisan reccende
        seo halige Godes cennestre.'

660   Zosimus hire to cwæð, 'And ne beþorftest þu nanre
        andlyfene oððe hræglunge?'

            Heo him andswarode and cwæð, 'Seofontyne gear,
        swa ic þe ær sæde, ic notode þære hlafa, and syððan be
        þam wyrtum leofode þe ic on þysum westene funde. Se
665   gegyrla witodlice þe ic hæfde sona swa ic Iordanem
f.132r oferfor mid swiðlicre ealdunge totorene | forwurdon, and
        ic syþþan mænigfeald earfeðu dreah, hwilum þære isihtan
        cealdnysse þæs wintres, hwilum þæs unmætan wylmes
        þære sunnan hæto. Ic wæs grimlice beswæled for þam
670   micclan byrne and eft for þære micclan forstigan
        cealdnysse þæs wintres, swa þæt ic foroft ofdune on þa
        eorðan, and forneah eallunga unastyrigendlic butan gaste
        læg.

            'Þus ic wæs lange on mænigfealdum and mislicum
675   nydþearfnyssum and on unmætum costnungum winnende
        and wraxligende, and me þa siþþan oþ þeosne
        andweardan dæg and mine earman sawle and minne
        lichaman þæt godcundlice mægen geheold, mid me sylfre
        symle smeagende of hu micclum yfelum heo me alysde.

---

646 þonne geseah] geseah þonne. geþohtas] *after this* ongunnon *is
written above the line in a later hand.*

within? When I felt such thoughts arising in me, which completely tormented me with the thought of intercourse, then I stretched myself out on the ground and drenched my cheeks with tears, because I hoped in truth that she would stand beside me, whom I [. . .] myself from the ground before that sweet voice shone upon me as usual and drove my troubled thoughts away from me. Constantly in truth I raised up the eyes of my heart to my guarantor in my necessity, begging her that in this desert she might help me to proper penitence, she who gave birth to the source of all chastity. And thus for the course of seventeen years, I have been, as I said before, struggling in all respects against perils of many kinds, until this present day; and the holy mother of God was my help and the guide of my ways.'

Zosimus said to her, 'And did you not need any food or clothing?'

She answered him and said, 'For seventeen years, as I have told you already, I used the loaves, and afterwards I lived on the plants that I found in this desert. The clothing I had at the time when I crossed over the Jordan wore out, torn to pieces with extreme old age, and afterwards I suffered hardships of many kinds, sometimes from the icy coldness of winter, sometimes from the intense scorching of the sun's heat. I was terribly seared from the great burning and again by the extreme frosty coldness of winter, so that very often I lay down on the ground, almost completely motionless without breath.

'So for a long time I was struggling and striving with many and various kinds of distresses and with inordinate temptations, and afterwards until this present day divine power has preserved me and my wretched soul and my body, while I have constantly reflected in myself from how many evils it

680 Soðlice ic eom afeded of þam genihtsumestan wistmettum minre fylle, þæt is mid þam hihte minre hæle,
and ic eom oferwrigen mid þam oferbrædelse Godes
wordes, se ðe ealle þincg befehð and befædmað. Ne
leofað na se man soðlice be hlafe anum ac of æghwilcum
685 worde þe forðgæð of Godes muþe.'*

(20) Zosimus þa witodlice gehyrende þæt heo þæra
haligra boca cwydas forðbrohte, ægðer ge of þam
godspelle and of manegum oþrum, and hire to cwæð,
'Eala modor, leornodest þu æfre sealmas oþþe oþre
690 halige gewritu?'

Ða heo þis gehyrde, þa smearcode heo wið his
weardes, þus cweðende: 'Gelyf me, ne geseah ic nænne
man buton þe, oððe wildeor, oþþe æniges cynnes nyten,
siððan ic Iordanen þæt wæter oferferde and ic hyder on
695 þis westen becom, ne ic stæfcyste witodlice ne leornode
ne þæra nanum ne hlyste þe þa smeadon and ræddon. Ac
Godes word is cucu and scearp, innan lærende þis
mennisce andgyt.

'And þis is se ende nu þæra þinga þe be me ge-
700 fremede synd. Nu ic þe halsigende and bidde þurh þæt
geflæscode Godes word þæt þu for me earmlicre
f.132v for|legenre gebidde.'

Ða heo þis cwæð, ða arn se ealda wið hire weardes
mid gebigedum cneowum, to þon þæt he hine on þa
705 eorþan astrehte, and mid wopegum tearum hlude
clypigende, 'Gebletsod sy God, se þe þa mænigfealdan
wundru ana wyrceað; and sy þu gebletsod, Drihten God,
þe me æteowdest þa wuldorfæstlicnysse þe þu on-
drædendum gyfest. Nu ic to soðan wat þæt þu nænne
710 þæra ne forlætest þe ðe gesecað.'*

Heo þa soðlice þone ealdan forene forfeng, and him
ne geþafode fulfremodlice on þa eorðan astreccan, ac
cwæð to him, 'Þas þincg þu gehyrdest, mann, eac ic þe la
halsige þurh þone Drihten Hælendne Crist urne Alysend
715 þæt þu nanum menn ne asecge, ær þan þe me God of
flæsces bendum alyse. Ac þas þincg ealle þus oncnaw-

had delivered me. Truly I am nourished to satiety with most abundant sustenance, that is, with the hope of my salvation, and I am clothed with the garment of the word of God, who embraces and encompasses all things. Man does not live by bread alone but from every word that comes forth from God's mouth.'

(20) Now when Zosimus heard that she produced sayings out of the holy books, both from the gospel and from many others, he said to her, 'O mother, did you ever learn the psalms or other holy scriptures?'

When she heard this, then she smiled towards him, speaking as follows: 'Believe me, I have never seen any person except you, neither wild beast nor animal of any kind, since I crossed over the river Jordan and came here into this desert; nor indeed have I learned letters or listened to those who studied and read. But God's word is living and keen, and teaches this human understanding from within.

'And this is the end now of all the things that were accomplished concerning me. Now I beg and beseech you through the incarnate word of God to pray for me, a wretched harlot.'

When she said this, then the old man hastened towards her on bended knees in order to throw himself to the ground, calling out loudly amidst his doleful tears, 'Blessed be God, who alone brings about wonders of many kinds; and may you be blessed, Lord God, who have revealed to me the glory that you grant to those who fear you. Now I truly know that you do not abandon any of those who seek you.'

She forestalled the old man, however, and did not let him prostrate himself fully on the ground, but said to him, 'The things that you have heard, sir, I implore you through the Lord Saviour Christ, our Redeemer, not to tell to anyone, before God releases me from the fetters of the flesh. But now that

enne,* far ham mid sibbe. And ic þe eft binnan geares
fyrste on þyssere ylcan tide æteowe, and þu me gesihst.
And do þu huru soðlice swa ic þe nu bebeode: þi halgan
720 Lenctenfæstene þæs toweardan geares efthwyrfende, ne
oferfar þu na Iordanem, swa swa gewuna synt of eowrum
mynstrum.'

Ða ongan eft Zosimus wundrian þæt heo swa ge-
wislice þæs mynstres regol cuðe, and he elles nan þincg
725 ne cwæð, þæt he God wuldrode, se þe mænigfealdlicor
gifað mannum, þonne he seo gebeden þam þe hine lufiað.

Heo þa eft cwæð, 'Onbid nu, Zosimus, swa swa ic ær
cwæð, on þinum mynstre, forðon witodlice þeah þu ær
wille faran ahwyder, þu ne miht. Þonne to þon halgan
730 æfenne þæs halgan gereordes, þæt is to þam halgan
Þurresdæge ær þam drihtenlican Easterdæge, genim
sumne dæl on gehalgodum fæte þæs godcundan lichaman
and þæs gelyffæstan blodes, and hafa mid ðe, and
geanbida min on þa healfe Iordanen þe to worulde be-
735 limpeð, oþþe ic þe to cume ða lyffestan gerynu to
onfonne. Soðlice, siþþan ic on þære cyrcan þæs eadigan
f.133r foreryneles | þæs drihtlican lichaman and his blodes me
gemænsumode ær ic Iordanen oferfore, næfre syððan ic
þæs haligdomes ne breac oððe þigde, and forþon ic bidde
740 þæt þu mine bene ne forseoh, ac þæt þu huru me bringe
þa godcundan and þa liffæstan gerynu to þære tide þe se
Hælend his ðegnas ðæs godcundlican gereordes
dælnimende dyde. Cyð þu eac Iohanne, þæs mynstres
abbude þe þu on bist, þæt he hine sylfne georne
745 besmeage and eac his heorde, forþon þær synd sume
wisan to gerihtenne and to gebetenne. Ac ic nelle þæt þu
him æt þysum cyrre þas þincg cyðe, ær þam þe God
bebeode.'

Þus cwæðende, heo eac fram þam ealdan gebedes
750 bæd, and to þam inran westene hrædlice efste.

---

731 Easterdæge] earster dæge.
737 me] ne.

everything has been disclosed, go home in peace. And within the space of a year I will appear to you again at this same time, and you will see me. And truly indeed, do as I now command you: when the holy fast of Lent comes round next year, do not cross over the Jordan at all, as people from your monastery usually do.'

Then Zosimus began to marvel again that she knew the rule of the monastery with such particularity, and he said nothing else, [except] that he glorified God, who when he is entreated gives so abundantly to people who love him.

Then she said again, 'Remain now, Zosimus, in your monastery, because in fact even though you may wish ahead of time to go anywhere, you will not be able to. Then on the holy evening of the Holy Supper, that is on the holy Thursday before the Lord's Easter Day, put into a consecrated vessel a portion of the Lord's body and of the life-giving blood, and bring it with you, and wait for me on the side of the Jordan that relates to the world, until I come to you to receive the life-giving sacramental elements. Truthfully, from the time when I participated in the Lord's body and his blood in the church of the blessed Precursor before I crossed over the Jordan, never since then have I partaken of or received the sacrament; and therefore I ask that you do not refuse my request, but rather that you bring to me the divine and life-giving sacramental elements at the time when the Saviour made his followers sharers in the divine Supper. Point out also to John, the abbot of the monastery where you are, that he should pay attention to himself and also to his flock, because there are some practices to correct and amend. But I do not want you to disclose these matters to him at this time before God tells you.'

Speaking thus, she also asked for a prayer from the old man, and rapidly hastened to the inner desert.

(21) Zosimus þa hine soðlice forð astrehte ond þa floras cyssende on þæt hire fet stodon, God wuldrigende and miccle þancas donde; and eftcyrrende, wæs herigende and blætsigende urne Drihten Hælendne Crist.

755 And he wæs eftcyrrende þurh þone ylcan siðfæt þæs westenes þe he ær þyder becom, and to þam mynstre ferde on þære ylcan tide þe heora Eastergewuna wæron togædere becuman. And eall þæt gear geornlice þa gesihðe forsweogode, læstra þinga geðrystlæcende aht

760 secgan þæs ðe he geseah, ac symle mid him sylfum geornlice God bæd þæt he him eft æteowde þone gewilnodan andwlitan, and he on mænigfealdum sworettungum þa lætnysse ðæs geares rynes* geanbidode.

Ða þa seo halige tid Lenctenfæstenes becom on þone
765 drihtenlican dæg þe we nemniað Halgan Dæg, þa gebroþru æfter þam gewunelican gebedum and sealmsangum ut foron, and he sylf on þam mynstre to lafe wearð, and þær gewunode for sumre lichamlicre mettrumnysse gehæft. And he eac swiðe georne gemunde

770 Zosimus þære halgan gebod, þa heo him sæde, þeah he ut faran wolde of his mynstre þæt he ne mihte. Swa-
f.133v þeahhwæðre, æfter naht mæne|gum dagum he hine þære seocnysse gewyrpte, and on þam mynstre drohtnode.

Soðlice, þa þa munecas ham cyrdon and on þam
775 halgan æfen þæs gereordes hi togædere gesamnodon, þa dyde he swa him ær beboden wæs and on ænne lytelne calic sende sumne dæl þæs unbesmitenan lichaman and þæs deorwurðan blodes ures Drihtnes Hælendes Cristes, and him on hand genam ænne lytelne tænel mid caricum

780 gefylledne and mid palmtreowa wæstmum, þe we hatað fingeræppla, and feawa lenticula mid wætere ofergotene, and on hrepsunge becom to Iordanes ofrum þæs wæteres, and þær sorgigende gebad þone tocyme þæs halgan wifes, þa heo þa þyder becom.

785 Zosimus nænige þinga hnappode, and geornlice þæt

---

751 ond] on, *underlined and preceded by large* 7 (= ond) *in a later hand.*

(21) Zosimus then stretched himself forward and kissed the ground on which her feet had stood, glorifying God and expressing many thanks; and as he went back he kept praising and blessing our Lord Saviour Christ. And he went back by the same path through the desert by which he had arrived there previously, and he got to the monastery at the very time when they were assembled together for their Easter observances.

And all that year he carefully kept silent about the vision, daring to say the least amount possible of what he had seen, but unceasingly within himself he prayed earnestly to God that he might show him that longed-for countenance again, and with frequent sighs he waited out the slowness of the year's course.

When the holy season of the Lenten fast came round, on the Lord's day that we call Holy Day [Sunday], the brothers went out after their customary prayers and psalms, while he himself was left behind in the monastery, and he remained there, detained by some physical illness; and he, Zosimus, remembered too, very well, the message of the saint, when she told him that even if he wanted to go out from his monastery he would not be able to. Nonetheless, after not many days he recovered from the illness and engaged in life in the monastery.

Now, when the monks returned home and gathered themselves together on the holy evening of the Supper, then he did as he had been instructed earlier and put into a small chalice a portion of the undefiled body and the precious blood of our Lord Saviour Christ, and he took in his hand a little basket filled with dried figs and with palm-tree-fruits, which we call finger-fruits [dates], and a few lentils soaked in water; and in the evening he came to the banks of the river Jordan, and sorrowing he waited for the arrival of the holy woman, when she would get there.

Zosimus did not doze at all, and eagerly surveyed the

westen beheold, and mid him sylfum smeagende þohte,
þus cweðende: 'Eala, hwæðer heo hider cumende syo,
and me ne gyme, and me eftcyrrende hwearf?'

790 Þus cwæðende and biterlice weop, and his eagan up to
þam heofone hæbbende, and eadmodlice God wæs biddende, þus cwæðende: 'Ne fremda þu, Drihten, þære
gesihðe þe þu me ærest æteowdest, þæt ic huru idel
heonone ne hwyrfe, mine synna on þreagunge berende.'

795 (22) Þus he mid tearum biddende,* him eft oþer
geþanc on befeoll, þus cweðende: 'And hu nu gif heo
cymð, hu sceall heo þas ea oferfaran, nu her nan scip nys
þæt heo to me unwurðan becuman mæge? Eala me ungesæligan, swa rihtwislicre gesihðe afremdad me.'

Ða he þis þohte, þa geseah he hwær heo stod on oþre
800 healfe þæs wæteres. Zosimus soðlice, hi geseonde, mid

---

788 eftcyrrende hwearf] *lightly underlined.*
789 Þus cwæðende] þus *and beginning of* cwæðende *lightly*
underlined.
792 þe] *the passage between* þe *and* þæra *(line 805) copied twice. The*
edited text follows the first copying. The second copying (B), which
shows disagreements (highlighted below in the apparatus), reads as
follows, in edited form:
þe þu me ærest æteowdest, þæt ic huru heonon idel ne hwyrfe,
mine synna onþreagunge ne bere [*an error for* berende (= *Latin*
portans)].'
Ðus mid tearum | [f. 134r] biddende, him eft oþer geþanc on
befeoll, þus cwæðende: 'And hu nu gif heo cymð, hu sceal heo þas
wættru oferfaran, nu her nan scip nis þæt heo to me unwurðum
becuman mæge? Eala me ungesæligan, swa rihtwislicre gesihðe
afremdad me.'
Ða he þis þohte, þa geseah he þær heo stod on oþre healfe þæs
wæteres. Zosimus soðlice, heo [*sic*] to geseonne, mid micclum
gefean wynsumigendum and God wuldrigende up aras, swaþeahhwæðere on his mode tweonigende hu heo mihte Iordanes wætru
oferfaran. Þa geseah he witodlice þæt heo mid Cristes rode tacne
Iordanes wæter bletsode. Soðlice, ealra þæra
792-93 idel heonone] B heonon idel. berende] B ne bere.
794 he] *not in B.*
795 cweðende] B cwæðende.
796 sceall] B sceal. ea] B wættru. nys] B nis.
797 unwurðan] B unwurðum.
799 hwær] B þær.
800 hi geseonde] B heo to geseonne.

desert, and he considered within himself and thought, saying this: 'O, will she come here and not notice me, and has she turned from me and departed?'

As he said this, he wept bitterly, and raising his eyes up to heaven he humbly prayed to God, speaking as follows: 'Do not keep me, Lord, from the vision which formerly you showed to me, so that I do not depart from here in vain, bearing my sins in reproach.'

(22) As he prayed tearfully, another thought occurred to him again, and he said this: 'And if she does come, how is she to cross this river, since there is no ship here so that she can come to me in my unworthiness? O unhappy me, kept away as I am from so righteous a sight.'

As he thought this, he noticed then where she stood on the other side of the river. Seeing her, Zosimus now rose up with

micclum wynsumigendum gefean and God wuldrigende
up aras, swaþeahhwæðere on his mode tweonigende hu
heo mihte Iordanes wæteru oferfaran. Þa geseah he
witodlice þæt heo mid Cristes rode tacne Iordanes
805 wæteru bletsode. Soðlice, ealra þæra nihte þeostru þa ðæs
monan byrhtnyss onlihte, sona swa heo þære rode tacn on
þa wætru drencte. Swa eode heo onuppan þa hnescan yða
wið his weardes, gangende swa swa on drigum. Zosimus
wundrigende and teoligende his cneowa to bigenne hire
810 ongeanweardes,* heo ongan of þam wættrum clypian and
forbeodan, and þus cwæð: 'Hwæt dest þu, abbud? Wite
þæt þu eart Godes sacerd and þa godcundan geryne þe
mid hæbbende.'

He þa sona hire hyrsumigende, up aras. Sona swa heo
815 of þam wæterum becom, þa cwæð heo to him, 'Fæder,
bletsa me.'

Witodlice, him an gefor swiðlic wafung on swa
wuldorfæstan wuldre, and þa þus cwæð: 'Eala þu
soðfæsta, god is se þe gehet him sylfum gelice beon þa þe
820 hi sylfe ær clænsiað. Wuldor sy þe, Drihten God, þu þe
me þurh þas þine þeowene æteowdest hu micel ic [. . .]*
on minre agenre gesceawunge on þam gemete þæra oþra
fulfremodnysse.'

Þus cweðende, ða bæd heo Maria þæt heo ongunne
825 þæt rihtgeleaffulnysse gebæd, þæt is *Credo in Deum*, and
þæræfter þæt drihtenlice gebæd, *Pater noster*. Þyssum
gefylledum, þa brohte heo þam ealdan sibbe coss, swa
swa hit þeaw is, and þær onfeng þam halgum gerynum
Cristes lichaman and blodes mid abrædedum handum.
830 And in þa heofon locigende and mid tearum geomr-
f.134v igende, and þus cwæð: 'Forlæt nu, | Drihten, þine
þeowene æfter þinum worde in sibbe faran, forþon þe

---

801 wynsumigendum gefean] *B* gefean wynsumigendum.
803 wæteru] *B* wætru.
805 wæteru] *B* wæter.
806 byrhtnyss] byrhnysse, *with* t *written above, and comma-like sign
below.*
817 him an] *Skeat; J* híman.

great happiness and joy, glorifying God, though he was uncertain in his mind how she would be able to cross the waters of the Jordan. Then, however, he noticed that she blessed the waters of the Jordan with the sign of the cross of Christ. Truly, the brightness of the moon lit up the darkness of the whole night, as soon as she plunged the sign of the cross into the waters. Thus she made her way towards him on top of the soft waves, walking as though on dry land. As Zosimus marvelled and made to bend his knees towards her, she began to call out and restrain him, and she spoke as follows: 'What are you doing, abbot? Remember that you are a priest of God and you have the divine sacramental elements with you.'

He obeyed her at once then and got up. As soon as she arrived from the waters, she said to him, 'Father, bless me.'

Now, extreme astonishment came upon him at so magnificent a glory, and then he said this: 'O righteous one, good is he who has promised that those who have first purified themselves will be like himself. Glory be to you, Lord God, who have shown me through this servant of yours how much in my own estimation I [am inferior] in comparison to the perfection of those others.'

When he had spoken thus, then she, Mary, asked that she might begin the prayer of true faith, that is *Credo in Deum*, and after that the Lord's Prayer, *Pater noster*. These having been completed, she offered the old man the kiss of peace, as is customary, and there she received the holy sacramental elements of Christ's body and blood, with outstretched hands. And looking towards heaven and sorrowing tearfully, she spoke as follows: 'Lord, let now your servant go in peace according to your word, for my eyes have seen your

mine eagan gesawon þine hælo.'*

And eft to þam ealdan cwæð, 'Miltsa me, abbud, and
835 gefyl nu oþer gebæd minre bene. Gang nu to þinum
mynstre mid Godes sibbe gereht, and cum nu ymb geares
rynu to þam burnan þe wytt unc ærest gespræcon. Ic þe
bidde for Gode þæt þu þis ne forhæbbe, ac þæt þu cume,
and þu me þonne gesihst, swa swa God wile.'
840 Þa cwæð he to hire, 'Eala, wære me gelyfed þæt ic
moste þinum swaðum fyligan and þines deorwurðan
andwlitan gesihðe brucan! Ac ic bidde þe, modor, þæt þu
me ealdan anre lytelre bene getyðige, þæt þu lytles
hwæthwegu gemedemige underfon me, þæs ðe ic hider
845 brohte.'

And þus cwæð: 'Do hider þone tænel þe ic me mid
brohte.'*

Heo þa sona mid hire ytemestan fingrum þære
lenticula, þæt syndon pysan, heo onhran, and on hire muð
850 sende þreora corna gewyrde, and þus cwæð, þæt þæs
gyfe genihtsumode þe þære sawle staðol unwemme
geheold. And heo cwæð to þam ealdan, 'Gebide for me,
and for mine ungesælignysse gemunde.'*

He sona hire fet mid tearum oþran, biddende þæt heo
855 on þa halgan Godes gesamnunga gebæde. And hine þa
alet wepende and heofende, and he ne geðyrstlæhte æniga
þinga heo to lettenne; heo æniga þinga gelet beon ne
mihte.

(23) Heo þa eft mid ðære halgan rode gedryncnysse
860 Iordanem oþhrinan ongan, and ofer þa hnescan yða þæs
wæteres eode, swa swa heo ær dyde þyderweardes.
Zosimus þa soðlice wearð micclan gefean cyrrende, and
færlice wearð mid micclan ege gefylled. Swiðlice hine
sylfne hreowsigende þreade þæt he þære halgan naman

---

836 gereht] *lightly underlined.*
839 gesihst] gesiht, *with* s *written above the line and comma-like sign below.*
844 underfon] underfoh.
860 oþhrinan] oþrinan, *with* h *written above the line and comma-like sign below.* ongan] *Skeat; not in* J.

salvation.'

And then she said to the old man, 'Have mercy on me, abbot, and carry out another prayer which I request. Go now to your monastery guided with the peace of God, and come then after the course of a year to the stream where the two of us first spoke together. I ask you in the name of God not to refuse this, but to come, and you will see me then, in accordance with God's will.'

Then he said to her, 'O that I might be allowed to follow in your footsteps and enjoy the sight of your precious face! But I ask you, mother, to grant a little request from me, an old man, namely that you condescend to accept from me some little of what I have brought here.'

And he said this: 'Pass to me here the basket I brought with me.'

Then at once she touched the lentils, which are peas, with the tips of her fingers, and she put the amount of three grains in her mouth, and said that this gift was sufficient to keep the condition of the soul undefiled. And she said to the old man, 'Pray for me, and protect me in my unhappiness.'

Straightaway amidst his tears he touched her feet, asking that she pray in respect of the holy church of God. And then weeping and sighing she left him, and he did not dare to hinder her in any respect; in no respect could she be hindered.

(23) Then she began to touch the Jordan again by dipping the holy cross in it, and she went over the soft waves of the river, just as she had done before on the way there. So Zosimus returned then with great joy, and he was suddenly filled with great awe. He sorrowfully blamed himself severely

865 ne axode; þeahhwæðere, hopode þæt he þy æfterfyligendan geare þæt gewiste.

(24) Þa æfter oferfarenum þæs geares ryne, becom on
þæt widgille westen and geornlice efste to þære
wuldorlican gesihðe, and þær lange hyderes and þyderes
f.135r secende for, oþþæt he sum swutol | tacn þære gewilnedan
gesihðe and wilnunge þære stowe undergeat, and he
geornlice mid his eagena scearpnyssum hawigende ge on
þa swiðran healfe ge on þa wynstran, swa swa se
gleawesta* hunta, gif* he þær mihte þæt sweteste wildeor
875 gegripan. Ða he þa styrigendlices nan þincg findan ne
mihte, þa ongan he hine sylfne mid tearum ofergeotan,
and mid upahafenum eagum gebæd and cwæð,
'Geswutela me, Drihten, þæt gehydde goldhord þe þu me
sylfum ær gemedemodest æteowan, ic bidde þe, Drihten,
880 for þinum wuldre.'

(25) Ða he þus gebeden hæfde, þa becom he to þære
stowe þær se burna getacnod wæs, þær hi ærest spræcon,
and þær standende on oþre healfe geseah swa swa
scinende sunne and þæs halgan wifes lichaman orsawle
885 licgende, and þa handa swa heo gedafenodon alegdon
beon, and eastweardes gewende. Ða sona þyder arn, and
hire fet mid his tearum þwoh; ne geþrystlæhte he soðlice
nan oþer þæs lichaman oðhrinan. And þa mid micclum
wope þære byrgenne gebæd geworhte, mid sealmsange
890 and mid oþrum gebedum þe to þære wisan belumpon. Þa
ongan he þencan hwæðer hit hire licode. Þa he þis ðohte,
þa wæs þær an gewrit on þære eorðan getacnod, þus
gecweden: 'Bebyrig, abbud Zosimus, and miltsa Maria
lichaman. Ofgif þære eorðan þæt hire is, and þæt dust to
895 þam duste geic.* Eac gebidde þeahhwæðere for me of
þyssere worulde hleorende on þam monðe Aprilis þære

---

865 ne] *Skeat; not in J.*
874 þæt] þæs.
894 lichaman] lichama.
895 geic] ge ic, *lightly underlined.* of] on, *changed to* of *by later hand.*
896 þyssere] þysserere, *with line through last two letters.* monðe]
monðe þe.

that he had not asked the name of the saint; however, he hoped that he would learn it the following year.

(24) Then when the course of the year had passed, he came into the vast desert and eagerly hastened to the glorious vision, and he travelled for a long time seeking hither and thither, until he he perceived some clear sign of the longed-for vision and the place of his desire, as he eagerly looked both to the right and to the left with the keenness of his eyes, just like the the most skilful hunter, seeing if he might be able to catch there the sweetest wild animal. When he could not find anything that moved, then he began to soak himself with tears, and with upraised eyes he prayed and said, 'Reveal to me, Lord, that hidden treasure of gold which formerly you condescended to show to me – I ask you, Lord, for the sake of your glory.'

(25) When he had prayed thus, he arrived then at the place where the stream was marked out, where they had first spoken, and he saw there situated on the other side what looked just like a shining sun and the body of the holy woman lying lifeless, and the hands were arranged as was proper for them to be, and it was turned to the east. He ran there at once then and washed her feet with his tears; in truth he did not dare to touch any other part of the body. And with much lamentation he performed a service for burial, with psalm-singing and other prayers that pertained to the occasion. Then he began to consider whether this would be pleasing to her. As he was considering this, there was a written message marked out on the ground, expressed as follows: 'Abbot Zosimus, bury and have mercy on the body of Mary. Commit to the earth that which belongs to it, and add dust to dust. Also pray for me, moreover, departing from this world on the ninth night

nigeþan nihte, þæt is Idus Aprelis,* on þam drihtenlican
gereorddæge, and æfter þam huslgange.'

(26) Þa se ealda þa stafas rædde, þa sohte he ærest
900 hwa hi write, forþan þe heo sylf ær sæde þæt heo næfre
naht hwilces ne leornode. Swaþeah, he on þam swiðe
wynsumigende geseah þæt he hire naman wiste, and he
swutole ongeat sona swa heo þa godcundan gerynu æt
f.135v Iordane onfeng, þære ylcan | tide þyder becom, and sona
905 of middanearde gewat; and se siðfæt þe Zosimus on xx
dagum mid micclum geswince oferfor, eall þæt Maria on
anre tide ryne gefylde, and sona to Drihtne hleorde.
Zosimus þa soðlice God wuldrode, and his agene
lichaman mid tearum ofergeat, and cwæð, 'Nu is seo tid,
910 earmincg Zosimus, þæt þu gefremme þæt þe beboden is.
Ac hwæt ic nu ungesælige, forþon ic nat mid hwi ic
delfe, nu me swa wana is ægþer ge spadu ge mattuc!'

Þa he þus on his heortan digollice spræc, þa geseah he
þær swilchwugu treow licgende and þæt lytel. Ongan he
915 þærmid delfan, witodlice swiðe georne. And seo eorðe
wæs swiðe heard, and ne mihte he adelfan, forþon he
wæs swiðe gewæced ægðer ge mid fæstene ge on þam
langan geswince, and he mid sworettungum wæs
genyrwed, and mid þære heortan deopnysse geomrode.
920 Þa he hine beseah, þa geseah he unmættre micelnysse
leon* wið þære halgan lichaman standan, and hit his
fotlastes liccode. Þa wearð he gefyrht mid ege þæs
unmætan wildeores, and ealre swiðost forþon þe þæt
halige wif him ær to cwæð þæt heo þær nænig wildeor ne
925 gesawe. Ac he hine sona æghwanon mid þære rode tacne

---

897 Aprelis] in capitals.
901 he] heo.
903 heo] he.
906 Maria] in capitals.
915-16 georne. And seo eorðe wæs] georðe 7 wæs.
916 he (first)] heo.
919 mid þære heortan deopnysse geomrode] cf. G mid swate and
hefiglice geomrode of þære heortan deopnysse.

of the month of April, that is, the Ides of April, on the day of
the Lord's Supper, and after partaking in the eucharist.'

(26) When the old man read those letters, he wondered at
first who had written them, since she herself had said formerly
that she had never learned any such thing. However, he
realized, rejoicing very much about it, that he knew her name;
and he perceived clearly that as soon as she had received the
divine elements of the sacrament at the Jordan, at that same
time she had come here and had at once departed from the
world; and the journey that Zosimus had travelled in twenty
days with much hardship, Mary had fully completed in the
course of one hour, and had immediately departed to the Lord.
Truly Zosimus glorified God then, and he soaked his own
body with tears, and said, 'Now is the time, Zosimus,
unfortunate wretch, for you to carry out what has been asked
of you. But what am I [to do] now in my unhappiness, for I do
not know what to dig with, since both spade and mattock are
so lacking to me.'

When he said this secretly in his heart, then he saw lying
there some bit of wood or other, and a small one at that. He
began to dig there, really very busily. But the ground was very
hard and he could not dig, for he was very much weakened
both with fasting and from the long toil, and he was oppressed
with sighs, and he groaned from the depths of his heart.

As he looked around him, he saw a lion of enormous size
standing beside the body of the saint, and it was licking the
soles of her feet. Then he became terrified with fear of the
enormous wild beast, and especially because the holy woman
had told him previously that she had not seen any wild beast
there. But at once he armed himself on all sides with the sign

gewæpnode and mid mægene þære licgendan. Þa ongan
seo leo fægnian wið þæs ealdan weard, and hine mid his
leoðum styrgendum* grette. Zosimus þa soðlice to þam
leon cwæð, 'Eala þu mæste wildeor, gif þu fram Gode
930 hider asend wære to þon þæt þu þissere halgan Godes
þeowene lichaman on eorþan befæste, gefyll nu þæt
weorc þinre þenunge. Ic witodlice for yldum gewæht
eom, þæt ic delfan ne mæg, ne naht gehyðes hæbbe þis
weorc *to begangenne, ne ic efstan ne mæg swa myccles*
935 *siðfætes hider to bringanne. Ac þu nu mid þære*
godcundan hæse þis weorc mid þinum clifrum do, oþþæt
wit þisne halgan lichaman on eorðan befæston.'

(27) Sona æfter his wordum seo leo mid hire clifrum
earmum scræf geworhte, swa micel swa genihtsumode
f.136r þære halgan lichaman to byrgenne; and he mid | his
tearum hire fet ðwoh, and mid forðagotenum tearum
mænigfealdlice bæd þæt heo for eallum þingode; and swa
þone lichaman on eorðan oferwreah, swa nacode swa he
hi ærest gemette, buton gewealdan þæs toslitenan
945 rægeles, þe he Zosimus hire ær to wearp, of þam Maria
sumne hire lichaman* bewæfde. And heo þa ætgædere
cyrdon, seo leo in þæt inran westen, swa swa þæt
mildeste lamb. Ða gewat Zosimus to his mynstre, God
wuldrigende and bletsigende and mid lofum herigende.
950 Sona swa he to þam mynstre becom, þa rehte he heom
eallum of frymðe þa wisan, and naht ne bediglode ealra
þæra þinga þe he geseah oððe gehyrde, þæt hi ealle
Godes mærða wurðodon, and mærsodon þære eadigan
forðfore dæg. Iohannes soðlice ongeat sume þa

---

926 mægene] *Skeat; J* mænege; *cf. G* gewæpnode mid gewisse
truwiende þæt hine ungederodne geheolde þæt mægn þæs licgendan.
934-36 *to begangenne . . . weorc*] *material in italics supplied from G;*
not in J, in which the preceding þis weorc *has been underlined.*
936 do] *G; not in J.*
940 lichaman] *G; not in J.*
941 tearum *(first)*] *followed by erasure of two-letter word.*
951 of] n *written above* f, *with comma-like mark below; G* of.
953 þære] *preceded by large capital* 7 *in left-hand margin, in later*
hand.

of the cross and with the power of the person lying there. Then the lioness began to fawn at the old man and to greet him with its moving limbs. Zosimus then said to the lion, 'O greatest wild beast, if you were sent here by God in order that you should commit the body of this holy servant of God to the earth, perform now the task of your duty. In truth I am weakened with old age, so that I cannot dig; nor have I anything suitable to carry out this task, nor am I able to rush away on so great a journey to bring anything here. But you do this task with your claws, in accordance with the divine command, until the two of us have committed this holy body to the earth.'

(27) Immediately after his words the lioness made a pit with the claws of its forelegs, as big as was suitable for burying the saint, while he washed her feet with his tears, and as he poured forth his tears he offered manifold prayers that she would intercede for all; and so he covered over the body in the earth, as naked as when he first met her, except for the protection of the torn garment which Zosimus had formerly thrown to her, with which Mary had covered some part of her body. And they went away together, the lion heading into the inner desert, just like the gentlest lamb. Then Zosimus departed to his monastery, glorifying and blessing God and extolling him with praises.

As soon as he arrived at the monastery he related the matter to them all from the beginning, and concealed nothing of all the things that he had seen or heard, so that they all exalted the glories of God and celebrated the day of the passing of the saint. John indeed perceived that some of the

955 mynsterwisan to gerihtanne, swa swa seo halige ær
     foresæde, ac he þa sona Gode fultumigendum gerihte.
     Zosimus on þam mynstre wæs drohtnigende an hund
     wintra, and þa to Drihtne hleorde. Wuldor sy urum
     Drihtne Hælendum Criste, þe leofað and rixað a on
960 worulda woruld. Amen.

---

956 gerihte] *G; not in J.*
960 Amen] *in capitals, with* n *stretched out to fill the whole line*
(AMEN *being the only word on this last line of the text). Text ends on
line 19 of f. 136r, with rest of the page (= 13 lines) blank; f. 136v also
blank*

practices of the monastery had to be corrected, just as the saint had previously mentioned, but with the help of God he immediately corrected them. Zosimus served in that monastery for a hundred years and then departed to the Lord. Glory be to our Lord Saviour Christ, who lives and reigns for ever, world without end. Amen.

COMMENTARY

5 *Paulus*: On Paul, see Introduction, n. 4.

11-14 *Soðlice . . . bediglige*: Tobit 12. 7.

12 *man cynnes*: Written as one word in J. Although the reading *man cynnes* makes tolerable sense, *cynnes* is probably a mistake for *cyninges*, corresponding to *regis* (Latin, line 5). Skeat reads *man mancynnes*.

16-18 *þæs slawan . . . on eorðan*: Cf. Matth. 25. 14-30.

45-46 *þæs ðe hi rehton, þæt he wære*: 'As they recounted, (that) he was'; note also *swa he sylf sæde Zosimus, þæt he sylf wære* (lines 55-56), 'as Zosimus himself said, (that) he himself was'. In these passages the first clauses seem to be parenthetical but are followed by subjunctive *þæt* noun clauses where we would expect principal clauses to occur. The unusual grammatical form may be due to scribal error (though in both cases O agrees with J), but see Bruce Mitchell, *Old English Syntax*, 2 vols (Oxford: Clarendon Press, 1985), § 1980, where comparable formulations are discussed.

50 *Eadige . . . geseoð*: Matth. 5. 8.

55-56 *swa he sylf sæde Zosimus, þæt he sylf wære*: See comment on lines 45-46.

56 *modorlicum beorðrum*: DOE comments (*beorþor*, 3), 'in the dative plural . . . erroneously rendering *ulnis* "arms" (? as if *vulvis*); perhaps "mother's womb" or "uterus"'.

68 *Ðas . . . þencendum*: On the use of 'absolute' phrases in the Old English *Life*, see Introduction, pp. 49-50.

69 *engel*: This word is not paralleled in texts of the Latin, which agree in having *quidam*, 'someone' (line 78).

99 *ac*: Superfluous conjunctions are a feature of our text. In view of the general grammatical precision of the *Life*, with its

self-conscious Latinate quality (see Introduction, pp. 43-50), these should be seen as due to scribal interference. This conclusion is borne out by the fact that there is disagreement between J, O and G in the incidence of such conjunctions.

And, in particular, often appears pleonastically in the *Life*, as in *Þus cwæðende and biterlice weop*, 'thus speaking (and) bitterly wept' (line 789), and *And in þa heofon locigende and mid tearum geomgigende, and þus cwæð*, 'And looking to the heavens and lamenting with tears (and) thus spoke' (lines 830-31); cf. also lines 631, 705, 751-54 etc. Note the following variants: *and æfter þysum* (J)/*æfter þisum* (O), '(and) after this' (line 58); *And he wæs þus sprecende* (J)/*þus sprecende* (O), '(And he was) speaking thus' (lines 61-62); *and ic me sylfe heom befæste* (J)/*forþam ic me sylfe heom befæste* (O), '(and/beacuse) I will give myself over to them' (in which neither conjunction seems satisfactory) (line 399); *ic cwæð to hire geornlice and unforbugendlice behealdende* (J)/*ic cwæð to hire geornlice unforbugendlice behealdende* (G), 'I spoke to her earnestly (and) beholding her unswervingly' (lines 491-92); *hawigende and eft clypigende* (J)/*hawiende clypode* (G)/*hawigende eft clypode* (O), 'gazing and crying out again/gazing cried out/gazing cried out again' (lines 559-60); *and aheardodon* (J)/*aheardodon* (O), '(and) became hard' (lines 602-3); *and ealre swiðost forþon* (J)/*ealre swiðost forþam* (G), '(and) especially because' (line 923).

113 *mete*: J lacking a noun to go with *ungeteorodne*, the most obvious candidate would appear to be *mete*, corresponding to Latin *cybum*, 'food' (line 128); Skeat, *þeaw*.

137 *gesetnysse*: The non-standard nominative -*e* spelling in abstract nouns of this kind is unusual in our text, but note also *neadþearfnysse* (line 160); and see A. Campbell, *Old English Grammar* (Oxford: Clarendon Press, 1959), § 592 (*f*).

150 *Dominus illuminatio mea et salus mea; quem timebo*: Psalm 26 (27). 1, 'The Lord is my light and my deliverance; whom shall I fear?' The Latin version gives the whole of this verse, adding *Dominus defensor uitae meae; a quo trepidabo*, 'The Lord is the defender of my life; whom shall I hold in dread?' (lines 159-60).

159 *[. . .]*: The deficiency here is perhaps due to the accidental omission of *þam þe* after *mid* (the scribe may have been distracted by the similar-looking *mid þam wyrtum þe* in the next line): *mid þam þe*, 'when', would correspond directly to Latin *quando* (line 169). If this suggestion is correct, *neadþearfnysse* should be taken as nominative (see comment on line 137).

166 *æghwilcne*: Evidently a mistake for *æghwilc*, probably attracted into the accusative because of the influence of the preceding *hine*.

207 *[. . .]*: There is no indication of omission in J, but a verb of perception appears to be required as does a direct object, corresponding to Latin *umbram*, 'shadow' (line 214).

236-37 *Geanbida min*: At this point Latin texts, except for C-C/C, have the further sentence *Sustine me infirmum et indignum*, 'Wait for me, a weak and unworthy one' (at line 242); the OE reflects the distinctive C-C/C omission.

282 *lare*: Unlike the J reading, G *are* directly corresponds to Latin *honore*, 'honour' (line 285).

283 *godcundlican*: Genitive plural. Campbell points out that in LWS -*an* sporadically appears as the ending for this case (*Old English Grammar*, § 656).

287 *dropum*: The J reading, unlike G *dropung*, 'dripping', directly reflects the Latin *guttis*, 'drops' (line 289).

291 *geongran*: Unlike the J reading, G *strengran* directly corresponds to Latin *fortiori*, 'stronger' (line 293).

293 *lufu*: Unlike the J reading, G *gyfu* directly corresponds to Latin *gratia*, 'grace' (line 294).

336 *þæt an*: The OE reflects the distinctive C-C/C reading *tantum*, 'only' (Latin, line 331). Most other Latin texts have *autem*, 'however'.

361-2 *Ic hæfde broþor and eðel on Egyptum*: J and O agree in this reading, which is not reflected in known Latin texts. The Latin reads *Ego, frater, patriam Egyptum habui*, 'I had Egypt, brother, as my homeland' (line 383).

384 *yrmðe*: Unlike the J reading, O *myrcðe*, 'pleasure', directly reflects Latin *placabile*, 'pleasing' (line 401).

414 *swingle*: Unlike the J reading, O *spinle* directly

corresponds to Latin *fusum*, 'spindle' (line 427). A few words later, *seldon* has no equivalent in the Latin; *seldon* looks like a curious addition, since, according to the Latin (lines 398-99), Mary often made her living by spinning coarse flax (not mentioned in the OE: cf. line 381).

432 *syllendan*: Unlike the J reading, O *nellendan* directly corresponds to Latin *nolentes*, 'unwilling' (line 444). There is some disagreement among Latin texts at this point, most omitting *nolentes* in line 444 (*nolentes* also having occurred in line 443). It is likely that the OE translator was contending here with a text similar to that of C-C/C.

442-43 *he nele . . . gehwyrfednysse bið*: Cf. Ezekiel 33. 11.

446 *lichaman*: Unlike the J reading, O *gelicum* directly corresponds to Latin *similibus*, 'similar' (line 456).

452-53 *seo symbelnyss becom þære halgan deorwurðan rode upahefennysse*: On the Feast of the Exaltation of the Cross (14 September), see Michael Swanton, *The Dream of the Rood*, 2nd ed. (Exeter: University of Exeter Press, 1996), pp. 44-46. The Feast of the Exaltation goes back to the Dedication of the Holy Sepulchre in 335, and remains a major feast of the eastern churches.

456 *cyrcan*: This is the church of the Holy Sepulchre, built on the traditional site of Christ's crucifixion and of his burial and resurrection. Dedicated by Constantine in 335, it was burned by the Persians in 614, but restored shortly afterwards. Holy Sepulchre was a particular focus for veneration of the cross, housing relics of the True Cross, before they were seized in 614; see, further, Introduction, p. 8.

473 *ongean stode*: The OE follows the distinctive C-C reading *est obvia*, 'is against' (line 481). C has *minitasset*, 'had threatened', while the most Latin texts have *quasi multitudo militaris est ima taxata*, which must be corrupt but might be translated 'as though there was a host of the most lowly ranked soldiers'; cf. Greek ὥσπερ στρατιωτικῆς πληθύος τεταγμένης εἰς τοῦτο, 'just as if a large company of soldiers were arrayed for this purpose' (*PG* 87.3, 3713B; trans. Kouli, p. 82).

490-1 *þære halgan Godes cennestran anlicnysse*: On the

theme of devotion to the Virgin, see Introduction, pp. 7-8.

521 *wearð þa gelæd*: Unlike the J reading, G *wearð onæled* directly corresponds to Latin *succensa*, 'inflamed' (line 519).

533 *gefylled*: This participle corresponds to the distinctive C-C reading *repleta*, 'filled' (line 529), rather than to the 'regular' Latin reading *reperta*, 'found' (C *inuenta*, 'found'); cf. Greek γεγένημαι, 'I came to be' (*PG* 87.3, 3713D).

575-76: *to Sanctes Iohannes cyrcan þæs Fulwihteres . . . ge-sette*: The mention of a church of St John the Baptist and of Mary washing herself in the Jordan before receiving the eucharist and beginning her new life develops a theme of symbolic baptism, with the Virgin Mary acting as Mary's sponsor and guide. The Jordan, 'holiest of all rivers' (OE, line 78), has a central place in the spiritual geography of the legend: see Andrew Scheil, 'Bodies and Boundaries in the Old English *Life of St Mary of Egypt*', *Neophilologus* 84 (2000), 137-56, at p. 145.

The *Life* of the eighth-century Anglo-Saxon monk and bishop Willibald includes an account of the travels of the saint and his brother Wynnebald in the Holy Land, during which they visited the monastery of St John the Baptist and the nearby church at the place on the Jordan where Christ was baptized by John. This church, not far from Jericho, can be identified as the one at which Mary stopped:

> [They] set out for the monastery of St John the Baptist, where about twenty monks were living. They stayed the night and then went forward about a mile to the Jordan, where our Lord was baptized. At this point there is now a church built up high on columns of stone; beneath the church, however, the ground is dry. On the very place where Christ was baptized and where they now baptize there stands a little wooden cross: a little stream of water is led off and a rope is stretched over the Jordan and tied at each end. Then on the Feast of the Epiphany the sick and infirm come there and, holding onto the rope plunge them-selves in the water. Our bishop Willibald bathed himself there in the Jordan. They passed the day there and then departed. (trans. C. H. Talbot, *The Anglo-Saxon Missionaries in Germany* (London: Sheed and Ward, 1954), pp. 153-77, at p. 165; *Vita*

Willibaldi Episcopi Eichstetensis, ch. 4, 'De Transitu Willibaldi', ed. O. Holder-Egger, Monumenta Germaniae Historica,
Scriptores 15.1 (Hannover: Impensis Bibliopolii Hahniani,
1887), 86-106, at p. 96).

617-18: *ic wan . . . wildeora lustum*: The corrector's alter-
ation of *manðwæra*, 'placid, gentle', to *manfullra*, 'wicked',
reflects dissatisfaction with this passage. The Latin source
probably had *mansuetis*, 'gentle', in mistake for *inmansuetis*,
'wild'. The Latin itself is confused at this point, reading *feris
inmansuetis et inrationabilibus eluctans desideriiis*, 'struggling
with wild beasts and irrational cravings' (lines 601-2) (C-C and
C have the 'regular' reading), even though Mary later (ch. 20)
says that she has not seen any animals. Cf. Greek θηρσὶν
ἀνημέροις ταῖς ἀλόγοις ἐπιθυμίαις πυκτεόυσα, 'struggling
with irrational desires, (as if) with wild beasts' (*PG* 87.3, 3716D-
3717A; trans. Kouli, p. 85 (my brackets)).

633 *hreafigende*: This can be interpreted as a variant form of
reafigende, which might just about mean 'greedy, eager', though
the sense is strained. BT, *Suppl.*, plausibly suggests that
hreafigende has been written for *hwearfigende*, 'wandering
about'.

643 *ondræde*: Translated as present tense by Skeat, but the
verb should be taken as in the preterite indicative, thus
conforming to the rule that *þa*, 'when', occurs only with the
preterite indicative: see Mitchell, *Old English Syntax*, § 2564,
and Mitchell's article 'Some Problems of Mood and Tense in
Old English', *Neophilologus* 49 (1965), 44-57, at pp. 46-47.

646 *[. . .]*: Although there is no break in the text, the sequence
is grammatically deficient: a feminine noun such as *gewilnunga*
appears to be required, corresponding to *desiderium*, 'craving'
(Latin, line 625).

649 *[. . .]*: Again, although there is no break in the text, the
sense of the OE fails at this point, lacking an equivalent to *quae
me fidedixerat, minaci me conpellatione exagitare furentem,
quasi preuaricanti, et paenas preuaricationis mihi inminentis iram
mucronis contra me agentem. Non enim antea surgebam*, 'who
had acted as my guarantor would truly stand by me and furiously

scold me with a threatening reprimand, as a violator of my duty, and that as a punishment for my violation of duty she would bring against me the anger of a menacing sword. Afterwards I used not to get up' (Latin, lines 628-32).

650 *stemn*: The OE follows the distinctive C-C/C reading *uox*, 'voice' (Latin, line 632), where all other known Latin texts have *lux*, 'light' (= φῶς, *PG* 87.3, 3717B).

684-85 *Ne leofað na . . . of Godes muþe*: Cf. Deuteronomy 8. 3, Matthew 4. 4.

709-10 *þu nænne . . . þe ðe gesecað*: Cf. Psalm 9. 11.

716-17 *þas þincg ealle þus oncnawenne*: An example of an absolute phrase in the nominative or accusative: see Introduction, pp. 49-50.

763 *rynes*: This follows the 'regular' Latin reading *cursus*, 'course', not the aberrant C-C *Rursus*, 'again' (line 724).

794 *Þus he mid tearum biddende*: A form of nominative absolute, though the occurrence of *him* in the principal clause means that the phrase is not truly absolute: see Introduction, pp. 49-50. In B (the phrase occurs in the passage copied twice) *he* is omitted.

809-10 *Zosimus . . . ongeanweardes*: A further occurrence of a nominative absolute: see Introduction, pp. 49-50.

821 *[. . .]*: There is no indication of omission, but a verbal phrase is lacking, corresponding to *inferior sim*, 'I am lower down, inferior' (Latin, line 772).

830-33 *Forlæt þu . . . þine hælo*: Luke 2. 29.

846-47 *And þus cwæð . . . brohte*: As a response by Mary to Zosimus's previous speech, the sense of this is illogical. Even if we take Zosimus as the speaker the sense remains unsatisfactory, since he is not in the habit of telling Mary what to do. There is no direct speech at the corresponding point in the Latin (lines 792-93).

852-53 *Gebide . . . gemunde*: The OE text is unsatisfactory both in the irregular forms of the verbs and in the overall construction. The original reading would have had a form of *gemunan*, 'be mindful of, remember', corresponding to Latin *memor esto* (line 798).

874 *gleawesta*: This follows the 'regular' Latin reading *scitissimus*, 'most skilful' (= Greek ἐμπειρότατος, *PG* 87.3, 3724A), rather than the distinctive C-C/C *citissimus*, 'swiftest' (line 816).

874 *gif*: The view that this should be taken as expressing the idea of purpose in a conditional clause (as proposed by Hubert Gibson Shearin, *The Expression of Purpose in Old English Prose*, Yale Studies in English 18 (New York: Henry Holt, 1903), p. 90) is supported by the Latin reading *sicubi* (N *sicut ubi*), 'if in any place' (line 816) (= Greek εἴ που, *PG* 87.3, 3724A). Mitchell suggests that *gif* here introduces a dependent question rather than a conditional clause (*Old English Syntax*, § 2812).

894-95 *Ofgif . . . þam duste geic*: Cf. Genesis 3. 19.

897 *Idus Aprilis*: Numeral *v* needed to give the correct date; cf. Latin *v idus Aprilis* (line 838) (= 9 April).

921 *leon*: As first pointed out by F. Delmas, 'Remarques sur la vie de Sainte Marie l'Égyptienne', pp. 38-39, the lion episode is modelled on ch. 16 of Jerome's *Life of St Paul of Thebes* (*PL* 23, 17-30; trans. Carolinne White, *Early Christian Lives* (Harmondsworth: Penguin, 1998), pp. 76-84), in which the aged Antony performs Paul's funeral rites in the remote desert. In Jerome's account there are two lions, which suddenly appear as Antony is lamenting that he has no spade with which to dig the earth and that he is too far from the monastery to go there to get one. Antony is terrified at the sight of the lions, but they act tamely towards him. They dig a grave with their paws, and afterwards lick Antony's hands and feet.

927-28 *mid his leoðum styrgendum*: The G reading *mid liþum styrungum*, 'with gentle movements', directly translates the Latin *blandis motibus* (line 869).

946 *lichaman*: Mitchell persuasively argues that this is accusative, agreeing with *sumne*, not partitive genitive (*Old English Syntax*, § 406).

VARIANT READINGS

O, *Incipit*, as transcribed by Wanley (see Introduction, pp. 15-16) (lines 1-3). 1 herigendlicestan] herigendlicestra. gehwyrfednysse] gehwyrfednesse. 3 gewinn] gewin. arwurðan Egyptiscan] arwyrðan Egiptiscan.

O, ff. 26 and 56 (lines 12-111). *Due to fire damage (see Intro-duction, p. 15), parts of the O fragments are not clearly legible, and some parts are completely illegible, so that a full collation is not possible. In particular, f. 56 is legible only in a few places in the top part of each side, and even then barely so. This leaf is not collated here.*[1] (f. 26) *Begins* is micel genyþerung. 13 genyðrung] genyþerung. mon] man. 15 forsuwige] forswugige. þa] þas. geræcednyssa] gerecednesse. Se me gecydde þæt ic on gefealle] þæt ic hine cyðe þyles þe ic gefealle. 16 genyðredan] geniþeredan. 17 þeowes] þeowes; *J* þeawas. talent] sceat *(?: in-distinct).* 18 ahydde on eorðan] on eorðan ahydde. 19 ungeleaf-ful] ungeleaful. 20 þissa] þas. gewurðe hit] geweorðe hit la næfre. 21 gerecednyssum] gerecednessum. 22 forsuwige] for-mirðrige þy les þe ic wið god gesyngige . . . *(some words lost at end of line).* 23 *rubric*] *omitted.* 25 wæs swiþe] swyþe. 26 fram] fram his. 27 getyd] getid. Se wæs gehaten Zosimus] and his nama his zosimus. 29 fram frymþe drohtnode] wæs fram frymðe drohtniende. forhæfednysse] hæftnysse. 32 fulfremednysse þæs]

---

[1] The electronic edition of MS Cotton Otho B. x currently being prepared by Kevin Kiernan, using ultraviolet imaging, will make possible a more com-plete collation of this text of the *Life of St Mary of Egypt*; see Linda Miller Cantara, 'St Mary of Egypt in BL Cotton Otho B. X: New Textual Evidence for an Old English Saint's Life' (MA diss., University of Kentucky, 2001), online at 'http://lib.uky.edu/ETD/ukyengl2001t00018/htlm/cantara.htm'.

fulfremednesse þes. þeowtscypes] leodscipes. 33 swilce wisan] swylce manige wisan. þær sylf] self þær. 34 geihte] geyhte. forþan] forþam. gewilnode] wilnode. 35 fulfremod] fulfremed. 36 munecas] manega munecas. 37 feorrum] feor. of] *omitted.* to him comon] coman. hi to his bysne and to his larum] hy to his bysenum and larum. 38 gewriðon] gewriðen. to þære onhyringe his forhæfednysse hi underðeoddon] to his geferrednysse hi underþeodan. 40 he *(first)] om.* on him hæbbende wæs] hæfde on him. 41 haligra] haliga. 42 awende] ut awænde. 43 gastbrucende] gastlice brucende. hæfde . . . wæs] hæfde þæt is þæt he næfre. 44 sealmsang, mærsung, and haligra gewrita smeagung] sealmsanga and haligra gewrita smeagunga. 45 swilce] swylce. 46 godcundan] godcunda. 47 æteowednysse] ætywednysse. 48 gesihþe] gesyhþe. 49 þincg] *om.* þe] *om.* 50 forðan] forþam. 52 heora] hira. lichaman symle] lichoman symble. 54 underfonde] underfonde; *J* to under. 55 swa] swa swa. 56 sylf] *om.* beorðrum] beoðrum. 57 fiftigðe] fifteowðe. 58 drohtnigende] drohtniende. and æfter þysum] æfter þisum. 59 geþancum] geþohtum. 61 lare ne bysene] lare ne bysne. And he wæs] *om.* 62 me mage] mage me. 63 niwes] nywes. 64 þæt] þe. *(f. 26v ends; f. 56 not collated.)*

G, f. 4 (lines 268-352). *Due to damage to the leaf (see Introduction, p. 15), many words and sequences of words in the first fragment of G are lacking or illegible. Letters in italics are indistinct or uncertain. Begins* ...s onfeng. 269 and gegyrede hire] *om.* 270 beheligenne] oferhelianne. 271 Heo þa] and heo ða hi. 276 on þa eorðan hine astrehte] on eorðan streccan *(following words lacking).* 277 ongean hi astrehte] ongean þam heo eac hi astrehte. 278 bæd] wilnode. 279 manega] manegra. 280 Zosime] Zosimum. biddenne] gebiddanne. 281 bletsigenne] bletsianne. forþan þu] forðam þe ðu. 282 lare] are. 283 gyfum þæra godcundlican, æt his] gyfum his godcundlicnesse and his. 284 þeowigende] *þeow*iende. 285 Ðas] Ða. gebrohton on] ongebrohton. 286 fyrhtu] fyrhto. 287 dropum] dropung. sworettan] sprecan. 288 eallunga] eallinga. on þam oreðe] and þam orðe. 290 forþam þu eart soðlice Godes þinen. Geþinga me nu, of þam geongran

dæle for þyssere worulde dead [*J* deað] gefremed] forðam þe þu
eart beforan drihtne geþungen and of þam strengran dæle þisse
worulde dead gefremed. 293 lufu] gyfu. 295 oncnawen] na on-
cn*awen*. 296 is hi [*J* he is] to getacnigenne] is hi to getacnienne.
297 þæt unbereafigendlice gebæd] þæt beþearflice *ge*bed. 299
ongan heo [*J* he] hire onemnþrowigan] ongann heo emþrowian.
300 se ðe is] om. 301 hælu tiligende] hælo tiliend. 302 Zosime]
Zosime *with* as *written above* e. andswarigende] andswarode.
303 arisan hi butu] arison hi buta. 304-52 *Ða ongan eft . . . adune
astrehte*] *see main text. Ends* adune a*strehte*.

O, ff. 16 and 17 (lines 354-456). *Begins (f. 16)* fram me. 354 þi]
ðy. swilc] þe. fleo] flyh. swaþeahhwæðere] swa hwæþere, *with*
þeah *written above*. 355 þe *(first)*] hit. forhælende] ne forhelende.
357 hwilcehwugu] hwylcehwugu. 359 biterlice] biterlican. 360
gereccan eall] reccan. 361 cwæðende] cweþende. 364 heora lufu]
hyra lufan. byrig] birig. 365 sceamað] scamað. gereccenne]
gemyndgianne. 366 fæmnhad] fæmnanhad. 368 underþeoded]
underþeod. sceortlice] scortlice. 369 areccenne] areccanne.
hraðor] raþor. 370 oncnawan] oncwan, *with* na *written above*.
þone] ðane. 371 lufe þæs geligeres] lufan forgeligres. Ac] *om*.
372 xvii] seofantyne. wintrum] wintran. meniu geondferde]
mænigo geondfor. 373 þam] ðan. forligeres] forligres. 374
gyfum] geofum. 375 aht gyfan] gyfon. 376 wæs swiðe onæled]
swa swiðe wæs onhæled. 377 þæt] *om*. 378 þy] þam. ic þe eð
mihte] ic mihte þe eð. 379 gewilnunga] gewilnunge. forligeres]
geligres. 381 symle] symble. forþon] forþan þe. ær] þe ær. 382
gewilnunga] gewilnunge. 383 adale] adele. forligeres] geligres.
384 yrmðe] myrcðe *(indistinct)*. 385 þæt swa] gif ic. 387 Ða ic
þus leofode] ic þa þus lufode. ic on sumere tide micele meniu
Affricana and Egypta] ic sumre tide on sumra healue miccle
mænigeo of affricana and of egypta. 389 færunga heora] færinga
hira. þone axode hwider [*J* hwæþer]] ic þone ahsode hwider. 390
mæniu] mænigeo. 391 þus] *om*. 392 wurðunga] weorþunge. 393
wurðian] æfter þæt wurðian. 394 Wenst] wast. me underfon
willan] willen me underfon. 396 færeht] færriht. 397 næbbe]
nabbe. færeht] færriht. syllanne] sellanne. 398 an þæra] me on an

þara. astigan] gestigan. þeah] þeah þe. 399 and ic] forþam ic.
heom] him. 400 hi *(first)*] him. for þam færehte] and þane wið
þam færrihte onfon. þæt hi me þe hrædlicor underfon] *om.* 401
abbud] abbud Zosimus. 402 gewilnode] wilnode. emwyrhtena]
emnwyrhtena. 403 þære] þam. wynlustas] wynlustes. *(some
words lost at end of f. 16v)* 405 gescyndnysse] gesceandnysse.
heora] hira. 407 gewemmað] wemmað. 408 soðlice] witodlice.
þa] on. ofergeotende] ofergeotendum. 409 sege] sege me. 411
gerecednysse [*J* gerynysse]] gerecednysse. 412 And þus cwæð]
heo þa togeycte þære ærran cyðnysse. Se geonglincg gehyrde
sona þæt bysmor] Se geongling þa soðlice gehyrende þæt
bysmorgleow. 413 and] *om.* 414 sona] soðlice. swingle] spinle.
417 hæbbenne] habbenne. 416 geseah gesamnode] gegaderade
geseah. 418 waruðe] weroðe. 418 licwurðe me þuhte to mines
lichaman luste] licwyrðe þæs þe me þuhte to mines lichaman
lustum. 419 unsceandlice [*J* sceandlice, un *having been erased*]]
unsceandlice. ic] on. 420 heora] hira. 421 eower færeld mid eow]
eowrum færelde. 422 na eow] eow na. And ic hi þa ealle] And hi
ealle. 423 ceahhetungum bysmerlicum] bysmer ceahhettungum
astyrede wurdon. 424 fracodlicum] fracoðlicum. 426 gebæra]
gebæro. 427 hreowan] reowan. 428 tunga] tunge. 429 asecgan]
gesecgan. eara] eare. mandæda] man. 430 wæron] *om.* and
(first)] oððe. gefremede] gefremede wæron. *(some words lost at
end of 17r)* 431 syngigenne] syngienne. 432 syllendan] nellendan. 433 sih tihtende] si tihtend. 434 lærende] lærend. 435
gehealden] gehealdan. forþan] forþam. wundrige] wundrie. 436
aðolode] aþolade. 437 untynde] ontynde. swa cwyce] cwucuwe.
439 forspillednysse] forspillendnysse. þæs] þær. 440 nænne ne
forlætað forwurðan] nænne nele forweorðan. 441 ealle hale
gedeð þe on hine gelyfað] ealle weorðan hale. forðon] forþam.
443 bið] anbit. 444 mid] *om.* 445 foron] foran. mænige] manige.
446 rode] rode *(not in J).* lichaman] gelicum. 447 fullicum]
manfullicum. gemængde [*J* gemægde]] gemængde. wyrsum [*J*
wyrcum]] wyrsum. 448 on þære sæ mid me] mid me on þære sæ.
449 swilce mænge ælðeodige] swylce mænega ælðeodie.
ceastergewarena] ceasterwaran. 451 gegaderigende] gegadriende.
452 halgan deorwurðan rode upahefennysse] halgan rode

deorwurðan upahafenes. 456 yrnan] urnan. *Ends* urnan, *with a few words lost after this at the end of f. 17v.*

G, f. 5 (lines 488-572). *Begins* weardre heortan. 488 heofende forðbringan] heofiende forðbrohte. 489 siccetunga] siccetunge. 492 and cweðende] *om.* 493 wuldorfæste] wuldorfæsta, *with* e *written above* a. 494 geara] geare. 495 þæslic] þeslic, *with* a *written above* e. þe] *om.* eom þæt ic] *om.* 496 sceawige and gebidde] bidde oððe gesceawie. 497 mænigfealdum] mænigfealdlicum. 498 oncnawan] oncnawe, *with* n *written above end of word.* 499 unwemmed] unwæmme. forþon] forþam. 500 swa besmitenre] besmitene. 501 ascunod [*J* ascimod]] ascunod. aworpen] awurpon. 502 swaþeahhwæðere] swaþeahhwæðre. forþan] forðam. wære mann forðy] wære forði mann. 503 þon] þam. 504 gecygede] gecigde. gefultuma] Gefultma. nu] *om.* 505 anegre ælces fylstes bedæled] anegra ælces oðres fylstes bedælede, *with* fylstes *altered from* fyltes. 506 geopenigenne] geopenienne. þære] *om.* 507 wurðe] beo. 509 femne geeacnodost] fæmne geeacnodest. eac swilce fæmne acendest] *om.* 511 wuldorfæste] wuldorfæsta, *with* e *written above* a. 513 untynede] untyned. 515 minne lichaman] me. 517 sona ic, halige fæmne] sona swa ic þu halga, *with* e *written above second* a *of* halga. suna] sunu, *with* a *written above second* u. mid þam] sona. 518 þissere] þisse. 520 geredst] gerecst. 521 wearð þa gelæd] wearð onæled. 522 hætu] hæto. oþhrinon] æthrinen. 523 þrystlæcende] *om.* 524 astyrede] astyrode. ðe] þæt, *with* þe ic me *written in margin.* 525 gebæd] gebed. me eft] ic me þa eft. 526 þincg] þing. utsceofe] utascufe. 527 þæs temples] þæs, *corrected to* þære *(om. temples).* and ic þa ineode] *om.* 529 byfigende] byfiende. eft] þa *(last word of f. 5r).* 530 dura geðeodde] duru geþydde. ingang] se ingang. swilc] swylce. 531 duru] *om.* 532 þæs siðfætes gegearwode] gerymde and. 534 gebiddan] to gebiddanne. 535 þære geliffæstan rode] þa liffæstan, *with* þære *written above* þa, *and* rode *written in margin.* Ða] and. 536 gerynu] rynu, *with* ge *written above.* symle geare is þa hreowsigendan] symle is geare his þa hreowsiendan. 537 sylfe] sylfne. þa flor] þam eorðan. 538-9 eorðan gecyste. Ða ic uteode] flor cyssende uteode. 539 of þære] þe. 540 halgan] halgan godes. anlicnysse] anlicnysse *(not in J)*. 542 fremsumesta] fremsumesta, *with* e *written above* a. hlæfdig] hlæfdige. 543 arfæstan] arfestan. æteowdest] ær æteowdest. 544 þe [*J* þu]] þe. ne [*J* me]] ne. geseah] geseah nu. 545 geseoð. Seo wuldor [*J* geseow seo wuldor]] geseoð . wuldor sy ðam. 547 hreowsunge] hreowsunga. 548 oððe areccan] oððe toareccan, *with* ne *added at end of word* (= to areccanne) *and* oððe *underlined.* 549 gefremmane] fremmanne. swa] swa swa. 551 latteow æteowod] latþeow. 552 beforan me] me beforan. 553 wæg] weg. læt] gelæt. 554 feorran] feorranne. stefne clypigende] stemne clypiende. 555 Iordane] iordanem. 556 gefærst and gemetst] gemetest. 557 minum þingum] minom ðingon (= O). 558 ongeat] ic ongeat. 559 halgan] halgan (= O; *not in J)*. anlicnysse hawigende] hawiende. and eft clypigende] clypode. 561 ðe] þa (= O). menniscum cynne] mancynne. 562 þu me] me nu. 563 þa] *om.* (= O). 564 for [*J* forð]] fór (O for). sum] sumne. and] þe. 566 gebohte] bohte. ða [*J* Ðær]] þa (O Ða). gehyððo] gehyðe (O gehyþe). 568 wæg] weg. 569 rihtlicost gelædde] ealra rihtost wære. Ða] *om.* wiste] wiste (= O; *not in J, in which* ongæt *is written above the line in a later hand)*. 570 axunga þære æscan towriðende [*J* towriðenne]] axunge þære æscan togewriðende. 571 siðfæt] siðfæc. *Ends* þæs dæges wæs u..., *with last few words illegible.*

O, f. 15 (lines 557-612). *Begins* gehyrde. 557 minum þingum] minon þingon (= G). 559 halgan] halgan (= G; *not in J)*. and eft clypigende] eft clypode. 560 middaneardes] middan, *with* eardes *written above.* 561 ðe] þa (= G). menniscum] mænniscon. 562 me] me nu. 563 þa] *om.* (= G). 564 for [*J* forð]] for (G fór). 565 penegas sealde] pæningas seald. me] *om.* 566 ða [*J* Ðær]] Ða (G þa). genoh gehyððo] gehyþe (G gehyðe). 568 se wæg] geweg. 569 rihtlicost gelædde] rihtor wære. Ða] *om.* þone] þane. wiste] wiste (= G; *not in J, in which* ongæt *is written above the line in a later hand)*. ic *(second)*] ic þider. 570 symle þa axunga þære æscan towriðende [*J* towriðenne]] symble þa ahsunge þære æscan towriþende *(indistinct)*. 573 gegyrnode] earnode. deorwurðan] *om.* 574 hi [*J* heo] hi þa. and þære æfenrepsunga genealæhte] *om.* 576 Fulwihteres] fulluhteres. 577 in Iordane] on iordanen. 578 ansynu þwoh] ansyne aþwoh. 579 gemænsumode] gemænsumede. liffæstan] liffæstum. 582 anes [*J* þæs]] anes. 584 morgen] mergen. 585 Sancta Marian] *om.* 588 symle] symble. God anbidigende [*J* gód anbidigenne]] god anbidigende *(indistinct).* 589 ealle] *om.* 590 þissere] þysse. 592 synt] synd. 593 eardodost] eardodest. 594 andswarode] andwyrde. Hit is] *om.* 595 feowertigum] feowertigon. þincð] þincð is. 596 byrig] birig. 598 hwilcum] hwylcum. 600 andswarode] andwyrde. Twægen healfa] Twegen healfe. 601 Naht] Ða æfter naht. 602 and] *om.* 603 notigende to sumere hwile] to sumere hwile notigende. 605 mihtst] mihtest. manegra] manigra. 606 lencgu] lengo. freode þone] gefreode þane. 608 Heo þa gedrefedu him] ðe gedrefedu Heo him. 609 swiðe] swyþe. sylf] self. gif] Ac. 610 gemynde] mynde. frecednysse] frecednyssa. ahrefnode] aræfnde. 611 unwislicra geþanca] unrihtwislic geþohta. gedrefedon] gedrefdon. þæt ic eft fram þam ylcum geþohtum sum geswinc þrowige] forþam þæt ic ondrede þæt ic from þam ylcan geþohtum . . . þrowige *(indistinct). Ends here, with some words lost at end of f. 15v.*

G, f. 6 (lines 919-60). *Begins* wæs genyrwed. 919 mid þære heortan deopnysse geomrode] mid swate and hefiglice geomrode of þære heortan deopnysse. 920 hine] hine færinga. unmættre] unmætre. 921 hit his fotlastes liccode] fetlastas licciende. 922 gefyrht mid ege] afyrht for þam ege. 923 and ealre] ealra. forþon] forþam. 924 ær] *om.* þær nænig] næfre þær nan. 925 æghwanon] *om.* þære] *om.* 926 gewæpnode and mid mægene [*J* mænege] þære licgendan] gewæpnode mid gewisse truwiende þæt hine ungederodne geheolde þæt mægn þæs licgendan. 927 his leoðum styrgendum] liþum styrungum. 929 leon] leonan. mæste] mæsta, *with* e *written above* a. 930 hider asend wære] asend come. þon] þam. þissere] þisse. 931 on] *om.* gefyll] gefyl. 932 for yldum gewæht eom, þæt ic] mid ylde gewæht. 933 hæbbe] habbende. 934 *to begangenne . . . weorc] here G supplies main text (not in J).* 936 do] do *(not in J).* oþþæt] þæt. 937 on eorðan befæston] eorþan befæsten. 938 Sona æfter his wordum] Mid þam soðlice

æfter þas halgan wordum. clifrum] *om.* 940 lichaman] lichaman
(not in J). byrgenne] byrgelse. and he] Se ealda þa soðlice. 941
hire] þære halgan. tearum *(second)*] benum. 943 on] mid. swa]
swa swa. 944 buton gewealdan] butan gewealden. 945 rægeles]
hrægles. þe he Zosimus hire ær towearp] þe hire ær Zosimus hire
towearp. of] mid. 946 sumne] sume. lichaman] lichaman limu.
heo] hi. 947 cyrdon] þanon cyrdon. seo] se. in] on. westen]
westen gewat. 948 mildeste] mildoste. Ða gewat Zosimus to his
mynstre] and zosimus to his mynstre gecyrde. 949 wuldrigende
and bletsigende] wuldriende and bletsiende. herigende] heriende.
950 þa] swa. 951 of [*in J corrected to* on] of. þa] ealle þa. 953
and mærsodon] and mid ege and lufan and micclan geleafan
mærsodon. 954 soðlice] witodlice se abbod. 956 fultumigendum
gerihte [gerihte *not in J*]] fultumiende gerihte and. 957 wæs
drohtnigende an hund wintra] drohtniende hundteontig geara
gefylde. 958 hleorde] mid sibbe leorde. 959 Drihtne] *last word
on f. 6r.* Hælendum] hælende. þe] Se ðe. a on worulda woruld]
on ealra worulda woruld a buton ende.

O, *Explicit*, as transcribed by Wanley (see Introduction, p. 16)
(lines 958-60). 959 þe leofað] se lyfað. a on worulda woruld] on
ealra worulda woruld.

APPENDIX: *VITA S. MARIAE EGYPTIACAE*

The following text of the *Vita S. Mariae Egyptiacae* (*BHL* 5415) is based on that in London, British Library, MS Cotton Nero E. i, Part I (ff. 179r-184v) (N), the earlier of two surviving copies of the 'Cotton-Corpus Legendary' (C-C) containing the life. As discussed in the Introduction, C-C is considered as providing a variant of *BHL* 5415 similar to that used by the Old English translator, though it would not have been identical to the translator's exemplar and existing copies of it are later than the Old English. The edition is not intended to provide a critical text, but obvious errors have been corrected and occasional emendations introduced with the support of readings in the other C-C manuscript, Salisbury, Cathedral MS 221 (ff. 195v-204v) (S), particularly where these throw light on readings in the Old English version. The apparatus details all textual differences between S and N, except for minor spelling variations (e.g. between *ae* and *e* and between *i* and *y*).

Also collated with the text of N is that in British Library, Cotton Claudius A. i (ff. 76v-84v) (C), a tenth-century manuscript which appears to have been in Anglo-Saxon England, though written on the Continent. The copy of the *Vita* in this manuscript shares many of the features of the C-C witnesses, though there are also significant contrasts.

In the following text, abbreviations have been silently expanded and modern punctuation and capitalization introduced. Spaced points enclosed in square brackets indicate evident unintentional scribal omission. 'E *caudata*' is written as *oe* where the latter would be orthographically correct, otherwise as *ae*. Numbers in brackets follow the chapter divisions of Rosweyde's text. | (accompanied by marginal annotation) indicates manuscript foliation.

INCIPIT UITA SANCTAE MARIAE
EGIPTIACAE: V IDUS APRILIS

Secretum regis celare bonum est; opera autem Dei reuelare
et confiteri honorificum est. Ita enim legitur angelum
dixisse Tobiae post oculorum amissionem gloriosamque
inluminationem et post illa transacta pericula ae quibus
5   liberatus consecutus est pietatem. Etenim regis non seruare
secretum nociuum et ualde periculosum est, et Dei gloriosa
sylere opera magnum est animae detrimentum. Propter quod
ego diuina tegere sylentio dubitans, et pigri inminens serui
metuens condempnationis iudicium, qui a domino talentum
10 accipiens, fodiens in terram abscondit, et datum ad
operationem celauit extra negotiationem, sacram ad me
prolatam narrationem nequaquam silebo. Sed nullus mihi sit
incredulus scribenti de ea que audiui, nec quisquam me
mentyri existimet, rei magnitudinem dubitans. Mihi enim
15 absit sacris mentyri rebus et adulterari uerbum ubi Deus
memoratur. Ei autem qui minima intelligit et indignus de
Dei magnitudine, qui carnem adsumpsit, et incredulus est
ista dicenti, non mihi pertinebit periculum. Si qui autem illi
sunt qui huius scripturae legerint textum gloriosamque rei

---

title] *in small red capitals; text begins on f.179ra. S precedes* INCIPIT
with HVIVS IMITABILIS CONVERSIONIS ACTVVMQUE ET
MORVM VITAM ET PENITENTIAE MAGNVM VIRILEQUE CERT-
AMEN VENERABILIS MARIAE EGIPTIACE QUALITER IN HER-
EMO EXPLEVERIT TEMPORA VITE DE GRECO TRANSTVLIT IN
LATINVM PAVLVS VENERABILIS DIACONVS SANCTAE NEA-
POLIS ECCLESIE; *C* INCIPIT CONVERSIO VIRILE ET MAGNVM
CERTAMEN VENERABILIS MARIAE EGYPTIACAE.
1 Secretum regis] *in large capitals, taking up whole column.*
6 nociuum] no uum, *with erasure of two letters.*
8 inminens] *CS; N* inminentem; *C has the order* pigri serui metuens
imminens.
13 scribenti] *C* scribendi. que] *S* quam.
19 rei] *in S inserted above line.*

THE LIFE OF ST MARY OF EGYPT:
APRIL 9

'It is a good thing to keep hidden the secret of a king; however, to reveal and acknowledge the works of God is glorious.' For it is read [Tobit 12. 7] that thus the angel spoke to Tobias after the loss of his eyes and his glorious enlightenment and when he pursued godliness after the passing of those dangers from which he had been set free. Indeed, not to preserve the secret of a king is injurious and extremely dangerous, while to remain silent about the glorious works of God is greatly harmful to the soul.

Because of this I hesitate to conceal in silence godly things: fearing the threatening sentence of condemnation against the lazy servant, who when he received a talent from his lord, dug a hole and hid it in the earth, and kept concealed without making use of it for trade that which he had been given for his use [cf. Matthew 25. 14-30], I will not at all keep silent about the sacred narrative which has reached me. But let no one disbelieve me as I write what I have heard, nor let anyone consider that I am lying, or be in doubt about the magnitude of the matter. Far be it from me to lie about sacred matters and falsify my account, where God is mentioned. It is to someone who understands very little and is unworthy of the greatness of God, who took on flesh, and to someone who is disbelieving of these matters that I relate, that the danger applies, not to me. But if there are people who read the text of this composition and refuse to believe sensibly the

20   admirationem sane credere rennuerint, et illis Dominus
*f.179rb*misereatur, quoniam et ipsi humanae | naturae infirma con-
siderantes inpossibilia decernunt ea que de hominibus
gloriosa dicuntur. Adsumam de cetero adnarrationem,
ipsam rem referens, que in hac nostra generatione facta
25   dinoscitur, quam sacer uir, diuina et agere et docere
educatus, enarrauit. Sed, ut supra dictum est, nullus haec ad
incredulitatem trahat, considerans inpossibile fieri in hac
nostra generatione tam grande miraculum: gratia per gene-
rationes in sanctas pertransiens animas amicos Dei facit et
30   prophetas, quemadmodum Salomon secundum Deum
edocuit. Tempus namque est sacre prodere narrationis
initium.

(1) In monasterio Palestinorum fuit uir uitae moribus et
uerbo ornatus, qui ab ipsis cunabulis monachicis est actibus
35   diligenter instructus et conuersationibus ueraciter educatus,
nomine Zosima. Et nullus nos estimet dicere Zosimam
illum in predicationis erroneae dogmatis accusatum secte
alterius. Alius enim hic et alius ille, et multa inter utrosque
distantia, licet unum uterque sortiti sunt uocabuli nomen.
40   Hic itaque Zosimas ab initio in uno Palestinorum con-
uersauit monasterio, et omnem pertransiens monachicum
disciplinam, in abstinentie opus omnium factus est
probatissimus. Omne sibi preceptum traditum canonis ab
his qui ab infantia educati sunt, luctam perfectae discipline
45   monachicae inreprehensibiliter conseruabat. Multa etiam et

---

20 rennuerint] *S* renuerit, *with* n *in S inserted above line as correction; C*
retinuerint.
22 decernunt] decertunt, *corrected to* decernunt *(= S), with* n *written*
above line; C decertant.
23 adnarrationem] *C* narrationem.
28 generationes] *C* regenerationes.
31 namque est] *CS; N* namque.
33 uitae] *C* uirtute et.
36 Zosima] *CS* Zosimas.
37 erroneae] *CS; N* errone e. dogmatis] *S* dogmate.
39 uterque] *CS; N* utque. sunt] *S* sint.
42 opus] *C* operae.
43 Omne] *CS* Omne enim.
44 luctam] *C om.*

glorious wonder of the story, may the Lord be merciful to them also, since they, thinking in terms of the weaknesses of human nature, judge imposssible the glorious things that are told about human beings.

I will proceed now to my story, relating a particular case which is recognized as having happened in this our own generation, which a devout man, trained both to perform and to teach godly things, recounted in detail. But, as it is said above, let no one draw these events into disbelief, thinking it impossible that so great a miracle should occur in this our generation: throughout the generations grace enters holy souls and 'makes them friends of God and prophets', as Solomon taught [Wisdom 7. 27] in accordance with the will of God.

It is now time to begin the narration of the holy story.

(1) In a monastery in Palestine there was a man adorned by the conduct of his life and by his speech, who from the very cradle was conscientiously trained in monastic customs and carefully instructed in their ways of life. His name was Zosimas. No one should assume that I am speaking of that Zosimas who was accused of erroneously preaching the doctrines of another sect. This was one person and that another, and there was a great difference between the two of them, even though they each shared the one name by which they were called.

This Zosimas, then, from his earliest days lived his life in a monastery in Palestine, and passing through all monastic training, in the work of self-discipline he became the most accomplished of all. Blamelessly he kept every precept of the rule handed down to him by those who had trained him from childhood in the contest of complete monastic self-discipline. He even also added, over and above, many practices of his own

ipse sibi adiciens superaddidit, cupiens carnem spiritui
subiugare. Nec enim in aliquo offendisse aliquando con-
probatur. Ita enim fuit monachis in cunctis perfectus
actibus, ut multotiens multi monachi de predictis locis
50 monasteriis et de longinquis partibus ad eum confluentes,
eius exemplis atque doctrinis se constringerent, et ad illius
imitationem abstinentie se multo magis subiugarent.

(2) Haec itaque in se omnia habens, a meditatione sacri
aeloquii numquam discessit, sed in stratu suo quiescens,
55 siue surgens, aut operam tenens manibus uel cybum, si
f.179va conueniebat ut sumeret, bonum | quod ille uti consueuerat
spiritaliter utebatur. Unum opus habebat intacitum numquam deficiens, psallere frequenter et meditationem facere
sacri eloquii. Multotiens enim ut adsereret diuine
60 inlustrationis dignus effectus est a Deo sibi uisiones
ostense. Et mirum non est nec incredibile: sic enim, ut ait
Dominus, 'Beati mundo corde, quoniam ipsi Deum uide-
bunt'; quanto magis qui suam purificauerint carnem sobrie
semper, animorumque per uigiles oculos diuine prospiciunt
65 inlustrationis, uisionis indicium hinc preparate futurae
bonitatis accipientes. Dicebat autem is ipse Zosimas ab
ipsis, ut ita dicam, maternis ulnis in hoc se esse monasterio
traditum, et usque ad quinquagesimum tertium annum in eo
cursum monachicum peregisse. Post haec autem pulsatus
70 est a quibusdam cogitationibus, quasi iam in omnibus esset
perfectus, alterius non indigens in nullo doctrina. Haec
autem, ut dicebat, in se cogitabat: 'Numquid est in terris

---

49 predictis locis] *S* predicti loci; *C* predictis locis et.
51 illius] *CS; N* alius.
56 bonum quod] *S* bono quo.
58 deficiens] *S; N* deficientes, *with dots under last three letters and* s
written above; C deficientem.
59 ut adsereret] *in S* ut *is written above* et.
61 ostense] *C* ostense sunt. sic] si *corrected to* sic, *with* c *written above
line.* ut] *C om.*
64 oculos] *S* oculi.
65 hinc preparate futurae bonitatis accipientes] *C om.*
68 annum] *not in S.*
71 nullo doctrina] *S* ullo doctrinae, ullo *preceded by erasure of one letter.*

desiring to subjugate the flesh to the spirit. Nor was he found at any time to have failed in any way. He was so perfect in all monastic observances that on many occasions many monks from monasteries in the aforementioned region and from distant parts flocked to him, bound themselves to his examples and teachings, and subjected themselves much more to imitation of his self-discipline.

(2) While he kept all these observances in himself, he never neglected meditating on the sacred discourse [of the Scriptures], but whether resting in his bed or getting up, or whether he held work or food in his hands – if it was appropriate for him to take it – whatever good thing he was accustomed to make use of, he would use in a spiritual manner. One task he had, unconcealed and never ceasing – to sing the psalms frequently and to engage in meditation on the sacred Scripture. On many occasions, as has been affirmed, he was made worthy through divine enlightenment that visions should be shown to him by God. And that is not strange or unbelievable, for thus, as the Lord says, 'Blessed are the pure in heart, for they shall see God' [Matthew 5. 8] – how much more those who have always purified their bodies temperately and who look for divine enlightenment through the vigilant eyes of their souls, receiving from this source a token of the vision of goodness that awaits them in the future.

This same Zosimas used to tell how he was entrusted from his mother's very arms, so to speak, to this monastery and how he pursued the monastic path in it up until his fifty-third year. After this, however, he was agitated by certain thoughts, namely that he might already be perfect in all things and needed no teaching from anyone else. These things, as he said, he would think to himself: 'Is there a monk on earth who might be able to

monachus qui nouum aliquid possit tradere mihi, aut
adiuuare me ualens in aliquo quo dignior sim, aut quod ego
75   in monachico non expleuerim opere? Numquid inuenitur
eorum qui solitudinem dilixerunt uir qui prior me in actibus
sit.'

Haec et his similia eo cogitante, adstitit quidam et dixit,
'O Zosima, bene quidem, et sicut possibile fuit homini,
80   decertasti, bene cursum monachi consummasti. Tamen,
nullus est in hominibus qui se perfectum esse demonstret.
Maior enim lucta presens quam illa que preteriit, licet tu
nescias. Ut autem cognoscas quante sint et aliae uie salutis,
egredere de terra et de cognatione tua et de domo patris tui,
85   ut Abraham ille patriarcharum eximius, et ueni ad monasterium quod iuxta Iordanem adiacet flumen.'

(3) Mox itaque secutus dicentem, egressus de monasterio in quo ab infantia conuersatus est, et perueniens ad
Iordanem omnium fluminum sanctiorem, dirigitur ab eo qui
90   uocauit eum in monasterio in quo illum Deus uenire
precepit. Pulsans igitur manu ianuam, loquitur prius
monacho qui ianuam obseruabat, et ille nuntiauit eum
f.179vb abbati, qui suscipiens eum, habituque | et specie religiosum
conspiciens, postquam flexit genu, ut mos est monachis,
95   accepta oratione, hoc eum interrogauit: 'Unde, frater,
aduenisti, et quamobrem apud humiles coniunxisti mona-
chos?'

Zosimas autem respondit, 'Unde quidem ueni non puto
necessarium dicere. Aedificationis quoque gratia, pater,

---

74 quo dignior sim] S; N quo dignior sit; C quod ignorem.
78 quidam et dixit] CS quidam et dixit ei; in S quidam written above line.
80 monachi] C monachicum.
81 demonstret] C demonstrat.
82 enim lucta] C est enim luctam. illa que] C illud quod.
85 ad] C in.
86 quod] CS; N quo.
87 egressus] C egressusque.
90 quo] C quod. Deus] C dominus.
93 suscipiens] C suscepit. habituque] C cum habitu.
94 conspiciens] C conspexit. flexit] CS flectit.
95 interrogauit] C interrogauit abbas dicens.

pass on something new to me, or have the power to help me in something in which I might be more worthy [*corrupted from* which I do not know], or which I have not fulfilled in monastic work? Is there not a man to be found among those who have loved the desert who is superior to me in his actions?'

When he was thinking these and similar things, someone came up and said, 'Zosimas, you have certainly fought well and as much as has been possible for a human being, and you have perfected the monastic path well. Yet there is no one in the human race who may prove himself to be perfect. Your present struggle will be greater than that which has gone before, even though you are not aware of it. But in order that you may understand how many other ways there also are leading to salvation, "Go out from your land and from your family and from the house of your father" [Genesis 12. 1], as did Abraham the great patriarch, and go to the monastery which lies near the river Jordan.'

(3) Directly then he followed the person speaking to him, and went out from the monastery in which he had lived from childhood. He arrived at the Jordan, which is holier than all rivers, and was guided by the person who had called him to the monastery to which God had commanded him to come.

Having knocked at the door with his hand, he spoke first to the monk on duty at the door, who announced him to the abbot. He received him in, recognizing from his dress and his appearance that he was in religious life. After he [Zosimas] had bent his knee, as is the custom with monks, and received his blessing, he [the abbot] questioned him thus: 'Where have you come from, brother, and for what reason have you come to us humble monks?'

Zosimas replied, 'I do not think it is necessary for me to say where I have come from. I have come for the sake of edification,

100   adueni. Audiui de uobis magnalia et laude digna, et posse
       Deo animam sociare.'
           Dixit autem ei abbas, 'Deus, frater, qui solus sanat
       animae infirmitatem, ipse te et nos doceat diuina mandata,
       et dirigat ad ea faciendum omnes que oportuna sunt. Homo
105   enim hominem aedificare non ualet nisi unusquisque ad-
       tendat semetipsum frequenter, et sobrio intellectu quod
       expedibile est operetur, Deum habens cooperatorem. Tamen
       quoniam, ut dixisti, caritas te Christi uidere nos humiles
       monachos perduxit, mane nobiscum, si ob hoc uenisti, et
110   omnes nos nutriat Pastor Bonus sancti spiritus sui gratia,
       qui animam suam dedit liberationem pro nobis, et proprias
       oues uocat ex nomine.'
           Haec dicente abbate, flectens iterum Zosimas genua,
       accepta oratione, respondit 'Amen', et mansit in eodem
115   monasterio.
           (4) Uidit autem ibi seniores actibus et uisione splen-
       dentes, spiritu feruentes, et Domino seruientes. Psallentes
       enim ibi erant, incessabiles totius noctis habentes stabilita-
       tem, et in manibus semper operatio, et in ore psalmi diuini
120   absque diminutione. Sermo ibi otiosus non proficiebat;
       cogitatio auri argentique aut rei alicuius apud illos non erat.
       Expensio anni totius, aut mensura, uel temporalis uite
       meditationes, doloribus congrue, nec nomen apud eos
       cognoscebatur. Sed unum erat primum solummodo, quod
125   festinabatur ab omnibus, ut unusquisque mortuus esset
       corpore, sic semel seculo et eis que in seculo sunt

---

100 Audiui] *C* Audiui quidem. posse] *C* possibile.
107 Deum] *C* dominum. Tamen] *C* tamen frater dilectissime.
108 quoniam] *S* quid. ut dixisti, caritas te] *C* dixisti quod te caritas.
110 sancti spiritus sui gratia] *C* gratia spiritus sancti.
111 liberationem] liberatio, *with* nem *written above.*
113 Haec] *C* Haec autem. flectens] *C* flens et flectens.
117 Psallentes] *C* Psalmodiae.
118 habentes] *corrected from* habens.
121 rei] *C* rerum.
122 aut mensura, uel] *C* mensurari debuit et.
123 congrue] *C* congruebant. nomen] *C* nomen alicuius secularis rei.
126 corpore, sic semel seculo] *C* seculo sic semel corpore. que] *C* qui.

father. I have heard great things concerning you, and worthy of praise, and things which are able to bring the soul close to God.'

The abbot said to him, 'Let God himself, brother, who alone heals the weakness of the soul, teach you and us his divine requirements, and let him guide everyone to do the things that are suitable. For one person cannot edify another unless each one constantly attends to himself and with a sober understanding occupies himself with what is right, with God as helper. However, since, as you have said, the love of Christ has led you to visit us humble monks, stay with us, if you have come for this reason, and may the Good Shepherd nourish us all by the grace of his holy spirit, he who "gave his life as a ransom" for us [cf. Matthew 20. 28, Mark 10. 45] and who "calls by name the sheep that belong to him" [John 10. 3].'

When the abbot had said this, Zosimas bent his knees again, received his blessing and said 'Amen', and he remained in the same monsatery.

(4) There he saw elders shining in their actions and appearance, fervent in spirit and serving the Lord. They would sing the psalms there, remaining unceasingly steadfast during the whole night, and they always had work in their hands and the divine psalms on their lips, without slackening. Idle talk had no place there. There was no thought among them of gold and silver or of any material thing. Their expenditure for the whole year was not known among them, nor was its measure, or considerations of temporal life with their consequent worries, or even the name of the year. But there was one primary goal above all, which was hastened towards by everyone, that each one of them should be dead to the body, having thus once and for all been

mortificatus et iam non uiuens. Cybum autem habebant
indeficientem diuinitatis eloquia; nutriebant uero corpus
130 necessariis pane et aqua, ut multo magis apud diuinam
caritatem apparerent efficaces.

(5) Hec Zosimas ut uidebatur prospiciens, aedificabatur
ualde, pretendens se ad perfectionem et crescere faciens
proprium cursum, cooperatores inueniens optime diuinum
135 inuocantes paradysum.

f.180ra   Transactis autem aliquot diebus, | adpropriauit tempus
quando sacra ieiunia Christianis traditum est celebrare, et
purificare seipsos ob diuine passionis resurrectionisque Dei
salutationem. Regia autem monasterii numquam aperi-
140 ebatur, sed semper erat clausa, et absque ulla perturbatione
monachi cursum suum explebant. Nec enim erat aperire
aliquando, nisi fortassis monachus propter aliquod opus
necessarium adueniebat. Solitarius enim erat locus iste et
plurimis uicinorum non solum inusitatus, sed incognitus.
145 Canon autem talis a priscis seruabatur temporibus, propter
quod, ut considero, Deus Zosimam in eodem perduxit
monasterio.

(6) Dehinc, ego referam qualiter ipsius monasterii seruabatur traditio. Dominica qua prima ieiuniorum ebdomada
150 nominari mos est, agebantur diuina sacramenta consuete, et
unusquisque particeps efficiebatur intemerati ac uiuifici

---

128 mortificatus] *C* mortificati. uiuens] *C* uiuentes.
129 indeficientem] *C* indeficientem uidelicet.
132 uidebatur] *C* uidit.
133 faciens proprium cursum] *C* proprium cursum optans.
135 inuocantes] *NS; C* innouantes.
138 seipsos] *C om.*
139 Regia] *C* porta.
142 propter . . . Solitarius] *C* aut aliquis solitarius propter aliquem
necessitatem adueniret.
143 enim erat] *C* erat enim.
144 incognitus] *C* et incognitus.
146 in eodem perduxit monasterio] *C* in eundem perduxit monasterium.
148 ipsius monasterii] *S* monasterii ipsius.
150 nominari] *CS; N* non mirari.

made dead rather than living to the world and to the things that are in the world. They had the inexhaustible food of the divine discourse [of the Scriptures]; and they fed the body with the necessities of bread and water, so that they might prove themselves all the more capable in works of divine love.

(5) When Zosimas observed these things, as seemed proper, he was greatly edified. He stretched himself towards perfection and acted to advance on his own path, finding co-workers who splendidly invoked [C renewed] divine paradise.

After some days had passed, the time approached when it is traditional for Christians to keep the sacred fast and to purify themselves in order to welcome the passion and resurrection of God. The courtyard into this monastery was never opened, but was always kept shut, and the monks fulfilled their way of life without any disturbance. Indeed it was not to be opened ever, unless perchance a monk arrived because of some necessary matter. For that locality was deserted and to most neighbouring people it was not only unfamiliar but unknown. Such a rule had been observed from early times, and it was for this reason, I believe, that God led Zosimas to that same monastery.

(6) I will now describe the nature of a tradition observed in this monastery. On the Sunday by which the first week of the fast is customarily called, the divine sacraments were performed in the usual way, and each person became a sharer in the undefiled

corporis et sanguinis Domini nostri Iesu Christi. Et solito
modicum cybi sumentes, congregabantur omnes in oratorium, et curuatis genibus factaque suppliciter oratione,
salutabant se inuicem monachi, et unusquisque genuflexo
155 publiciter amplectabantur abbatem, postulantes orationem,
ut haberent ad inchoatum certamen cooperatorem et comita-
torem. Haec ita se habentibus, fores monasterii patefiebant,
et, psallentes consona uoce, 'Dominus inluminatio mea et
salus mea; quem timebo? Dominus defensor uitae meae; a
160 quo trepidabo?', et cetera, exibant omnes, unum multotiens
aut duos monasterii custodes relinquentes, non ut custodi-
rent ea quae intus erant reposita – non enim erant apud illos
aliqua furum congrua – sed ne oratorium absque diuina
reliquerent solempnia. Unusquisque autem se annonabat
165 prout poterat aut uolebat. Nam unus portabat corpori ad
mensuram sufficiens, alius caricas, alius palmarum fructus
dactilos, alius uero legumina aquis infusa, alius nihil preter
corpus proprium et uestimentum quo utebatur: nutriebatur
autem, quando necessitas nature exigebat, herbis que nasce-
170 bantur per solitudinem. Canon autem erat unusquisque sibi
ipsi et lex absque preuaricatione, ut non cognosceret aliquis
f.180rb consocium qualiter abstinebat, aut quomodo agebat. |

Iordanem enim mox transmeantes longe ab inuicem se
sequestrabant, et nullus se iungebat ad socium, ciuitatem

---

151 corporis . . . cybi] *in S inserted above line*. Et] *inserted above line; et
also in CS.*
152 congregabantur] *S* congregabant.
155 publiciter] *C* suppliciter. amplectabantur] *in S* e *is inserted above
second* a; *C* amplectabatur.
158 uoce] *C* uoce dicentes.
160 trepidabo] *C* trepidabo dum adpropriant super me nocentes. exibant]
C exiebant.
163 furum] *C* fenorum.
164 solempnia] *C* sollempnibus. annonabat] *C* onerabat.
168 nutriebatur] *S* nutriebat; *C* nutriebantur.
169 exigebat] *CS (S corrected from* exiebat, *with* g *inserted above); N*
exiebat.
171 ipsi] *CS* ipse. absque] ipse, *with* absque *written above*. non] *not in S.*
172 qualiter abstinebat] *C* uel qualiter abstinerat. quomodo] *corrected
from* quo, *with* modo *inserted above line*. agebat] *C* ageret.

and life-giving body and blood of our Lord Jesus Christ. And when they had taken a little food as usual, they gathered in the chapel, and on bended knees and with a prayer of supplication, the monks greeted each other in turn, and after genuflecting, each one without exception embraced the abbot, asking for his blessing, so that they would have a co-worker and companion for the struggle which was about to begin. After these proceedings, they opened the doors of the monastery and they all went out, singing with one voice, 'The Lord is my light and my deliverance; whom shall I fear? The Lord is the defender of my life; whom shall I hold in dread?' [Psalm 26 (27). 1], etc. They often left one or two behind as guards of the monastery, not in order to guard the things which were kept inside – for there were no belongings among them of interest to thieves – but so that they would not leave the chapel without the divine solemnities. Each one provided for himself according as he was able or wished. For one brought with him sufficient food in proportion to the needs of his body, another brought dried figs, another dates, which are the fruit of palm-trees, yet another beans soaked in water, and another nothing except his own body and the clothes he wore: he would nourish himself, when the necessity of nature demanded, with the grasses that grew in the desert. There was one single rule for each of them, and a law without exception, that no one should get to know how his fellow exercised abstinence or in what manner he got on.

As soon as they had crossed the Jordan, they separated far away from each other, and none of them associated with a companion, for they regarded the desert as their city. But if one

175 estimantes solitudinem. Sed si unus ex ipsis a longe uenientem ad se aliquem uidebat, mox declinabat de itinere et
ad aliam partem pergebat. Uiuebat autem sibi et Deo,
psallens frequenter et constituto gustans tempore cybum. Ita
omnia ieiunia celebrantes, reuertebantur ad monasterium
180 ante diem uiuificum resurrectionis Domini et Saluatoris,
Domini nostri Iesu Christi, que festa dominica cum ramis
palmarum celebrare sancta accepit aecclesia. Reuertebantur
autem, unusquisque habens proprii laboris testem agricolam
propriam conscientiam, cognoscentem qualiter operatus est
185 et qualia laborum semina seminauit, et nullus ullomodo
interrogabat quomodo aut qualiter laboris certamina
consummasset.

(7) Hic est itaque huius monasterii canon, et ita perfecte
et optime custodiebatur. Unusquisque enim, ut dictum est,
190 per solitudinem Deo iungebatur, et in semetipso decertabat,
ne hominibus placeret, sed soli Deo. Illa enim quae propter
homines fiunt ut hominibus placeant aguntur, non solum
non proderunt facientibus, sed et multo damno etatis
agentibus efficiuntur obnoxia.

195 Tunc itaque Zosimas consueta monasterii lege trans-
meauit Iordanem, modicum quid pro corporis necessitate
deportans congrua, et uestem qua utebatur, et canonem
quidem celebrabat, solitudinem pertransiens, et tempore
aesce necessitatem soluebat nature. Sedebat autem nocte in
200 terra, modicum quiescens, et somnum ad modicum gustans,

---

177 partem] *inserted above line.* Uiuebat] *C* uiuebant.
178 psallens] *C* psallentes. gustans] *C* gustantes.
181 Domini nostri Iesu Christi] *C adds* et saluatoris mundi. que festa
dominica] m *erased at the end of* que *and* festa; *C* quam festam
dominicam.
182 aecclesia] *CS; N* aecclesiam.
186 quomodo] *corrected from* quo, *with* modo *inserted above line.*
192 homines] es *over erasure.*
193 multo damno etatis] *S* multae *for* multo; *C* multa dampna etiam.
194 efficiuntur] *S* efficientur.
197 et canonem quidem celebrabat] *C* iuxta canonem quidem.
199 soluebat] ac fiebat, *underlined, and* soluebat *written above; CS*
faciebat.
200 terra] *C* terra nuda.

of them saw anyone coming towards him from a distance, immediately he turned away from his path and proceeded in a different direction: he lived for himself and for God, singing the psalms frequently and taking food at the proper time.

When they had in this way kept the whole fast, they would return to the monastery before the life-giving day of the resurrection of the Lord and Saviour, our Lord Jesus Christ, which the holy church is accustomed to celebrate on the festal Sunday with branches of palms. They would return, however, each one having as the (only) witness of his own labour that husbandman, his own conscience, which knew how he worked and what seeds of his labours he sowed; and no one in any way asked how or in what manner he accomplished the struggles of his labour.

(7) This then was the rule of this monastery, and it was kept perfectly and splendidly. Each one, as it is said, was united to God by means of the desert, and fought within himself not to please men, but God alone. For those things which are done for the sake of men and are performed in order to please men, not only do not benefit those who do them, but also bring about dangers to those who perform them, with much harm in the world.

Then indeed Zosimas, following the customary law of the monastery, crossed over the Jordan, carrying a very little for his bodily needs, and the clothes which he wore, and he kept the rule as he travelled through the desert, and fulfilled the necessities of nature at the proper time for eating. He would sit on the ground at night, resting a little and taking a little sleep wherever evening

quodcumque eum uespertinum repperiebat tempus. Diluculo autem properare incipiebat, semper incessabile habens
idem propositum, in desiderium enim habens, ut dicebat,
introire in solitudinem, sperans inuenire aliquem patrem in
205 ea habitantem, qui eum posset aliquod aedificare, sicut
desiderabat, et sine cessatione iter agebat, ac si apud
aliquem manifestum festinans.

f.180va   Uiginti autem dierum exiens iter, cumque sexte hore |
tempus aduenit, stetit modicum ab itinere, et conuersus ad
210 orientem agebat solitam orationem. Consueuerat enim
constituta diei tempore figere itineris cursum, et stans
psallere, et genu flexo orare. Dum autem psalleret, et in
caelum intentis inspiceret obtutibus, uidit a parte dextra, ubi
stans sextam orabat, umbram quasi humani corporis
215 apparentem, et prius quidem turbatus est, fantasiam alicuius
spiritus existimans se uidisse, et contremuit. Signo enim
crucis se muniens, et a se timorem proiciens – iam enim et
orationis eius finis instabat – conuertens oculos, uidit
aliquem in ueritate properantem ad partem occidentis.
220 Mulier autem erat quod uidebatur, nigerrimo corpore pre
solis ardore denigrata, et capillos capitis habens ut lana
albos, modicos et ipsos, non amplius quam usque ad cerui-
cem descendentes.

    (8) Hoc itaque Zosimas uidens, et desiderate dulcedinis
225 gauisus effectus gloriae uisionis, coepit festinanter currere
in eam partem, ubi et illud quod apparuit festinabat. Gaudebat enim gaudio magno: non enim uiderat in spatio dierum

---

201 quodcumque] *C* quocumque.
203 idem] i *written over three-letter erasures in NS; C* eundem.
desiderium] *C* desiderio. ut dicebat] *C* dicebat se uelle.
205 aliquod] *S* aliquo; *C om.*
208 cumque] *C* cum.
209 aduenit] *C* adueniret. ab] *in S inserted above line.*
211 tempore] *CS; N* tempora.
212 psallere] *S* sallere, *with* p *inserted on line at beginning of word.*
214 sextam] *C* sexta.
216 et] *C om.*
218 conuertens] *C* conuertensque.
224 desiderate . . . uisionis] *C* pro desiderio gloriosae uisionis effectus est
letus; *S* desiderata dulcedine *for* desiderate dulcedinis.

time found him. At dawn he would begin to hasten, always having the same unceasing purpose, for he had in himself a longing, as he said, to enter into the desert, hoping to find some father living in it, who might be able to edify him in some way, as he wished, and he pushed forward on his journey without ceasing, as if hurrying to visit some renowned person.

After he had continued on his way for twenty days, and when the time of the sixth hour arrived, he stopped for a while on his journey, and turning to the east he said his usual prayer; for he was accustomed at the appointed time of day to fix the course of his journey, to stand and recite the psalms and to kneel in prayer. While he was reciting the psalms, however, and was looking to heaven with an intent gaze, he noticed to the right of where he was standing and performing the prayers of the sixth hour the shadow appearing of what seemed to be a human body, and at first he was alarmed, imagining he had seen a phantom of a spirit of some kind, and he began to tremble all over. He defended himself with the sign of the cross and shook off his fear – he had already got to the end of his prayer – and turning his eyes he saw that there really was someone hastening in a westerly direction. It was a woman that he saw, extremely blackened in her body from the intensity of the sun, and with the hair of her head as white as wool, and sparse at that, not reaching any further than to her neck.

(8) When Zosimas saw this, he rejoiced at the longed-for loveliness of this vision of glory, and he began quickly to run in the direction in which that which appeared also hastened. He rejoiced indeed with great joy: for he had not seen the sight of a human being in the period of those days, nor the form of any

illorum speciem hominis, aut animalium, aut uolucrum,
bestiarumque formam. Desiderabat igitur cognoscere quae
230 uel qualis bestia esset que uidebatur, sperans quoniam
maiorum alicuius efficeretur prospectus. Illa autem, ut uidit
econtra Zosimam uenientem, cepit fugiens currere apud
inferiorem solitudinem. Zosimas autem aetatis senectam
obliuiscens, et laborem non reputans itineris, tetendit
235 rapidissimo cursu, desiderans se coniungere fugienti. Hic
enim sequebatur; illa autem prosequebatur. Erat autem
Zosime cursus uelocior, et paululum efficiebatur
propinquior. Ubi autem adpropinquauit, ut iam etiam uox
possit audiri, coepit has uoces emittens clamare Zosimas
240 cum lacrimis, 'Cur me fugis decrepitum peccatorem, serue
Dei? Uere, sustine me, quicumque es, per Deum pro cuius
f.180vb nomine hanc inhabitas solitudenem. | Sustine me per spem
quam habes pro tanta laboris remuneratione. Sta, et tribue
orationem et benedictionem seni, per Deum, qui neminem
245 aliquando proicit.'

Haec cum lacrimis Zosima postulante, uenerunt currentes in quendam locum, in quo quasi aridus torrens
designabatur, in quo fuisse considerauit torrentem. Sed
locus ille talem conuenit habere similitudinem quo enim in
250 terra illa apparebat. Ut uenerunt itaque in predictum locum,
illud quod fugiebat descendit, et iterum ascendit in partem
aliam. Zosimas autem clamans et nusquam progredi ualens,
stetit in alia parte loci, qui speciem habere uidebatur torrentis, et addidit lacrimas lacrimis, et suspiriis suspiria

232 apud] S ad.
235 se] C om.
236 prosequebatur] C precedebat.
241 me] C om.
242 me] C om. spem] C spiritum.
243 tanta] C tanti.
249 quo] CS quomodo.
250 Ut uenerunt itaque] C itaque ut uenerunt.
251 illud quod fugiebat] C illa quae fugebat.
252 nusquam progredi ualens] C ultra progredi non ualens.
254] addidit lacrimas lacrimis] addidit lacrimis, with lacrimas inserted
above.

beasts, whether animals or birds. He desired therefore to find out which and what sort of creature it was that appeared, hoping that the sight of some kind of even greater things might ensue.

She, on the other hand, when she saw Zosimas coming, began to run in haste towards the depths of the desert. Zosimas, however, forgetting his old age and not worrying about the exertion of the journey, proceeded very quickly on his course, desiring to join up with the one who fled. He followed, while she went on ahead. But Zosimas's course was the swifter, and bit by bit he got to be closer. When he got close enough for his voice to be heard, Zosimas began calling out tearfully in these words: 'Why do you flee from me, a worn-out sinner, servant of God? Wait for me, whoever you are, for the sake of God, in whose name you dwell in this desert. Wait for me, for the sake of the hope you have of reward for your toils, which are so great. Stop, and grant your blessing and benediction to an old man, for the sake of God, who never casts anyone aside.'

With Zosimas entreating thus amidst his tears, they came running to a certain place, in which it seemed a dried-up river was marked out, where he thought a river to have been – anyway, that place looked as if it had such an appearance where it came into sight in that landscape. When they came, then, to the aforementioned place, the creature that fled went down and climbed up the other side again. Zosimas, however, calling out and unable to get anywhere further, stood at the other side of the place which seemed to have the appearance of a river, and he added tears to tears and increased sighs with sighs, so that she

255 ampliauit, ut multo magis ex propinquo stridorem luctus
audiret.

(9) Tunc illud corpus quod fugiebat uocem talem emisit:
'Abba Zosimas, ignosce mihi propter Dominum, quoniam
manifestare me tibi conuersa non possum: mulier enim sum,
260 et omnino corporeo tegmine nuda, ut ipse uides, et corporis
turpitudinem habens intectam. Sed si uis peccatrici mulieri
orationem uere tribuere, proice mihi de indumentis quibus
circumdatus es, ut possim muliebrem infirmitatem operire,
conuertens ad te, et tuas accipiam orationes.'

265 Tunc tremor nimiusque metus et mentis excessus accepit
Zosimam, audiens scilicet quia eum ex nomine uocauerit
Zosima. Strenuus enim erat uir ille ualde, et diuinitatis dono
prudentissimus, et ut cognouit quia ex nomine uocasset eum
quem numquam uiderat, de quo nec umquam audierat, nisi
270 manifestissimae providentiae gratia fuisset inlustrata, fecit
cum festinatione quod iussum est ei, et exuens se pallio quo
erat indutus, terga uersus, proiecit ei. Illa autem accipiens,
in quantum potuit tegens partem corporis quam oportet plus
tegere ceteris, precincxit se, et conuersa ad Zosimam, ait ei,
275 'Quid tibi uisum fuit, abba, peccatricem uidere mulierculam? Quid queris a me uidere aut discere? Tantum non
pigritasti laborem pertolerare?'

Ille autem in terra prostratus poscebat benedictionem
secundum morem accipere. Prostrauit autem se et ipsa, et

---

255 ut multo magis] C cum autem.
257 Tunc] C om. fugiebat] C fugebat tunc. emisit] C emisit dicens.
262 de indumentis quibus] de *inserted in margin;* C indumentum quo.
263 operire, conuertens] C operiens conuerti.
266 uocauerit] *last five letters underlined and* sset *written above;* CS
uocauerit.
267 Zosima] C zosimam.
268 ut] C om. uocasset] C aliter non uocasset.
269 uiderat] C ante uiderat. de quo nec umquam audierat] C nec audierat.
270 manifestissimae] CS; N manifestissimi.
276 discere] C disscere.
277 pertolerare] C pertolerare o abba.
279 se] C se in terram. et uterque iacens in terra] C Vterque iacebant in
terra. unus . . . deposcens] C unus ex una parte benedictionem deposcens
et illa ex alia parte.

heard all the more the grating sound of his lamentation from the vicinity.

(9) Then that body which fled sent forth this utterance: 'Father Zosimas, pardon me for the sake of the Lord, since I cannot turn and show myself to you: for I am a woman and completely naked of bodily covering, as you yourself see, and I have the shame of my body uncovered. But if you really wish to grant the prayer of a sinful woman, throw me part of what you are wearing, so that I can cover up my womanly weakness and may turn to you and receive your blessings.'

Then trembling and excessive dread and a loss of his mental self-possession overcame Zosimas, because of course he heard that she called him by the name Zosimas. He was a very alert man and most sagacious by the gift of God, and when he realized that she called him by name whom she had never seen and of whom she had never heard, unless she had been enlightened by the grace of the most manifest providence, he hastily did what she told him. He took off the cloak he had been wearing, and with his back turned he threw it to her. She took it and girded herself round, covering that part of the body which ought to be covered more than others, and turning to Zosimas, she said to him, 'Why did it seem good to you, father, to see a common sinful woman? What do you seek to see or learn from me? Did you not hesitate to put yourself to such trouble?'

He, however, throwing himself down, asked to receive her blessing, according to the custom. But she also threw herself

f.181ra uterque | iacens in terra, unus ex alio benedictionem de-
poscens, et non erat aliud ab alterutro audiri nisi tantum
'benedic'.

(10) Post multarum autem horarum spatium, dixit mulier
ad Zosimam, 'Abba Zosimas, tibi conpetit benedicere et
285 orare. Tu enim presbiterii honore suffultus es et plurimis
iam annis sancto adsistis altari, et donis diuinitatis Christi
secreta rimaris.'

Haec uerba Zosimam in magnum timorem et certamen
magis inducebant, et tremens senex sudoris guttis
290 infundebatur. Dicit autem ei defectus et quasi halitum iam
conclusus, 'Manifesta iam quid es ex ipsa uisione, O
spiritalis mater, quoniam tu ad Dominum profecta es, et
fortiori parte seculo mortua es. Manifestata autem plus
omnium tributa tibi gratia, ut me uocares ex nomine, quem
295 numquam uidisti. Sed quia gratia non ex dignitate cog-
noscitur sed ex animarum actibus significare consueta est,
ipsa benedic propter Dominum, et orationem tribue indigentiae tuae perfectionis.'

Stabilitati autem senis conpassa, dixit, 'Benedictus
300 Deus, qui salutem procurat animarum.'

Et Zosima respondente 'Amen', surrexerunt utrique de
terra, et ait mulier seni, 'Homo, quamobrem ad me
peccatricem uenisti? Tamen quoniam quidem te gratia
Spiritus Sancti direxit, ut aliquod ministerium exhibeas
305 meae exiguitatis corpori congruum, dic mihi, quomodo

---

284 Abba] *C* o abba.
286 altari] *CS* altario.
290 defectus] *C* abbas zosimas fatigatus. halitum] *S; N* alium; *C* alite.
292 Dominum] *C* deum.
293 fortiori] *CS; N* fortior. Manifestata autem] *C* Manifesta autem quia.
294 omnium tributa] *C* omnibus hominibus attributa est. ut] *C* quia. ut . . .
gratia] *in S inserted in right-hand margin.* uocares] *C* uocasti.
297 orationem . . . perfectionis] *C* orationem tuae perfectionis tribue
meae indigentiae.
299 Stabilitati . . . dixit] *C* Compassa stabilitati senis dixit.
302 Homo] *C* o homo.
305 corpori] *C* corporis. quomodo] *preceded in N by* quomodo
imperatores.

down, and they both lay on the ground, each one asking blessing from the other, and nothing was to be heard from either of them, except only, 'Bless me.'

(10) After a space of many hours the woman said to Zosimas, 'Father Zosimas, it is fitting for you to bless and to pray, for you are borne up by the office of the priesthood, and for many years you have served at the holy altar and you probe the secrets of the divine gifts.'

These words brought Zosimas all the more into great fear and conflict; the old man trembled and was suffused with drops of sweat. Fainting away and practically unable to breathe, he said, 'It is clear now what you are from your appearance, O spiritual mother: that you have set out on a journey to the Lord and to the greater part are dead to the world. The grace granted to you is revealed above all in that you called me by my name, whom you have never seen. But since grace is not identified by official rank but is accustomed to be indicated by the actions of the soul, you yourself bless me for the sake of the Lord, and grant the prayer of one in need of your perfection.'

Taking pity on the old man's persistence, she said, 'Blessed be God, who oversees the salvation of souls.'

With Zosimas responding 'Amen', they both arose from the ground, and the woman said to the old man, 'Why, sir, have you come to see me, a sinful woman? But since in fact the grace of the Holy Spirit has guided you so that you may perform a service relating to my poor self, tell me, how is the most Christian

hodie Christianissima regitur tribus, quomodo imperatores,
quomodo sanctae aecclesiae pascitur grex?'

Zosimas autem respondit hoc uerbum: 'Mater, tuis
orationibus sanctis pacem stabilem Deus largitur. Sed
310 suscipe indigni monachi consolationem, et propter Dominum ora pro omni mundo, et pro me peccatore, ut non huius
cursus ityneris labor sine fructu mihi efficiatur tantae
solitudinis uia.'

Et illa respondit ad eum, 'Te quidem oportet, abba
315 Zosima, sacerdotii, ut dixi, habens honorem, pro me et pro
omnibus orare. In hoc enim et uocatus es, sed quia obedi-
entiae preceptum habemus, quod mihi a te iussum est, bona
faciam uoluntate.'

Et haec dicens, ad orationem conuersa, et eleuatis oculis
320 in excelso manibusque extensis, coepit orare motu tantum
f.181rb labiorum in silentio; | uox penitus non audiebatur ut
intellegi posset. Unde et Zosimas nulla potuit ex ipsa
oratione agnoscere. Stabat enim, ut dicebat, tremens, terram
conspiciens, et nihil ullomodo loquens. Iurabat autem,
325 Dominum testem uerbi proponens, quoniam ut uidit eam
perseuerantem in orationis constantia, paululum eleuatis ab
aspectu terre oculis, uidit eam eleuatam quasi cubitum
unum a terra, et in aere pendentem orare. Hoc autem ut
uidit, nimio pauore correptus, prostrauit se in terram,
330 sudoreque suffusus et nimium per nimium perturbatus, nihil
dicere presumebat, in seipso tantum dicebat, 'Domine,
miserere.'

(11) In terra autem prostratus iacens, scandalizabatur in

---

306 quomodo] N quo.
308 hoc uerbum] C dicens. Mater] C o mater.
309 largitur] S largitus est; C largitus est mundo.
320 motu tantum] S tantum motu.
321 uox] C et uox.
323 dicebat] CS; N dicerat.
325 Dominum] CS deum.
328 pendentem] S pedentem, *with* n *inserted above line.*
330 nimium per nimium] S nimium, *followed by erasure, the resulting*
space corresponding to that required for per nimium.

community getting on these days, and how the emperors? How is the flock of the holy church being looked after?'

Zosimas replied as follows: 'In accordance with your holy prayers, God has granted a stable peace. But accept the encouragement of an unworthy monk, and for the sake of the Lord pray for the whole world and for me, a sinner, so that the hardship of the course of this journey may not prove fruitless for me, my passage across such a desert.'

And she replied to him, 'It is you in fact who ought to pray for me and for all, since, as I have said, you hold the office of the priesthood. You were called to this office; but since we have the requirement of obedience, I will do with good will what you have asked.'

After these words she turned round for prayer, and with her eyes raised on high and her hands stretched out she began to pray in silence, with only her lips moving; the voice from within was not heard so that it could be made out. Hence Zosimas was unable to understand anything of that prayer. He stood, as she spoke, trembling, staring at the ground, and saying nothing at all. He swore, however, declaring the Lord as witness of his word, that as he watched her keeping on with her continuing prayer, lifting his eyes from the ground a little, he saw her raised up about one cubit from the ground and praying suspended in the air. When he saw this, seized with overwhelming terror he threw himself on the ground, and, suffused with sweat and exceedingly alarmed indeed, he did not dare to say anything, except that he said within himself, 'Lord, have mercy.'

(11) Lying prostrate on the ground, however, he was snared

mente putans ne spiritus esset, qui fingit orare. Conuersa
335 autem mulier, erexit monachum ita dicens: 'Quid te, abbas,
cogitationes tue perturbant scandalizare in me, quia spiritus
sum, et fictam facio orationem? Satisfactus esto, homo,
peccatricem me esse mulierculam, tamen sacro sum circum-
data baptismate, et spiritus non sum sed fauilla et cynis et
340 totum caro, et nihil spiritalis fantasiae aliquando uel ad
mentem reducens.'

Haec dicens, signo crucis signat frontem suam oculos-
que et labia, simulque et pectori uexillum crucis infigens,
ita dixit: 'Deus, abba Zosimas, de aduersario et inmissioni-
345 bus eius liberet nos, quoniam multa super nos est inuidia
eius.'

Haec audiens, senex prosternit se, et adprehendit pedes
eius, dicens cum lacrimis, 'Obsecro te per Dominum
Ihesum Christum, uerum Deum nostrum, qui de uirgine
350 nasci dignatus est, pro quo hanc induta es nuditatem, pro
quo has carnes ita expendisti, ut nihil abscondas a seruo tuo,
qui es, et unde, uel quando et ob quam occasionem solitudinem hanc inhabitasti, sed omnia quae circa te sunt edicito
mihi, ut Dei magnalia facias manifesta. Sapientia enim
355 abscondita et thesaurus occultus que utilitas in utrisque,
sicut scriptum est? Dic mihi omnia propter Dominum. Non
f.181va enim pro gloriatione aliquid dicis | aut ostentatione, sed ut
mihi satisfacias peccatori et indigno. Credo enim Deo, cui
uiuis, et cum quo conuersaris, quoniam ob huiuscemodi rem
360 directus sum in hanc solitudinem, ut ea que circa te sunt

---

334 esset] *in S inserted above line.*
337 sum] *S* sim, *corrected from* sum. homo] *C* o homo.
340 nihil] *C* nihil de me. aliquando uel ad mentem reducens] *C* ad tuam
reducas mentem.
342 suam] *C; N* suum; *S* suum *altered to* suam.
343 et] *erased in S.* infigens] *CS* infingens.
344 Zosimas] *CS* Zosima.
350 nuditatem] *C* nuditatem et.
354 Sapientia] Scriptum est enim sapientia.
355 que] *CS; N* quem.
356 sicut scriptum est] *C* utique nulla. Non] *C* nec.
358 Credo enim Deo] *C* Crede enim per illum.

in his mind with the thought that she might be a spirit, which pretended to pray. But the woman turned round and raised up the monk, speaking as follows: 'Why, abbot, do your thoughts disturb you so that you are confounded about me, thinking that I am a spirit and am performing a false prayer? Be assured, sir, that I am an ordinary sinful woman, though one protected by holy baptism; and I am not a spirit but ashes and dust and wholly flesh, bringing nothing of spiritual delusion to the mind at any time.'

As she said this, she made the sign of the cross on her forehead and on her eyes and lips, and impressing the mark of the cross on her breast she spoke thus: 'May God free us, abbot Zosimas, from the enemy and his attacks, since his ill-will towards us is great.'

Hearing this, the old man fell prostrate and took hold of her feet, saying amidst his tears, 'I implore you by the Lord Jesus Christ, our true God, who deigned to be born from a virgin, him for whose sake you have clothed yourself in this nakedness and for whose sake you have thus worn out this flesh of yours, that you conceal nothing from your servant – who you are, and where you came from, and when and for what reason you came to dwell in this desert – but tell me everything concerning yourself, so that you may make manifest the wonderful works of God. As is written [Ecclesiasticus 20. 32], "Wisdom that is hidden and treasure that is hoarded up, what profit is in them both?" Tell me everything for the sake of the Lord. For you do not say anything out of boasting or ostentation, but in order to give assurance to me, a sinner and an unworthy one. I trust in God, for whom you live and in whose company you dwell, that I have been guided into this desert for a reason of this kind, that God may make

Deus faciat manifesta. Non enim nostre uirtutis est iudiciis
resistere Dei. Nisi fuisset acceptabile Christo Domino
nostro manifestare te, et qualiter decertasti, nec te ipsam
permiserat uideri ab aliquo, nec me confortaret tantam
365 properare uiam, nusquam ualentem progredi, aut potentem
de cellula mea procedere.'

(12) Haec eo dicente, sed et alia plura, eleuans eum
mulier dixit, 'Uere erubesco, abba meus, ignosce, dicere tibi
turpitudinem meorum actuum. Tamen nudum meum corpus
370 uidisti, denudabo tibi et opera meorum actuum, ut cognoscas quantae turpitudinis luxuria et confusione et
obprobrio repleta est anima mea. Non enim, ut tu ipse
considerasti, propter aliquam gloriam meam, quae circa me
sunt, nolo narrare. Quid enim potero gloriare, que diabolo
375 uas fui aelectionis effecta? Scio autem quia si coepero
narrare ea que sunt de me, fugies a me quemadmodum quis
fugiet a facie serpentis, auribus non sustinens audire ob
inexpedibilia quae sum operata. Dicam tamen, nihil negans,
sed uerius referam, subplicans te prius ut non deficias orare
380 pro me, ut misericordiam merear et inueniam in die iudicii.'

Et senex suffusus lacrimis flebat. Tunc coepit mulier
narrare ea que de se erant, ita dicens:

(13) 'Ego, frater, patriam Egyptum habui. Parentibus
autem meis uiuentibus, duodecimum gerens aetatis annum,
385 affectum illorum spernens, in Alexandriam ueni. Et
quomodo quidem uirginitatem meam in primis uiolauerim,
et qualiter indesinenter et insatiabiliter uitio libidinis iacui
subiugata, erubesco considerare. Hoc enim nunc breue est

361 iudiciis] *CS; N* iudicis.
362 Domino] *CS* deo.
363 nec] *C* non. ipsam] *CS; N* ipsum.
369 Tamen] *C* Tamen, *with* quia *added above line.*
371 luxuria et confusione] *C* luxuriae confusione.
374 nolo narrare] *C* narrabo tibi.
376 ea] *CS; N* e *caudata.*
377 facie] *C* faciet.
385 in] *erased in S.*
388 Hoc enim nunc breue] *C* haec enim nunc longum.

manifest your story. For it is not in our power to resist the judgements of God. If it had not been pleasing to Christ our Lord to make you known, and in what way you have engaged in your struggles, he would neither have permitted you to be seen by anyone nor would he have given me the strength to hasten on such a journey, who never was fit to travel on foot or able to leave my cell.'

(12) When he had said this and much else, the woman raised him up and said, 'Truly I blush – forgive me, my father – to tell you the foulness of my acts. Since you have seen my naked body, I will also lay bare to you the doings of my acts, so that you may know with what filth in my rankness and shame and dishonour my soul is filled. It is not, as you yourself thought, out of any pride on my part that I am unwilling to relate my story. For what will I be able to boast about, I who by choice turned into a vessel for the devil? I know that if I begin to relate my story, you will flee from me in the way anyone will flee from the face of a serpent, and you will not endure to listen with your ears because of the insufferable things with which I was occupied. I will speak, however, denying nothing. I will narrate truly, entreating you first not to cease praying for me, so that I may merit and find mercy on the day of judgement.'

And the old man wept, suffused with tears. Then the woman began to relate her story, speaking thus:

(13) 'My homeland, brother, was Egypt. While my parents were still alive and I was twelve years old, I rejected their love and came to Alexandria. And how in fact I desecrated my virginity in the first place, and in what manner I kept going, incessantly and insatiably subjected to the vice of lust, I blush to contemplate. This can now be stated briefly. I will tell you it

dicere. Illud autem citius dicam, ut cognoscere possis
390 insatiabilem uitii mei ardorem, quem in amorem habui
f.181vb stupri. Decem et septem eo amplius annos, ignosce, |
publice populo transegi in incendo iacens luxuriae. Non
propter alicuius donum perdidi uirginitatem, neque enim ab
aliquibus dare uolentibus aliquid accipiebam quippiam. Hoc
395 enim libidinis furore succensa considerabam, ut amplius
concurrere ad me gratis facerem, implens stupri mei sceleris
desiderium. Neque enim consideres quia pro diuitiis nihil
accipiebam; mendicans enim uiuebam, aut multotiens
stuppam filando. Desiderium, ut dixi, habebam insatiabile,
400 ita ut indesinenter me luxuriae sterquilinio uolutarem. Et
hoc erat mihi placabile, et hoc existimabam uitam, si indesinenter naturae iniuriam peregissem.

'Hoc modo mihi uiuenti, uidi in quodam estus tempore
Lybiorum et Egiptiorum multitudinem concurrentem quasi
405 ad mare. Repperi itaque aliquem et interrogaui, "Ubi putas
festinant uiri isti qui currunt?" Dixit autem mihi, "In
Hierosolimam omnes ascendunt ob sancte crucis exaltatio-
nem, que post aliquos dies solito celebratur." Dixi autem ei
et ego, "Putas suscipiant me, si uoluero abire cum ipsis?" Et
410 ille dixit, "Si habes naulum, nullus te prohibebit." Dixi ei,
"Uere, frater, naulum uel sumptum non habeo. Uadam
autem et ascendam in unam nauium quam conduxerunt, et

---

389 autem] *C* autem tamen.
390 habui stupri] *C* stupri habui.
391 septem] *C* septem et. ignosce] *C* ignosce mihi abba quia.
392 populo transegi] *C* me pro populo commiscui.
397 enim] *C om.*
398 aut multodiens stuppam filando] *C* aliquando stuprando.
400 luxuriae] *C* in luxuriae. Et hoc erat mihi] *C* Hoc autem mihi erat; *S has* mihi erat.
403 estus] *C* estatis.
405 aliquem] *C* aliquem iuuenem.
408 aliquos] *C* aliquot.
409 suscipiant] *CS* suscipient.
410 prohibebit] *C* prohibet.
411 sumptum] *CS; N* suptum. Vadam autem] *C* tamen uadam.
412 nauium quam conduxerunt] *C* nauem illorum.

rather quickly, so that you may be able to understand the insatiable burning of vice in me, which I kept up in my love of debauchery. I spent more than seventeen years, forgive me, openly, with the crowd, sprawling in the fire of lust. I did not lose my virginity on account of anyone's gift, nor used I to accept anything from people who wished to give me something. Indeed, inflamed with the frenzy of desire, I was deliberate about this, so that I might make them flock to me all the more, without payment, satisfying my yearning for the sin of my debauchery. Nor should you think that I accepted nothing because of my wealth; I lived by begging, or often by spinning coarse flax. As I have said, I had an insatiable yearning, to the extent that unceasingly I wallowed in the dungheap of lust. And this was pleasing to me, and this I considered life, if unceasingly I might have inflicted injury on nature.

'While I was living in this way, one time in summer I saw a crowd of Libyans and Egyptians rushing as though towards the sea. I met someone and asked him, "Where do you think those men who are running are hurrying to?" He said to me, "They are all going up to Jerusalem for the Exaltation of the Holy Cross, which is traditionally celebrated in a few days." And I said to him, "Do you think they would take me, if I wished to go with them?" And he said, "If you have the passage money, no one will stop you." I said, "In truth, brother, I don't have passage money or expenses. I will go, though, and board one of the ships which they have hired, and even though they don't want to, they will

licet noluerint, enutrient me; memetipsam eis tradam.
Corpus enim meum in potestatem habentes, pro naulo
415 accipiant." Propterea autem cum eis uolui ambulare – abbas
meus, ignosce – ut multos haberem operatores in meae
libidinis passionem.

(14) 'Dixi tibi, mi domine senex, ignosce mihi: ne
compellas me meam dicere confusionem. Contremesco
420 enim, nouit Dominus. Maculant enim et te et ipsum aerem
isti sermones mei.'

Zosimas autem lacrimis terram infundens respondit ad
eam, 'Dic propter Deum, O mater mea, dic, et ne preter-
mittas sequentia tante salutiferae narrationis.'

425 Illa autem adiungens priori narrationi, addidit haec: 'Ille
autem adulescens sermonum meorum audiens scurilitatem,
ridens discessit. Ego autem fusum quem manu tenebam
proiciens – hunc enim sic post tempus conueniebat me
tenere – cucurri ad mare ubi illos perspexi currentes, et uidi
f.182ra iuuenes aliquos stantes | in litore, numero quasi decem, satis
corpore motuque acerrimos ad id quod michi erat placabile
optimos uisos; erant autem et alii iam qui in naues
ascenderant. Inpudenter autem, ut mihi consuetudo erat, in
medio eorum me inreuerenter dedi, dicens, "Accipite et me
435 uobiscum quo pergitis: non enim ero uobis inplacabilis."
Sed et alios sordidiores proferens sermones, omnes ad
ridendum commoui.

---

413 enutrient . . . tradam] *C* tamen memetipsam eis tradam. enutrientque
me.
415 Propterea . . . ignosce] *C* O abba meus ignosce mihi quia cum eis
uolui ambulare; *for* abbas meus *S has* abbas mi, *with* s *of* abbas *partly
erased.*
420 Maculant enim] *C* quia maculant. et *(first)*] *in S inserted above line.*
424 sequentia] *followed by erasure of* m.
425 haec] *C* haec dicens.
428 proiciens] *C* proiciens a me, *in which* a *has been added above.* hunc
enim sic post tempus conueniebat me tenere] *C om.* sic] si; *S* si. *changed
to* sic, *with* c *inserted above line.*
431 ad] *C* et ad.
432 alii iam qui] *C* alii multi qui iam.
436 ad ridendum] *C; N* arridendum; *S* aridendum, *corrected to* ad
ridendum, *with* r *altered to* d, *and* r *written above.*

feed me; I will give myself over to them. When they have my body in their power, they will accept it instead of passage money." It was for this reason that I wished to travel with them – forgive me, my father – that I should have many companions in the passion of my lust.

(14) 'I have said to you, my aged lord, forgive me: do not compel me to tell my shame. I tremble all over, the Lord knows. These words of mine are defiling both you and the very air.'

Zosimas, soaking the ground with his tears, replied to her, 'Tell, for the sake of God, O my mother, tell, and do not interrupt the flow of such a salvation-bringing narration.'

Then she took up her previous narration and added the following: 'When that youth heard the scurrilousness of my words, he went off laughing. Then I threw away the spindle I was holding – for it suited me to carry this about after a time – and I ran to the sea where I observed the people running, and I saw some young men standing on the shore, about ten in number, certainly vigorous enough in body and movement, seemingly perfect for what I had in mind; and there were others too, who had already gone on board the ships. Shamelessly, as was my wont, I thrust myself brazenly into the midst of them, saying, "Take me also with you where you are travelling: I will not be unpleasing to you."

'But when I uttered other words which were even filthier, I made everyone laugh.

'Illi autem inrubicundum motum meum uidentes, accipientes me in nauiculam portauerunt. Exinde autem
440 nauigationem coepimus. Quae autem post haec acta sunt,
quomodo tibi enarrare potero, homo? Que lingua dicere
potest, aut auris ualet audire, ea que in nauigio uel in itinere
facta sunt, quomodo et nolentes ad peccandum miseros ego
conpellabam nolentes? Non est narrabilis uel inenarrabilis
445 nequissima species cuius non sum infelicibus magistra
sceleris effecta. Ergo nunc satisfactus esto, quia stupesco
quomodo meas mare illud sustinuit iniquitatum luxurias,
quomodo non aperuit terra os suum, et in infernum
uiuentem demersit me, quae tantas in laqueum induxi
450 animas. Sed, ut arbitror, meam Dominus, qui neminem uult
perire, sed omnes fieri saluos, requirebat paenitentiam. Non
enim uult mortem peccatoris, sed longanimiter expectat
sustinens conuersionem.

'Sic namque cum magna festinatione ascendimus Hiero-
455 solimam, et quantas quidem dies ante festiuitatem in
ciuitate commoraui, similibus nequissimis uacaui operibus,
magisque peioribus. Non enim sufficiens fui iuuenibus
mecum in mari luxuriantibus et in itinere, sed et alios
multos peregrinos et ciues in mei scelere actus congregans,
460 coinquinaui seducens.

(15) 'Quando autem uenit sanctae exaltationis festiuitas
pretiosae crucis, ego quidem, sicut et prius, preibam,
iuuenum inlaqueans et capiens animas. Uidi autem primo

---

439 me] *in S inserted above line.*
441 quomodo] *CS; N* quo. homo] *C* o homo.
443 et] *C* etiam. nolentes] *word erased in S.*
447 quomodo] *CS; N* quo.
448 quomodo] *CS; N* quo.
449 quae] *CS; N* qui.
450 animas] *CS; N* animus. Dominus] *C* deus.
455 quantas] *CS* quantos.
456 commoraui] *C* commorata sum.
459 scelere] *C* sceleris.
460 seducens] *C* subiacens.
462 preibam] *C* pergebam.

'When they saw my scandalous behaviour, they accepted me and brought me onto their little ship. Thereupon we began our voyage. But how will I be able to tell you, sir, the things that took place after that? What tongue can tell, or what ears are fit to hear, those things which were done in the ship or on the voyage? – how I compelled even unwilling wretches into sinning, unwilling though they were. There is no basest form of vice, speakable or unspeakable, of which I did not become the mistress for those unfortunates. Be assured now, therefore, that I am amazed how the sea tolerated the lustfulness of my sins, how the earth did not open its mouth and plunge me alive down into hell, since I had lured so many souls into the snare. But, in my judgement, the Lord, who wishes no one to perish but all to be saved, sought my repentance. For he desires not the death of the sinner, but enduring patiently he awaits his conversion [cf. Ezekiel 33. 11].

'Thus, then, with great speed we arrived at Jerusalem, and during the days I spent in the city before the festival, I devoted my time to similar wicked activities, and much worse. For I was not contented with the young men who had acted lasciviously with me on the sea and on the journey, but in the sinfulness of my behaviour I drew together many pilgrims and townspeople, and I seduced and corrupted them.

(15) 'Then when the festival of the Exaltation of the precious Holy Cross arrived, I was going about, as before, ensnaring and capturing the souls of young men. I saw, though, in the early

diluculo omnes ad aecclesiam una [. . .] currentibus, et ueni
465 cum illis in atrium templi. Et cum aduenisset hora diuinae
crucis exaltationis, inpingebam et inpingebar, repellabar
quodammodo. Festinans ingredi cum populo conanter usque
f.182rb ad ia|nuam templi cum his qui ingrediebantur, cum magno
labore et tribulatione adpropinquabam et ego infelix.
470 Quando autem ianuam ingredi ueniebam, illi quidem omnes
sine inpedimento ingrediebantur, me autem diuina aliqua
uirtus prohybebat, non indulgens introitum. Mox igitur
repulsa, eiciebar foras, et sola eiecta inueniebar in atrio
stans. Considerans autem per muliebrem inpotentiam mihi
475 hoc euenire, iterum aliis me inmiscendo, uim mihi
quodammodo faciens introeundi, sed etenim laborabam in
uacuum.

(16) 'Ut enim limina uestigio contingebam, omnes
interius recipiebantur, nullum inpedimentum habentes; me
480 autem solam non recipiebat, sed quasi multitudo militaris
est obuia, ut mihi ingrediendi aditum clauderet. Ita me
repentina aliqua prohibebat uirtus, et iterum inueniebar in
atrio. Hoc ter et quater passa, et facere conans et nihil
proficiens, desperans de cetero et amplius nusquam progredi
485 ualens – factum quippe fuerat corpus meum a ui com-
primentium ualde confractum – recedens itaque discessi, et
steti in quodam angulo atrii templi, et uix aliquando ob
quam causam prohibebar uidere uiuificum lignum in cogi-
tatione reduxi. Tegit enim mentem et cordis mei oculos
490 intellectus salutis, recogitans quia squalida actuum meorum

---

464 una [. . .] currentibus] CS unanimiter concurrentes. abii et ego
currens cum currentibus.
467 conanter] C conante.
468 his] C his autem. magno labore et] C magna laboris.
470 ueniebam] C uolebam.
475 inmiscendo] C inmiscui. mihi] C om.
476 etenim] C om.
481 est obuia] C minitasset. ingrediendi] C ingredienti.
483 passa] C passa sum.
487 steti] CS; N steteri.
489 Tegit] C tetigit; S tegit, corrected to tetigit, with ti inserted above.

dawn all the people together [running] to the church [and I too went running with those who were *(material in square brackets supplied from CS)*] running, and I came with them to the forecourt of the temple. And when the hour of the divine Exaltation of the Cross arrived, I pushed and was being pushed, and was somehow driven back. Hastening to enter with the crowd by attempting to get up to the door along with those who were entering, I too drew near, wretched me, with great effort and tribulation. But when I came to enter by the door, all of those people indeed went in without hindrance, but some divine power restrained me, not granting me entry. Pushed straight back, then, I was thrown outside and found myself standing alone, thrown out, in the forecourt. Assuming that this happened to me because of my womanly weakness, I again joined in with the others and used my strength in order to get in somehow, but in fact I was labouring in vain.

(16) 'When I touched the threshold with the sole of my foot, although all were accepted inside without encountering any hindrance, me alone it did not accept, but it was as though a host of soldiers was in my way, to block my passage to get in. Thus some sudden force was preventing me, and again I found myself in the courtyard. When I had experienced this three or four times, attempting to make headway but not succeeding, giving up further hope and unable to progress any further at all – for my body had become badly injured with the force of the squashing together – I withdrew therefore and went off; and I stood in a particular corner of the courtyard of the temple, and after hardly any length of time the reason why I was prevented from seeing the life-giving cross came into my mind. For the knowledge of salvation touched my mind and the eyes of my heart: I reflected that the filthy vices of my acts barred my passage to get in.

scelera mihi introeundi aditum obserrabant. Coepi namque
flens nimium conturbari et pectus tundere, atque suspiria de
profundo cordis proferens, gemens eiulans, prospexi in loco
in quo stabam sursum imaginem sanctae Dei genitricis
495 stantem, et aio, ad eam intentissime et indeclinanter
adtendens, "Domina uirgo, que Deum uerum secundum
carnem genuisti, scio enim scio quia non est condecens nec
oportunum sic horridam adorare imaginem tuam uel con-
templari tantis pollutis sordibus oculis, que semper esse
500 uirgo dinosceris et casta, que corpus et animam habes
mundam et inmaculatam. Iustum enim est luxuriosam me a
_f.182va_ tua purissima castitatis munditia | abominari et proici.
Tamen, quoniam, ut audiui ob hoc effectus est Deus homo,
quem ipsa digna genuisti, ut peccatores uocaret ad
505 penitentiam, adiuua me solitariam et nullum habentem
adiutorium; praecipe et mihi licentiam tribue aecclesie
patefactum ingredi aditum. Non efficiar aliena a uisione
pretiosissimi ligni, in quo afixus est Deus homo, quem
uirgo concypiens, ipsa uirgo peperisti: proprium sanguinem
510 dedit pro mea liberatione. Iube, domina, et mihi indigne ob
diuinae crucis salutationem ianuam patefieri, et te ex te
genito Christo dignissimam do fideiussorem quia numquam
ultra meam carnem coinquinabo per horrida inmyxtionum
ludibria, sed mox ut filii tui, uirgo sancta, uidero lignum,
515 seculo et actybus eius cum omnibus quae in eo sunt statim
renuntio, et continuo egredior ubicumque ipsa ut fideiussor
me duxeris."

---

491 obserrabant] _in S the first_ r _is partly erased; C_ obseruabant.
493 eiulans] _C_ et eiulans.
495 intentissime] _C_ intendens.
498 adorare] _C_ me adorare.
501 Iustum] _CS; N_ Lustum.
502 purissima] _C_ purissimae.
504 ipsa digna] _S_ digna ipsa.
505 me] _C om._
506 tribue] _C_ tribue ut.
507 ingredi] _C_ ingrediar.
508 afixus] _S_ affixus; _C_ afixus est.
510 pro] _in S inserted in left-hand margin._
512 do] _CS; N_ deo.

Weeping then, I began to feel very great distress and to beat my breast. And as I brought forth sighs from the bottom of my heart, groaning and wailing, I noticed high above me in the place where I stood an icon of the holy mother of God standing, and I looked towards her most intently and unswervingly, and said, "Virgin lady, who gave birth to the true God according to the flesh, I know, truly I know, that it is not decent or appropriate for so frightful a woman to reverence your icon or to look upon you with eyes polluted with such defilements, you who have been distinguished as ever-virgin and pure, who keep your body and soul clean and without stain. It is fitting that I in my lechery should be detested and spurned by the most pure cleanness of your chastity. However, since I have heard that the reason that God, to whom you were worthy enough to give birth, became man, was to call sinners to repentance, help me who am alone and have no helper; order and give me leave to go into the open entrance of the church. Let me not be made a stranger to the precious wood upon which was fastened God and man, whom you yourself conceived as a virgin and gave birth to as a virgin: he gave his own blood as a ransom for me. Command, lady, that the door may be opened to my unworthy self also, so that I may pay homage to the divine cross; and I name you as my guarantor [of my vow], you who were most worthy for Christ to be born of you, that never more will I pollute my body through the dreadful mockery of fornication, but as soon as I see the cross of your son, holy virgin, I will forthwith renounce the world and its works, along with everything that is in it, and I will at once set off to wherever you yourself lead me as my guarantor."

(17) 'Haec dicens, et quasi aliquam satisfactionem re-
cipiens, fidei succensa calore, et de pietatis uisceribus Dei
520 genitricis praesumens, moui me de eodem loco in quo stans
feci orationem, et ueniens, iterum ingredientibus me miscui,
et ultra non erat qui me repelleret neque qui me prohiberet
adpropinquare ianue, quibus in templum introiebant.
Accepit ergo me tremor ualidus et extasis, et tota ex
525 omnibus tremebunda turbabar. Itaque coniungente me ad
ianuam, cuius mihi prius aditus claudebatur, quasi omnis
uirtus que me prius ingredi prohibebat, post autem ingrediendi uiam prepararet: ita absque inpedimenti dolore
introiui, et sic intra sancta sanctorum gaudio repleta sum, et
530 pretiosi ac uiufici ligni crucis adorare mysterium digna
habita sum. Et tunc uidi Dei sacramenta et qualiter est
paratus suscipere poenitentes. Tunc proiciens me pronam in
terram, et sanctum illum exosculans pauimentum, exibam.

'Currens autem illa quae me fidedixit, uenire stans,
535 coniunxi iterum in illum locum ubi fidedictionis
f.182vb conscriptum est cyrographum, et genu curuans coram | uultu
sancte uirginis Dei genitricis, his inprecata sum uerbis: "Tu
quidem, O semper benignissima domina, tuam ostendisti
pietatis misericordiam; tu indigne supplicatione non pro-
540 iecisti; uidi gloriam quam peccatores merito non uidemus:
gloria omnipotenti Deo, qui per te suscepit peccatorum
paenitentiam. Quid amplius peccatrix et misera ualeo
recordari aut enarrare? Tempus est iam implere quam fide-
dixi, fide dilectionis tua placita. Nunc ubi tibi conplacet,

---

523 quibus in] *in S* quibus *altered to* qui *by erasure;* C per quam.
introiebant] *in S altered to* introibant *by erasure.*
528 uiam] C uiam et introitum. ita] C *om.*
529 introiui] C *om.* gaudio repleta] C inuenta. et] C ac.
532 pronam] C prona.
534 Currens autem illa quae me fidedixit] C Cucurri autem ad eam quae
me in fide suscepit. uenire stans] C *om.*
535 coniunxi iterum in illum locum] C coniunxique iterum me illo loco.
fidedictionis] C fige dictionis.
537 uirginis] *in S corrected from* uirgis, *with* ni *inserted above line.*
inprecata] C precata.
544 dilectionis] C electionis. tibi] C *om.*

(17) 'Speaking thus, and receiving, as it were, some kind of assurance, I was inflamed with the heat of faith, and trusting to the mercy of the heart of the mother of God, I moved myself from that same place in which I stood to make my prayer, and I came and again joined myself to those who were going in; and there was no longer anyone who pushed me back or who prevented me from approaching the door by which they entered the temple. A strong trembling came over me, therefore, and a sense of amazement, and, shivering all over because of everything, I was totally agitated. Then I reached the door to which entry had previously been barred to me, and it was as though all the force that had previously prevented me from entering now prepared the way for my entry: thus I went in without the trouble of impediment, and so I was filled with joy inside the holy of holies, and I was deemed worthy to pay reverence to the mystery of the life-giving wood of the cross. And then I saw the sacraments of God and how he is prepared to receive penitents. Then, after I had thrown myself down to the ground and kissed that holy floor, I went out.

'I ran to her [*following C*] who acted as my guarantor, coming to a stop when I reached that place where the bond of surety had been signed, and bending my knee before the face of the holy virgin mother of God, I prayed in the following words: "O ever-most-gracious lady, you have shown me the mercy of your love; you have not rejected the supplication of an unworthy woman; I have seen the glory which we sinners do not see by our own deserts: glory be to the omnipotent God who through you accepts the repentance of sinners. What more can I a sinner and a wretch call to mind or relate? It is time now for me to fulfil what I have undertaken in agreement with your surety of love. Now

545 dirige me. Esto mihi salutis ducatrix et ueritatis magistra,
precedens me in uiam que ducit ad paenitentiam."

'Et haec dicens, audiui uocem alicuius a longe claman-
tis, "Iordanem si transieris, bonam inuenies requiem."

'Ego autem hanc audiens uocem, et pro me hanc factam
550 fuisse credens, lacrimans exclamaui, et ad Dei genitricis
ymaginem prospiciens uociferaui, "Domina, regina totius
orbis, per quam humano generi salus aduenit, noli me
derelinquere."

'Et haec dicens, de atrio sum templi egressa, et festinan-
555 ter ambulabam. Exeunte autem me, uidit quis et dedit mihi
tres nummos, dicens, "Accipe haec, nonna." Ego autem
accypiens, tres ex eis panes comparaui, et hos accepi
benedictioni meae itineris congruos. Interrogaui autem eum
qui panes uendebat, "Unde et qualis uia esse noscitur,
560 homo, que ad Iordanem ducit?" Et cognoscens portam
ciuitatis que in illa latera pergit, currens et iter agebam
plorans.

(18) 'Interrogationi autem interrogationem adnectens,
reliquum diei consumpsi iter properans. Erat autem hora
565 iam diei tertia quando pretiosam merui sanctam uidere
crucem, et sole iam ad occasum declinante, aecclesiam
beati baptistae Iohannis positam iuxta Iordanem repperi, et
in eodem templo ingressa, adorans, continuo in Iordanem
descendi, et ex illa sancta aqua manus et faciem laui.
570 Communicaui autem uiuifica et intemerata Christi Domini
sacramenta in eadem sancti precursoris et baptiste Iohannis

---

546 me] *not in S.*
555 uidit] *C* uidit me.
556 nonna] *C* omnia.
560 homo] *C* o homo.
561 currens] *in S inserted in right-hand margin.*
562 plorans] *C* et plorans.
564 Interrogationi . . . properans] *C om.*
565 merui] *in S corrected from* meru, *with* i *inserted above line.*
566 sole] *CS; N* sola.
567 beati] *CS; N* beate. repperi] *S, in which it is inserted in left-hand margin CN.*
568 ingressa] *C* egressa. Iordanem] *C* iordanen.
569 ex] *added above line.*

direct me to go wherever it pleases you. Be for me the guide to salvation and the mistress of truth, going before me on the road which leads to repentance."

'After I had said this, I heard the voice of someone calling out from afar, "If you cross over the Jordan, you will find good repose."

'Hearing this voice, and believing it to have been directed at me, I cried out weeping, and I looked at the image of the mother of God and exclaimed, "Lady, queen of the whole world, through whom salvation came to the human race, do not abandon me."

'After I had said this, I went out from the courtyard of the temple and hurriedly strode off. As I was leaving, someone saw me and gave me three coins, saying, "Take these, nun." I accepted them and bought three loaves with them, and I took these as a blessing suitable for my journey. I asked the man who was selling bread, "Do you know from where the road goes that leads to the Jordan, sir, and what is it like?" And finding out the gate of the city which leads to those parts, I set out running on my journey, and weeping.

(18) 'Adding enquiry to enquiry, I spent the rest of the day hastening on my journey. It had already been the third hour of the day when I merited seeing the precious holy cross, and when the sun was now setting in the west I found the church of the blessed John the Baptist, situated by the Jordan; and I went into that same temple and worshipped, and without delay went down to the Jordan and in that holy water I washed my hands and face. I received communion, partaking in the life-giving and undefiled sacrament of Christ the Lord in that same basilica of the holy

basilica, et tunc unius panis medietatem commedi, et ex aqua Iordanis bibi, in terra nocte quiescens. Lucescente in crastino, in partem aliam transiui, et iterum petii ducatricem *f.183ra* meam ut me dirigeret ubi ei pla|citum esset. Deueni autem in hanc solitudinem, et a tunc usque hodie elongaui fugiens, expectans Deum meum, qui saluos facit a pusillo animo et procella eos qui conuertuntur ad ipsum.'

Zosimas autem dixit ad eam, 'Quot anni sunt, O domina
580   mea, ex quo hanc inhabitas solitudinem?'

Respondit mulier, 'Quadraginta septem anni, ut considero, sunt ex qua sancta ciuitate egressa sum.'

Dixit autem Zosimas, 'Et quid inuenire ad hesum potuisti, aut inuenis, O mi domina?'

585   Respondit mulier, 'Duos semis quidem panis Iordanem transmeaui deportans, qui post modicum arefacti quasi lapides obduauerunt, et modicum quid usque ad aliquos annos comedens transegi.'

Dixit autem Zosimas, 'Et sic absque dolore transisti
590   tanti temporis longitudinem? Nihil repentine inmutationis conturbantis te sensisti calorem?'

Et illa dixit, 'Rem nunc me interrogas quam dicens ualde contremesco. Si ad commemorationem uenero tantorum quae sustinui periculorum et cogitationes que
595   inique perturbauerunt me, timeo enim ne et iterum ab eisdem aliquam tribulationem patiar.'

Dixit Zosimas, 'Nihil relinquas, o domina, quod non indices. Semel enim in nocte manifesta cognouimus

---

572 ex aqua] *CS; N* aqua.
574 ducatricem] S ductricem.
575 ei] *C om.*
581 considero] *CS; N* considera.
582 ex qua] *S* qua, *with* a *corrected to* o, *inserted above cancelled* a; *followed by* a, *also inserted above line (i.e.* quo a*); C* ex quo ex.
583 hesum] *in S the* h *is partly erased.*
590 Nihil] *CS* et nichil.
593 contremesco] *C* intremesco.
597 o domina] *CS; not in N.*
598 in nocte manifesta] *C* in hoc te manifestari; *cf. R* in hoc te manifestam.

precursor and baptist John, and I ate half of one of the loaves and drank from the water of the Jordan, and I rested on the ground that night. At first light the next day I crossed over to the other side, and again I asked my guide that she would direct me to go wherever it pleased her. And then I came to this desert, and from then until today "I have fled afar off", and "I have awaited my God, who delivers from faint-heartedness and from the storm" [Psalm 54 (55). 8-9] those who turn unto him.'

Then Zosimas said to her, 'How many years has it been, O my lady, since you lodged in this desert [cf. Psalm 54 (55). 8]?'

The woman replied, 'It has been forty-seven years, I think, since I came out from the holy city.'

Then Zosimas said, 'And what have you been able to obtain for food, O my lady, or what do you find?'

The woman replied, 'I crossed over the Jordan carrying two and a half loaves of bread, which dried up after a short time and became hard as stones, and for some years I survived eating some little of them.'

Then Zosimas said, 'And did you live in this way without trouble for such a long passage of time? Did you experience no feelings of passion from your sudden disturbing change?'

And she said, 'Now you are asking me a thing which I shudder terribly to speak about. If I recall to mind such dangers as I have undergone and the thoughts which have wickedly disturbed me, I fear that I will again suffer some affliction from the same things.'

Zosimas said, 'Do not leave out anything, O lady, which you do not tell about. Once and for all I know tonight the evident

ordinem, omnia a te indiminute oportet nos edocere.'

600 (19) Illa autem dixit ei, 'Crede, abbas, decem et septem annis feris inmansuetis et inrationabilibus eluctans desideriis. Dum cybum sumere initiabam, desiderio mihi erant carnes; concupiebam pisces quos Egyptus habebat; desiderabam uinum delectabile mihi; erat ualde in desiderium eo
605 quod multum illud uterer dum essem in seculo; multum enim delectabar in uinum et superabundantius ad ebrietatem bibebam. Et nunc mihi hic aquam autem omnino gustandi non habens uehementissime urebar, et non sustinebam necessitatis periculum. Fiebat autem mihi et de luxuriosis
610 canticis nimium desiderium, perturbans et reducens ad memoriam demoniorum cantica decantare, quae in seculo didiceram. Mox autem lacrimans et pectus meum manu percutiens, meipsam ad memoriam reducebam de con-
f.183rb uenientia fidedictionis quam feceram, | egrediens contra
615 hanc solitudinem. Ueniebam autem per cogitationem ante imaginem sanctae Dei genitricis, que me in sua fide suscepit, et ante illam plorabam, ut effugaret a me cogitationes quae meam miserrimam animam affligebant. Quando autem superflue dolenter lacrimabam, et uiriliter pectus meum
620 tundebam, tunc uidebam lumen undique circumfulgens me, et serenitas mihi quaedam stabilis mox fiebat.

'Cogitationes autem que ad fornicationem iterum conpellebant me, quomodo enarrari possum tibi? Abba, ignosce, ignis intus infelix corpus meum nimius succen-
625 debat, et omnem me per omnia exurebat, et ad desiderium

---

600 abbas] *in S* s *is erased.*
604 erat ualde . . . bibebam] *C* multum enim delectabar in uinum et superhabundandius usque ad hebrietatem biberam. et nunc erat ualde in desiderio eo quod multum ullud uterer dum essem in seculo.
605 illud] *S* illo, o *on erasure and followed by another erased letter.*
607 Et] *C om.* autem] *CS om., S having erasure.*
613 ad memoriam] *C om.*
615 autem] *C om.*
616 me in sua fide suscepit] *C* in sua fide suscepit me.
618 meam] *CS; not in N.*
623 quomodo] *CS; N* quo. enarrari] *CS* enarrare. possum] *S; CN* possunt. Abba] *C* o abba.

order; it is fitting that you teach me without omission everything about yourself [*considerable corruption of NS text is evident at this point, leading to unsatisfactory sense*].'

(19) Then she said to him, 'Believe me, father, I struggled for seventeen years with wild beasts and irrational cravings. While I would begin to eat food, my yearning was for meat; I craved for the fish that Egypt is endowed with; I longed for wine, which was delectable to me. I had an especial yearning for it because I used to enjoy it greatly when I was in the world; for I used to delight much in wine and would drink it very copiously indeed, to the point of drunkenness. And now not having even any water to drink here, I was burning up most terribly, and could not endure the danger with regard to the [lack of] necessities.

Then also an excessive yearning for lascivious songs affected me, agitating me and bringing it into my memory to sing the songs of devils, which I had learned in the world. Soon, however, I would start to weep and would beat my breast with my hand, and I would remind myself about the commitment I made before going out to face this desert. In my mind I would come before the icon of the holy mother of God, who received me as my guarantor, and I wept before her, asking that she would drive away from me the thoughts that were afflicting my wretched soul. When I was shedding tears profusely in my sorrow and beating my breast vigorously, then I would see a light shining around me everywhere, and a certain steady tranquility would soon come upon me.

'But how can I tell you about the thoughts which were urging me again towards fornication? Forgive me, father, a fire fiercely burned my unhappy body from within and raged throughout my whole being, and it dragged me towards a craving for sexual

mixtionis trahebat. Dum mihi ergo talis ascenderet cogitatio, prosternebam meipsam in terram, et lacrimis terram infundens, ipsam ueraciter mihi adstare sperans quae me fidedixerat, minaci me conpellatione exagitare furentem,
630 quasi preuaricanti, et paenas preuaricationis mihi inminentis iram mucronis contra me agentem. Non enim antea surgebam de terra nisi prius illa dulcissima uox inluminaret me solito, et cogitationes perturbantes me effugaret. Semper itaque cordis mei oculos ad illam fideiussorem meam sine
635 cessatione erigebam, deprecans eam auxiliari mihi in hac solitudine et penitentie. Habui adiutorium et cooperatricem ipsam quae genuit castitatis auctorem, et sic decem et septem annorum curriculum, periculis multis, ut dixi, eluctans, a tunc ergo usque hodie adiutorium meum Dei genitricis
640 mihi adstitit, uirgo per omnia et in omnibus me dirigens.'

Dixit autem Zosimas, 'Non exhybuisti cybum aut uestimentum?'

Et illa dixit, 'Panes quidem illos, sicut iam dixi, expendens decem et septem annos, deinceps nutriebar herbis
645 que inueniebantur per solitudinem. Indumentum autem quod habui transmeato Iordane nimia uetustate scissum et consumptum est. Multa ergo glaciali frigore et incendio aestus ardore necessitate sustinui: concremata estus
f.183va incendio et nimio frigoris corpore gelu rigescens | et
650 tremens, multotiens in terram cadens absque spiritu iacerem

---

627 meipsam] in S the ipsam is inserted above line.
628 ipsam] CS; N ipsa.
629 fidedixerat] C in fide superat, with superat altered to susceperat. me] not in S, which has erasure instead.
630 preuaricanti, et] S preuaricantem, followed by erasure of et.
631 agentem] in S corrected to agens by erasure and overwriting.
634 cordis mei oculos] C oculos cordis mei.
635 eam] CS; N eum.
637 quae genuit] S quem genut, with genut corrected by insertion of i above line.
639 adiutorium meum] C adiutrix mea. genitricis] S; N genitris; C genitrix.
641 exhybuisti] C exhibuisti tibi; R habuisti.
647 Multa . . . estus incendio] C multo ergo glacialis heimis frigore et incendii ardore necessitate concermata estu.

intercourse. Therefore, when such a thought arose in me, I would throw myself to the ground and water the earth with my tears, trusting that she who had acted as my guarantor would truly stand by me and furiously scold me with a threatening reprimand, as a violator of my duty, and that as punishment for my violation of duty she would bring against me the anger of a menacing sword. Afterwards I used not to get up from the ground until that most sweet voice [*recte* light] shone upon me as usual and drove away the thoughts that were troubling me. Always and constantly then I would raise up the eyes of my heart to that guarantor of mine, imploring her to help me in this desert and in my penitence. I have had as my help and my assistant her who gave birth to the source of chastity; and thus having struggled with many dangers, as I have said, over the course of seventeen years, from then until today the help of the mother of God has stood by me, the Virgin guiding me through all things and in all things.'

Then Zosimas said, 'Did you not provide yourself with food or clothing?'

And she said, 'I used those loaves, as I have already said, for seventeen years, and since then I have been nourished by the grasses I found through the desert. The clothing I wore when I crossed over the Jordan became torn and worn-out with extreme age. I endured much by necessity, therefore, in the icy cold and in the burning of the heat: I was scorched with the burning of the heat and stiff and shivering in my body with the extreme freezing of the cold, [to the extent that] many times I collapsed onto the ground and lay without breath and motionless. Struggling with

et inmobilis. Multis et diuersis necessitatibus et tempta-
tioniibus inmensis eluctans, a tunc et usque in hac die
uirtutis Dei multis modis miseram animam meam et corpus
custodiuit. Recordans enim de qualibus malis liberauit me
655 Dominus, aesca enutrior inconsummabili, et satietatis
possideo epulas spem salutis meae. Nutrior autem et
cooperior tegmine uerbi Dei, qui continet omnia. Non enim
in solo pane uiuit homo; et non habentes operimentum
petrae circumdati sunt tegmine, hi qui se peccati
660 expoliauerunt tunica.'
     (20) Audiens autem Zosimas quoniam scripturarum
testimonia proferabat ex Moysi uidelicet libris et beatissimi
Iob seu Psalmorum, dixit ad eam, 'Psalmos, O mater,
didicisti, uel alios libros scripturae sancte legisti?'
665   Illa autem hoc audiens, subridens dixit ad eum, 'Crede
mihi, non uidi hominem ex quo Iordanem transiui nisi te
hodie, sed neque feram aut aliud qualecumque animal, ex
quo in hanc deueni solitudinem. Litteras autem numquam
alicubi didici, sed neque sallentem aut legentem aliquem
670 auscultaui. Sermo autem Dei uiuus et efficax est; intel-
lectum intrinsecus docet humanum. Huc usque finis eorum
quae mea sunt. Nunc autem obsecrans quaeso te per in-
carnationem Verbi Dei ut ores pro me luxuriosa.'
     Et cum haec dixisset, cucurrit senex ut genu flexo se in
675 terram prosterneret. Uociferans, cum lacrimis exclamauit,
'Benedictus Deus qui facit mirabilia magna solus, gloriosa
et uehementer stupenda, quibus non est numerus. Benedictus es, Domine Deus, qui ostendisti mihi quanta largyris
tymentibus te. Uere enim non derelinquis querentes te,
680 Domine.'
     Illa autem adprehendens senem, non permisit in terram

---

652 a tunc . . . uirtutis] *in* S hac die *altered superscript to* hanc diem; C A
tunc ergo usque hodie uirtus.
659 petrae] *CS; N* petere. circumdati] *C* circumdate.
665 subridens dixit ad eum] *S* dixit ad eum subridens.
670 est] *C om.*
674 flexo] *CS (S altered from* flexu); *N* flexu.
676 Benedictus . . . numerus] *C om.*

many conflicting distresses and great temptations, from then until this day the power [*reading* uirtus] of God has protected my wretched soul and body in many ways. For when I recall from what evils the Lord has set me free, I am nourished with inexhaustible food and I enjoy as a satiating banquet the hope of my deliverance. I am nourished with and I am clothed by the covering of the word of God, who encompasses all things. For "man does not live by bread alone" [Deuteronomy 8. 3; Matthew 4. 4], and all who have no clothing are enclosed with a covering of stone, if they have divested themselves of the garment of sin [cf. Job 24. 7-8].'

(20) When Zosimas heard that she was citing the testimony of the Scriptures, namely from the books of Moses and of the most blessed Job and of the Psalms, he said to her, 'Have you learned the Psalms, O mother, or have you read other books of holy Scripture?'

Hearing this, she smiled and said to him, 'Believe me, I have not seen a human being since I crossed over the Jordan, except you today, not even a wild beast or any other kind of animal since I came to this desert. I never learned to read anywhere, nor did I even listen to anyone chanting psalms or reading. The word of God is living and powerful [cf. Hebrews 4. 12]; it teaches human understanding from within.

'This brings me to the end of my story. But now I implore and beg you by the incarnation of the Word of God that you pray for me, a lascivious woman.'

And when she had finished speaking, the old man ran to throw himself on the ground on bended knee. He called out, exclaiming amidst his tears, 'Blessed is God, who alone performs great wonders, glorious things and exceedingly amazing, of which there is no number [cf. Job 5. 9; 9. 10]. Blessed are you, Lord God, who have revealed to me how much you bestow on those who fear you. Truly indeed, Lord, you do not abandon those who seek you [cf. Psalm 9. 11].'

She grasped hold of the old man, however, and would not let

perfecte prosterni, sed dixit ei, 'Haec quae audisti, homo,
obtestor te per Dominum Saluatorem nostrum Ihesum
Christum, uerum Deum nostrum, nemini dixeris
685 quoadusque Deus de uinculo carnis absoluat me. His
omnibus acceptis, uade in pace, et iterum hoc eodem
tempore adueniente anno apparebo tibi, et uidebis me, Dei
f.183vb nos | gubernante gratia. Fac autem propter Dominum quod
tibi iniungo: in sacris ieiuniis recurrentibus anni uenturi non
690 transeas Iordanem, ut consuetudinem habetis agere in
monasterio.'

Stupebat autem Zosimas, audiens quoniam et canonem
monasterii inscia quasi que nosset edicebat. Nihil aliud
clamabat nisi gloriam Deo, qui maiora quam petitur dilige-
695 ntibus se largitur. Illa autem dixit, 'Sustine, ut dixi, abbas,
in monasterio, neque enim etsi exire uolueris quoquam,
ualebis. Uespere autem sacratissimae Dominicae caene, accipe diuini corporis et uiuifici sanguinis portionem in sacro
uase dignoque tanti mysterii, et affer et sustine me in parte
700 Iordanis quae coniungitur seculo, et ueniens uiuifica
accipiam dona. Ex quo enim in aecclesia beatissimi
precursoris, priusquam transirem Iordanem, communicaui,
deinceps usque nunc numquam communicaui, numquam
usque nunc sanctificationis huius usa sum portyone. Et ideo,
705 deprecor, meam petitionem ne rennuas, sed per omnia affer
mihi ipsa diuina atque uiuifica mysteria ea hora, qua
Dominus discipulos caene diuinae partycipes fecit. Iohanni
autem abbati monasterii in quo habitas edicito, "Adtende
tibi ipsi et gregi tuo. Aliqua enim fiunt ibi emendatione
710 indigentia." Sed nolo te haec nunc ei dicere, sed quando tibi

---

682 homo] *C* o homo.
684 nemini] *C* ut nemini.
685 Deus] *C om.*
687 anno] *C* futuro anno.
688 quod] *CS* quod nunc.
695 abbas] *S* abba.
699 et affer] *C* afferens.
703 deinceps usque nunc numquam communicaui] *in C added in margin;*
S omits nunc.
709 tibi ipsi] *C* ipsi tibi.

him throw himself right to the ground, but said to him, 'These things that you have heard, sir, I entreat you through our Lord and Saviour Jesus Christ, our true God, not to tell to anyone until God releases me from the bonds of the flesh. Now that you have heard all this, go in peace, and I will appear to you again at the same time next year, and you will see me, if the grace of God guides us. But in the name of God do what I enjoin upon you: when the time of next year's holy fast comes round, do not cross over the Jordan, as it is your custom to do in the monastery.'

Zosimas was amazed when he heard her mentioning the rule of a monastery unfamiliar to her as though she knew it. He spoke nothing else except the glory of God, who bestows more than they ask on those who love him.

Then she said, 'Stay in the monastery, as I have said, father, and indeed even if you wish to go out anywhere you will not be able to. On the evening of the most holy Lord's Supper put a portion of the divine body and life-giving blood in a holy vessel, and one worthy of such a mystery, and bring it and wait for me on that side of the Jordan that adjoins the secular world; and when I come I will receive the life-giving gifts. For from the time when I received communion in the church of the blessed Precursor before I crossed over the Jordan, from then until now I have never received communion, never until now enjoyed a portion of this sacred mystery. And for that reason, I beseech you, do not refuse my request, but bring to me without fail those divine and life-giving mysteries at that hour when the Lord made his disciples participants in the divine Supper. Say too to John the abbot of the monastery in which you live, "Take care for yourself and your flock. For there are some things happening there in need of correction." But I don't wish you to mention this

preceperit Deus.'

Haec dicens, orationem a sene postulans, ad interiorem solitudinem uelocius festinauit.

(21) Zosimas autem prosternens se osculabatur terrae
715   solum in quo eius uestigia steterant. Dans gloriam, inmensas gratias agens, reuersus est laudans et benedicens Dominum nostrum Ihesum Christum. Iterum autem remeans eiusdem solitudinis iter quo uenerat, coniunxit in monasterio eo tempore quo consueuerant hi qui in eodem
720   morabantur. Et totum quidem annum illum tacuit, minime audens quippiam dicere ex his que uiderat. In seipso autem deprecabatur Deum, ut iterum ei ostenderet desiderabilem uultum. Suspirabat autem, anni considerans tarditatem.

Rursus quando autem aduenit sacra ieiuniorum initiata
725   prima Dominica, mox post solitam orationem alii quidem psallentes exierunt; ipse autem modica febris infirmitate detentus, mansit in monasterio. Recordatus est autem
f.184ra Zosimas sanctae illius | sibi predictum, quia 'neque uolens exire ualebis'. Aliquantis autem elapsis diebus, ab infirmi-
730   tate subleuatus, in monasterio conuersabatur.

Quando autem monachi sunt reuersi et coniuncti uespere sacratae caene dominicae, fecit quod iussum est, et mittens in modico calicae intemerati corporis portyonem et pretiosi sanguinis Domini nostri Ihesu Christi, Dei nostri, posuit in
735   canistro caricas modicas et palmarum fructus, id est dactylos, et parum lenticulae infuse aquis, et uenit tarde hora iam uespere, et ad labium Iordanis sedebat, aduentum prestolans sancte. Beatissima illa tardante muliere, Zosimas non dormitauit, sed sollicite adtendebat solitudinem, sus-
740   tinens quod uidere desiderabat. Dicebat autem senex in

---

715 gloriam, inmensas] *C* gloriam deo inmensasque.
717 nostrum] *C om.*
718 coniunxit] *S* coniunxit se; *C* coniunxit et uenit.
719 monasterio] *C* monasterium.
724 Rursus] *C* cursus (*end of previous sentence*).
726 modica febris infirmitate] *CS; N* modicam febris infirmitatem.
727 mansit] *C* mansit intus.
735 caricas] *CS; N* caritas.

to him now but when God tells you.'

When she had said this, she asked for a prayer from the old man and hastened rather quickly into the interior of the desert.

(21) Zosimas then threw himself down and kissed the soil of the ground where her footsteps had been. Glorifying and giving infinite thanks, he returned praising and blessing our Lord Jesus Christ. He made his way back again by the same desert route by which he had come, and he arrived at the monastery at the time that was customary for those who lived there. And all that year indeed he remained silent, daring to say the least amount about what he had seen. Within himself, however, he beseeched the Lord to show him again the longed-for countenance. He would sigh as he considered the slowness of the year.

When the first holy Sunday at the beginning of the fast arrived again, soon after their accustomed prayer the others went out, singing psalms; he, however, was detained by a slight illness of fever and remained in the monastery. He remembered that holy woman's prediction that 'you will not be able to go out even if you wish'. Then after a few days had passed, he recovered from the illness and engaged in life in the monastery.

When the monks returned and assembled on the evening of the Lord's sacred Supper, he did what he had been told: he put in a small chalice a portion of the undefiled body and precious blood of our Lord Jesus Christ, our God, and he placed in a basket a small amount of dried figs and fruits of palms (that is, dates) and a few lentils soaked in water; and he came at a late hour, when it was already evening, and sat on the bank of the Jordan, awaiting the arrival of the saint. Although the most blessed woman was late, Zosimas did not fall asleep but anxiously watched the desert, waiting for what he longed to see. The old man spoke to himself and said, 'Has she come and not

semetipso dicens, 'Numquid ueniens, non me inuenit, re-
uersa est?'

    Haec dicens, lacrimans flebat, et oculos eleuans in
celum, suppliciter Deum deprecabatur, dicens, 'Non me
745 alienes, Domine, uidere iterum quam uidere me tribuisti.
Non uadam uacuus, peccata mea portans increpatione.'

    (22) Haec orans cum lacrimis, alia in eum cogitatio
incidit: 'Quid itaque et si uenerit, faciet? Quomodo transiet
Iordanem, quia nauicula non est? Qualiter ad me indignum
750 perueniat? Heu, me infelicem! Heu, quis me tam iuste
speciei alienauit?'

    Haec sene cogitante, ecce sancta illa aduenit, et in parte
alia fluminis stetit, unde uenerat. Zosimas autem uidens
eam, surrexit gaudens et exultans nimis, glorificans Deum.
755 Lucta autem certaminis in eius fluctuabat cogitationis
intentione, quia non potuit Iordanis transire fluenta. Et
respiciens senex, uidit eam uexillo crucis aquas Iordanis
signantem. Totius tunc noctis tenebras splendor inluminabat
lune, quia tempus recursus illius erat. Statim autem ut
760 signum crucis inpressit, ascendit super aquas, et ambulans
super liquidem equoris fluctum, ueniebat quasi per solidum
iter. Zosimas autem stupens, et genuflectere nitens, clamans
desuper aquas prohibuit, dicens, 'Quid facis, abbas, quia et
sacerdos Dei es, et diuina portas mysteria?'

765   Qui statim oboediuit dicenti. Illa autem descendente de
aquis, dixit seni, 'Benedic, pater, benedic.'

    Ille autem cum magna festinatione respondit – stupor

---

741 ueniens . . . inuenit] *C* uenit et non me inueniens, *with* inueniens
altered from inueni; *in S* ueniens *is followed by* quia *inserted above line.*
744 dicens] *CS; N* deum. Non me] *CS; N* nonne.
748 Quomodo] *CS; N* quo.
749 est] *C* adest.
750 perueniat] *C* perueniet.
754 glorificans] *C* et glorificans.
755 Lucta] *C* luctam.
756 potuit] *C* potest.
757 uexillo] *CS (in S altered from* uexillum?*); N* uexillum.
759 ut] *in C added above.*
762 Clamans] *C* clamans illa.
767 Ille] *S (altered from* illa?*); C* illae; *N* illa.

found me, and turned back?'

After he had said this, he wept tearfully, and raising his eyes to heaven he earnestly entreated God, saying, 'Do not keep me away, Lord, from seeing again her whom you vouchsafed me to see. Let me not depart empty-handed, bearing my sins with reproach.'

(22) As he was praying thus amidst his tears, another thought came to him: 'What will she do, even if she does come? How will she cross over the Jordan, since there is no boat? How may she reach me in my unworthiness? Alas, unhappy me! Alas, who has kept me from her beauty which is so righteous?'

As the old man was thinking this, behold, that saint arrived and stood on the other side of the river from whence he had come. When Zosimas saw her he rose up rejoicing and exulting greatly, glorifying God. But a conflicting thought fluctuated in contention in the anxiety of his mind, that she could not cross the flow of the Jordan. And when he looked again, he saw her making the sign of the cross over the waters of the Jordan – at that time the brightness of the moon lit up the darkness of the whole night, because it was the time of its return. Straightaway then, when she had made the sign of the cross, she rose upon the waters, and walking on the liquid waves of the surface, she came on her way as though on a solid path. Zosimas was amazed and he made to kneel. She restrained him, calling out from on the waters and saying, 'What are you doing, father, for you are a priest of God and you are carrying the divine mysteries?'

At once he obeyed the one speaking to him. She stepped off the water and said to the old man, 'Bless me, father, bless me.'

He answered with great haste – for extreme amazement had

f.184rb enim nimius inua|serat eum in tam gloriosum miraculum –
et dixit, 'Uere non mentitur Deus, qui pollicitus est sibi
770 similes esse eos qui semetipsos purificant. Gloria tibi,
Christe Deus noster, qui ostendisti mihi per hanc ancillam
tuam quantum meae considerationis inferior sim mensurae
uere perfectionis.'

Haec eo dicente, postulauit mulier sanctum dicere fidei
775 simbolum, et sic dominicam inchoaret orationem. Et
expleto 'Pater noster qui es in caelis', sicut mos est, pacis
osculum optulit seniori. Et sic uiuifica mysteriorum sancta
suscipiens dona, in caelis extensis manibus, ingemescens
cum lacrimis, ita clamauit: 'Nunc dimittis, Domine,
780 ancillam tuam secundum uerbum tuum in pace, quia uide-
runt oculi mei salutare tuum.'

Et seni dixit, 'Ignosce, abbas, et aliud meae petitionis
imple mandatum. Uade nunc ad monasterium, Dei pace
gubernatus; recursum autem anni aduenientis, iterum ueni
785 in illo torrente in quo tecum sum prius locuta. Per omnia
non omittas, sed propter Dominum ueni, et uidebis me
iterum qualiter Deus uoluerit.'

Ille autem respondit ad eam, 'Utinam esset possibile
nunc tua sequi uestigia, et tui pretiosissimi uultus uisione
790 frui! Oro, mater, ut unam senis petitiunculam facias, et
modicum cybi ex eo quod huc attuli, digneris accipere.'

Et haec dicens, ostendit ei quod secum detulerat cani-

---

768 in tam] *CS; N* iteram. gloriosum miraculum] *C* glorioso miraculo.
769 mentitur] *CS; N* mititur.
772 meae considerationis] *S* mea consideratione, *last letter having been
altered in both words.*
775 dominicam] *CS; N* dominica.
778 ingemescens] *S* ingemiscens.
779 Domine] *CS; N* deus.
782 meae] *CS; N* me, *followed by comma-like correction sign.* petitionis]
C petionis, *with* ti *added above.*
784 recursum] *S* recursu; *C* rursum. aduenientis] *in C* recursu *added
above.*
788 respondit ad eam] *C* respondens it ad illam.
789 sequi uestigia] *C* uestigia sequi.
790 petitiunculam] *CS; N* petiti uinculam.
791 huc] hic, *marked for correction; S* hic; *C* huc.

overwhelmed him at such a glorious miracle – and said, 'Truly God does not lie, who has promised that those who purify themselves will be like himself. Glory be to you, Christ our God, who has shown me through this handmaid of yours how far in my own regard I am below the measure of true perfection.'

After he had said this, the woman asked him to recite the holy Creed of faith and then to begin the Lord's Prayer. And when he had finished 'Our father who art in heaven', as is customary she offered the kiss of peace to the old man. And so when she had received the life-giving holy gifts of the eucharist, she reached up her hands to the heavens and amidst sighs and tears she cried out as follows: 'Now, O Lord, you let your handmaid depart in peace according to your word, for my eyes have seen your salvation' [Luke 2. 29].

And she said to the old man, 'Forgive me, father, and fulfil another request which I ask. Go now to your monastery, guided in the peace of God; and when next year comes round, come again to that river at which I first spoke with you. At all costs do not fail, but come for the Lord's sake, and you will see me again in the way that God wishes.'

He then replied to her, 'I wish it were possible now to follow in your footsteps and enjoy always the sight of your most precious face. I ask, mother, that you fulfil one little request of an old man, and deign to take a little of the food which I have brought here.'

As he was saying this, he showed her the basket he had with

strum. Illa autem extremis digitis lenticulis contigit, et tres
tollens granos proprio intulit ori, 'Sufficere', dicens,
795 'gratiam spiritus ut custodiret anime substantiam inmaculatam.'

Tunc dicit seni, 'Ora pro me propter Dominum, et meae
infelicitatis memor esto semper.'

Ille pedes eius sanctos contingens, cum lacrimis postu-
800 lans deprecabatur ut oraret pro aecclesia et imperio et pro
se. Dimisit abire flens et eiulans; non enim audebat eam
multum detinere, que nec, si uellet, poterat detineri.

(23) Illa autem iterum crucis inpressione Iordanem
signans, ascendit. Ambulans super liquidum Iordanis
805 elementum, transiuit sicut antea ueniens fecerat. Senex
autem reuersus est, cum gaudio et tremore nimio repletus.
Semetipsum reprehendebat, paenitens, quia nomen sanctae
ut cognosceret, non inquisiuit. Sperabat tamen hoc
aduenienti consequi anno.

810 (24) Transacto eodem anni cursu, uenit iterum in uastam
solitudinem deserti, expletis omnibus secundum consuetudinem, et festinans ad gloriosam illam uisionem
intuendam; perambulans autem solitudinis iter, et inueniens
_f.184va_ aliqua cupiti loci | indicantia signa, dextra leuaque
815 aspiciens, intuitu oculorum deducens, inlustrans ubique
sicut citissimus uenator, sicut ubi suauissimam repertam

---

793 lenticulis] _C_ lenticulas.
794 tres tollens granos] _CS_ tria tollens grana, _C having_ tres _corrected to_
tria.
798 infelicitatis] _CS; N_ infelicitati.
801 Dimisit] _in S preceded by_ et _inserted above line._ eam multum
detinere] _C_ multum detinere eam.
803 inpressione] _CS; N_ in passione.
804 Ambulans] _in S preceded by_ et _inserted above line as correction._
806 cum] _C om._
807 Semetipsum] _CS; N_ semetipsam.
808 inquisiuit] _S; CN_ inquisiuit sicut antea ueniens fecerat, _repeating
phrase from line 805._
810 Transacto] _C_ Transacto autem.
815 intuitu] _CS_ intuitum.
816 sicut _(second)_] _CS_ si.

him. She touched the lentils with the tips of her fingers and took three of the beans and put them in her own mouth. 'The grace of the spirit is enough', she said, 'to keep the substance of the soul undefiled.'

Then she said to the old man, 'Pray for me for the sake of the Lord, and be ever mindful of my unhappiness.'

He took hold of her holy feet and amidst his tears he asked and implored her to pray for the church and the empire and for himself. He let her go, weeping and lamenting; for he did not dare to hold back for long one who could not be held back, even if he wanted to.

(23) She again made the sign of the cross over the Jordan and rose onto it. Walking on the liquid element of the Jordan, she crossed over just as she had done when she was coming. The old man went back then, filled with joy and great trembling. He blamed himself regretfully that he had not asked the name of the saint, so that he might learn it. He hoped, however, that he would get to know it the next year.

(24) When the course of the year had passed, he came again into the vast solitude of the desert. Having done everything according to custom, he hurried to gaze upon that glorious vision. He made his way along the desert path and when he came upon some signs indicating the place he desired, he looked to the right and to the left, narrowing in with the gaze of his eyes and scanning everywhere like the swiftest hunter [to see] if anywhere

conprehenderet feram. Ut autem nihil nullomodo uidit
quoquam mouentem, coepit seipsum lugens infundere lacrimis. Tunc eleuans oculos, orans dicebat, 'Ostende mihi,
820 Domine, absconditum thesaurum quem mihi peccatori
manifestare dignatus es. Ostende mihi, obsecro, Domine, in
corpore angelum, cui totus conparari indignus est mundus.'

(25) Haec orando, peruenit ad locum qui in similitudine
fuerat designatus torrentis, et in extrema eius stans uidit in
825 partem superiorem splendentem solem, et aspiciens, uidit
sanctae mortuum iacens corpus, et manus, ut oportet, sic
conpositas, et ad orientem corpus iacens aspiciens. Currens
autem, lacrimis lauit beatissimae pedes, non enim aliud
corporis eius membrum audebat contingere. Lacrimans
830 autem aliquandiu, et psalmos dicens tempori et rei
congruentes, fecit sepulturae orationem, et dicebat sibi ipse,
'Forsitan non conplacet sancte hoc fieri.'

Haec eo cogitante, designata scriptura erat in terra, ubi
haec legebatur: 'Sepeli, abba Zosima, misere Mariae
835 corpusculum. Redde terrae quod suum est, et puluere adice
puluerem. Ora tamen pro me propter Dominum, transiente
mense Farmothi secundum Egiptios, qui est secundum
Romanos Aprilis die nona nocte, id est v idus Aprilis,
salutifere passionis, post diuinae et sacrae caene
840 communionem.'

(26) Has senex litteras cum legisset, cogitabat quidem

---

817 comprehenderet feram] S; N comprehendere; C comprehendere
feram posset. nullomodo] S ullomodo, *initial* n *having been erased.*
820 Domine] CS; N deus. quem] CS; N que.
821 obsecro, Domine] S; N obsecro deus; C domine obsecro.
824 designatus] CS; N designa.
825 partem superiorem] C parte superiore.
826 iacens] S *(corrected from* iacentem*)*; CN iacentem.
827 aspiciens] S *(corrected from* aspicientem*)*; CN aspicientem.
830 psalmos] S salmos, *with* p *inserted on line at beginning of word.*
834 legabatur] C *corrected to* legabantur. misere] C sepeli misere.
Mariae] *in small capitals.*
837 secundum] CS; N ad sanctam.
838 die nona nocte, id est v idus Aprilis] SC; *not in* N.
839 salutifere passionis] C die salutiferae passionis id est parasceue.

he might catch a most sweet wild animal which he had found. Since he did not see anything moving at all anywhere, he began to lament and to drench himself with tears. Then he raised his eyes and said in prayer, 'Show to me, Lord, the hidden treasure which you have deigned to reveal to me, a sinner. Show to me, I implore you, Lord, the angel incarnate, to whom the whole world is unworthy to be compared.'

(25) While he was praying thus, he reached the place which looked as though it had been a river, and standing at the end of it, he saw the shining sun in the part further up, and as he looked he beheld the body of the saint lying dead; and he saw that the hands were put together in the proper manner and that the body lay facing the east. He ran up to her and bathed the feet of the most blessed one with his tears – for he did not dare to touch any other part of her body. After weeping for some time and saying psalms appropriate to the season and the occasion, he offered a prayer of burial, and he said to himself, 'Perhaps it is not pleasing to the saint for this to happen.'

As he was thinking this, there was writing marked out on the ground, where it read as follows: 'Father Zosimas, bury the little body of the wretched Mary. Give back to the earth what belongs to it, and add dust to dust [cf. Genesis 3. 19]. For the sake of the Lord pray for me, who passed away in the month of Farmothi according to the Egyptians, that is, according to the Romans April, on the ninth day, that is the fifth day before the ides of April, on the night of the salvation-bringing Passion, after receiving the communion of the divine and sacred Supper.'

(26) When the old man had read this writing he wondered at

prius quisnam esset qui scripsit: illa enim, ut ipsa dixerat,
litteras ignorabat. In hoc tamen ualde exultans gaudebat,
quia eius sanctum didicit nomen. Cognouit ergo quia mox
845　ut diuina mysteria in Iordane participauit, eadem hora in
locum illum uenit ubi mox de hoc mundo transiit, et idem
iter quod Zosimas per dies uiginti ambulans uix
consummauit laborans, unius horae cursu Maria con-
sumpsit, et statim migrauit ad Dominum. Glorificans autem
850　Deum Zosimas, et lacrimis corpus eius infundens, 'Tempus
est', inquid, 'miser Zosimas, quod iussum est, perfice. Sed
quid faciam infelix, quia unde fodere non habeo? Sarculus
deest, rastrum non habeo, nihilque pre manibus habens ex
f.184vb omnibus.' |
855　　Haec eo in corde suo secrete dicente, uidit paruum
lignum et permodicum iacens, quod adsumens, cepit fodere.
Ualde enim dura erat terra et ualde fortissima, et
nequaquam ualebat senex fodere eam, quia et ieiunio confectus et longi itineris fatigatione nimis erat defectus.
860　Laborabat enim, et suspiriis nimis urgebatur, et sudoribus
medefactus, ingemuit grauiter ex ipso cordis sui profundo.
Et respiciens, uidit ingentis forme leonem iuxta corpus

---

842 esset] *S* eset, *corrected to* esset, *with* s *inserted above line.*
844 ergo] *CS* uero; *N* ergo.
845 Iordane] *S* ordane, *corrected to* iordane, *with* i *inserted above line.*
846 locum illum] *S* loco illo. idem iter quod] *CS (with letter erased
before* idem *in S); N* eidem iter que.
851 iussum] *S* iustum.
852 fodere] *C* fodiam.
853 nihilque] *S* nichil, *in which the* l *has been written above partly erased*
q, *followed by two further erased letters.*; habens] *S* habes, *corrected to*
habens, *with* n *inserted above line.*
856 iacens, quod] *S (iacens having been corrected); N* iacentem quem;
CN iacentem quem.
857 Ualde . . . eam] *in S written in right-hand margin, with erasure of a
three- or four-letter word in main text and an insertion mark referring to
the text in margin.* fortissima] *C* fortis.
859 defectus] *C* fatigatus.
860 nimis urgebatur] *S* urgebatur nimiis; *C* nimiis urgebatur *(nimiis
corrected in from* nimis).

first who then it had been who wrote it, since she, as she had said, was ignorant of letters. However, he rejoiced with great exultation because he learned her holy name. He realized, in consequence of this, that as soon as she had participated in the divine mysteries at the Jordan, at the same hour she had come to this place, where she soon passed away from this world. And the same journey which Zosimas had scarcely covered in a laborious walk of twenty days, Mary had completed in the course of one hour, and she had immediately departed to the Lord. Glorifying God and soaking her body with tears, Zosimas said, 'It is time, wretched Zosimas, to perform what has been asked. But what shall I do, unhappy as I am, since I have nothing with which to dig? There is no spade, I do not have a mattock; indeed I have nothing at all at hand.'

As he was saying this secretly in his heart, he saw a small little piece of wood lying there. He picked it up and began to dig. The earth was very hard and very firm indeed, and the old man was not at all able to dig it, since he was exhausted with fasting and was very much enfeebled with weariness from his long journey. He kept toiling and pushed himself on with much sighing, and drenched with sweat he groaned deeply from the bottom of his heart. And as he looked up he saw a lion of enormous size standing beside the body of the saint, and it was

sanctae stantem, et eius plantas lambentem. Uidens autem
contremuit pre pauorae grandissime fere illius, precipuae
865 quia audierat sanctam feminam illam dicentem quia
numquam aliquam feram uiderat. Signo autem se crucis
confirmans, armauit undique, credens quia inlesum eum
custodire ualet uirtus iacentis. Leo autem coepit annuere
seni, blandis eum motibus salutans. Zosimas autem dixit
870 leoni, 'Quoniam a Deo missus uenisti, O maxime ferarum,
ut huius Dei famule terre corpus commendetur, exple opus
officii.'

Et iussit sepelire eius corpusculum: 'Ego enim senectute
confectus non ualeo fodere, sed nec congruum quid habeo
875 ad hoc opus exercendum, et iterum ityneris tanti longitudinem properare non ualeo ut adferam. Tu diuino iussu
hoc opus cum ungulis facito, ut commendemur terrae hoc
sanctum corpusculum.'

(27) Continuo autem, iuxta senis sermonem, leo cum
880 brachiis fecit foueam, quantum ad sepeliendum sanctae
corpusculum sufficere possit. Senex uero lacrimis pedes
sanctae abluens, et multipliciter effusa prece exorans pro
omnibus eam nunc amplius exorare, operuit terra corpusculum, adstantem leonem, nudam, sicut eam prius reppere-
885 rat, et nihil aliud habens nisi illud scissum uestimentum,
quod ei iam [. . .] Maria tegit corporis sui membra. Tunc
recedunt pariter, et leo quidem in interiora solitudinis quasi
ouis mansueta abscessit. Zosimas autem reuersus est, benedicens et magnificans Deum, et ymnum laudis decantans

---

863 autem] *C* autem zosimas.
865 sanctam] *C* sanctam illam.
871 opus officii] *C* officium funeris.
873 corpusculum] *C* corpusculum dicens.
875 longitudinem] *C* longitudine.
880 ad] *S* a, *corrected to* ad, *with* d *inserted above line.*
884 adstantem leonem] *S* adstante leone; *C om.* nudam] *C* nudum
sanctae.
885 habens] *S* habentem. illud] *C* illum.
886 iam [. . .] Maria] *S* iam antea proiecerat zosimas; ex qua aliqua
maria; *C* iam antea proiecerat zosimas. ex quo aliqua maria. tegit] *CS; N*
tetgit.
889 magnificans] *C* glorificans.

licking the soles of her feet. When he saw it he trembled out of terror at that huge beast, especially since he had heard that holy woman saying that she had never seen any wild animal. Strengthening himself with the sign of the cross he armed himself all on all sides, trusting that the virtue of the one lying there would be able to preserve him unharmed. The lion began to make nodding motions towards the old man, however, greeting him with fawning movements. Zosimas said to the lion, 'Since you have come, O greatest of wild beasts, sent by God in order that the body of this handmaid of God may be commended to the earth, carry out the task of your duty.'

And he commanded it to bury her little body: 'For I am exhausted by old age and do not have the strength to dig. I do not even have anything suitable for carrying out this task, and I have not the strength to cover the distance of such a journey in order to bring something. By divine command, you perform this task with your claws, so that we may commend this holy body to the earth.'

(27) Immediately then, in accordance with the word of the old man, the lion made a pit with its forelegs, big enough to do for burying the body of the saint. The old man bathed the feet of the saint with his tears, and pouring forth his prayers he repeatedly beseeched her to intercede now even more for all people; and with the lion standing by he covered the body with earth, naked, just as he had previously met her, wearing nothing else but that torn garment which [Zosimas had previously thrown to her, with which *(following S)*] Mary covered the parts of her body. Then they went away at the same time, and the lion disappeared into the inner desert like a tame sheep. Zosimas meanwhile turned back, blessing and praising God, and he kept

890   Christo Deo nostro.

Ueniens autem in cenobium, omnia eis ab initio retulit.
Nihil abscondit ex his omnibus que uidit et audiuit, ut
omnes audientes magnalia Dei, nimio stupore admirarentur
et cum timore et amore magna fide celebrarent beatissime
895   sanctae transitus diem. Iohannes autem abbas inuenit
quosdam emendari corripiendos iuxta sanctae illius
sermonem, et hos miserante Deo conuertit. Zosimas autem
in eodem degens monasterio, impleuit annos centum, et
tunc migrauit ad Dominum in pace, gratia Domini nostri
900   Ihesu Christi, cum quo Patri gloria et honor et imperium,
una cum sancto et uiuificatore et adorando Spiritu, nunc et
semper et in secula seculorum. Amen.

---

890 Deo] *C* domino.
891 Ueniens] *C* Venientes. retulit] *C* recurrit et.
892 audiuit] *C altered from* audit, *with* ui *written above.*
894 magna] *C* magno, *with* et *added above.* beatissime] *C* beatissimi.
896 emendari] *in S there are points under all letters, indicating excision.*
C emendatione.
898 eodem] *C* eo, *altered to* eodem, *with* dem *written above.*
899 gratia . . . Amen] *after* Amen *C has* EXPLICIT CONVERSIO
VIRILEQUE ET MAGNVM CERTAMEN VENERABILIS MARIAE
AEGYPTIACAE.
900 Christi, cum . . . Amen] Christi *completes 183vb writing space, the
remainder written in bottom margin.*
901 adorando] *CS; N* adorandum. nunc] *in S inserted above line.*

singing a hymn of praise to Christ our God.

When he came to the monastery, he related everything to them from the beginning. He concealed nothing out of all the things he had seen and heard, so that all who heard marvelled with amazement beyond measure at the wonders of God, and in awe and love celebrated with great faith the day of the passing of the most holy saint. John the abbot found certain people in need of censuring, whom he should chastise, in accordance with the word of that holy saint, and with the mercy of God he converted them. Zosimas completed a hundred years, living in that same monastery, and then he journeyed to the Lord in peace, by the grace of our Lord Jesus Christ, with whom let there be glory and honour and dominion to the Father, together with the life-giving and adorable Holy Spirit, now and always, for ever and ever. Amen.

GLOSSARY

This Glossary provides citations and descriptions of all forms of words that occur in the edited text. For frequently-occurring forms, the first two instances are cited. In distinguishing *Đ* and *Þ*, head-words and citations follow the usage of the text, but subsequent line references ignore variations between these two letters. *Æ* is treated as a separate letter and follows *A*; *Đ/Þ* comes after *T*. Head-words with *ge-* prefix are listed under *G*. The symbol ~ indicates that the head-word should be supplied; * after a line number indicates a restored or emended form. With adjectives, forms should be taken as 'strong' unless it is specified otherwise.

The following grammatical abbreviations are used (for other abbreviations employed here, see pp. x-xii):

a.	accusative	n.	nominative
adj.	adjective	nt.	neuter
adv.	adverb	neg.	negative
anom.	anomalous	num.	number, numerical
art.	article	p.	plural
conj.	conjunction	part.	participle
correl.	correlative	pers.	person, personal
cp.	comparative	poss.	possessive
d.	dative	pp.	past participle
def.	definite	prep.	preposition
dem.	demonstrative	pres.	present
f.	feminine	pret.	preterite
g.	genitive	pron.	pronoun
imp.	imperative	refl.	reflexive
impers.	impersonal	rel.	relative
ind.	indicative	s.	singular
indecl.	indeclinable	sbj.	subjunctive
indef.	indefinite	sp.	superlative
inf.	infinitive	sv.	strong verb
infl.	inflected	undecl.	undeclined
inst.	instrumental	uninfl.	uninflected
interj.	interjection	v.	verb
interrog.	interrogative	w.	with
intrans.	intransitive	wk.	weak
m.	masculine	wv.	weak verb

A

ā, *adv.*, always, for ever: 960.

ābǣdan, *wv.1*, require, demand: ābǣde *pret.ind.3s.*, 160.

abbud, *m.*, abbot: *n.s.*, 280, 372 etc.; abbod, 91, 251, 272; abbot, 317G, 340G, 349G; ~es *g.s.*, 145; ~e *d.s.*, 81, 744; abbode *d.s.*, 102.

āblinnendnyss, *f.*, ceasing, cessation: ~e *d.s.*, 120.

ābrǣdan, *wv.1*, stretch out: ābrǣdedum *pp. (d.p.f.)*, 829.

ac, *conj.*, but: 18, 73, etc.

ācennan, *wv.1*, give birth to: ācendest *pret.ind.2s.*, 494, 503, 510; ācende *3s.*, 655.

adal, *m.*, filth, mire: ~e *d.s.*, 383.

ādelfan, *sv.3*, dig: *inf.*, 916.

ādrēogan, *sv.2*, put up with, endure: ādrēogende *pres.part.*, 626; ādruge *pret.sbj.3s.*, 436.

ādrūwian, *wv.2*, dry up: ādrūwodon *pret.ind.3p.*, 602.

ādūne, *adv.*, down: 352G.

āfanded, *adj. (pp. of* āfandian, test*)*, accomplished, excellent: ~esta *sp.n.s.m.*, 30.

āfēdan, *wv.1*, feed, support: āfēdað *pres.ind.3p.*, 399; āfēded *pp.*, 680.

Affricane, *proper name (p.)*, Africans: ~a *g.*, 388.

āflȳman, *wv.1*, put to flight, drive away: āflȳmde *pret. sbj.3s.*, 636, 651.

āfremdian, *wv.2*, alienate: āfremdad *pp.*, 798.

āfyrhtan, *wv.1*, frighten: āfyrht *pp.*, 209.

āgen, *adj.*, own: *a.s.n.*, 510, 514; ~e *a.s.m.*, 908; ~es *g.s.nt.*, 175; ~um *d.s.m.*, 174; ~re *d.s.f.*, 822.

āgēotan, *sv.2*, pour forth, shed: āgēat *pret.ind.3s.*, 510.

āhabban, *wv.3*, refrain from, hold oneself back from: āhæbbende *pres.part.*, 199.

āheardian, *wv.2*, harden: āheardodon *pret.ind.3p.*, 603.

āhebban, *sv.6*, raise up: āhōf *pret.ind.1s.*, 653.

āhrefnian, *wv.2*, endure: āhrefnode *pret.ind.1s.*, 619.

āht, *nt.*, anything *(w.g.)*: *a.s.*, 63, 375 etc.; ~es *g.s.*, 375.

āhwyder, *adv.*, (to) anywhere: 729.

āhȳdan, *wv.1*, hide, conceal: āhȳdde *pret.ind.3s.*, 18.

āhyldan, *wv.1*, incline, sink: āhylde *pret.ind.3s.*, 574.

ālǣtan, *sv.7*, leave: ālēt *pret.ind.3s.*, 855.

ālecgan, *wv.1*, lay, arrange: ālegdon *pret.ind.3p.*, 885.

Alexandria, *proper name*, Alexandria: ~n *d.s.*, 364.

ālȳsan, *wv.1*, free, deliver: ālȳse *pres.sbj.3s.*, 349G, 716 ālȳsde *pret.ind.3s.*, 679.

ālȳsednyss, *f.*, redemption, deliverance: ~e *d.s.*, 511.

Ālȳsend, *m.*, Redeemer: *a.s.*, 714.

amen, *interj.*: 302, 960.

an: *see* on.

ān, (i) *adj.*, a certain, a, one: *n.s.nt.*, 892; *a.s.n.*, 43, 957; ~e *a.s.f.*, 554; ~es *g.s.m.*, 582*; ~re *g.s.f.*, 843, 907; ~um *d.s.m.*, 684; *d.s.n.*, 24, 28; *d.p.f.*, 115; ǣnne *a.s.m.*, 776, 779; alone, only: *n.s.nt.*, 110, 131, 336G; ǣnne *a.s.m.*, 159; (ii) *pron.*, one, a certain one: *a.s.nt.*, 398; ǣnne *a.s.m.*, 151.

āna, *indecl. adj.*, alone: 91, 472 etc.

anbrincgelle, *f.*, incitement: anbrincgellan *d.s.*, 350G*.

and, *conj.*, and: 2, 9 etc.

andbidian, *wv.2*, wait for, expect: andbidigende *pres. part.*, 589*.

andgyt, *nt.*, understanding, knowledge: *a.s.*, 698; ~e *d.s.*, 96; andgit *n.s.*, 485.

andlyfen, *f.*, food: ~e *g.s.*, 661.

andswarian, *wv.2*, answer: andswarigende *pres.part.*, 302; andswarode *pret.ind. 3s.*, 312G, 391 etc.

andweard, *adj.*, present: ~an *a.s.m.wk.*, 588, 657, 677.

andwlita, *m.*, countenance, face: ~n *a.s.*, 346G, 762; *g. s.*, 842; *d.s.*, 541.

andwyrdan, *wv.2*, answer: and-wyrde *pret.ind.3s.*, 86.

āneg, *adj.*, alone, solitary: ānegre *d.s.f.*, 505.

anlīcnyss, *f.*, image, likeness: ~e *a.s.*, 491, 496, 540*; *d.s.*, 559, 634.

ānmōdlīce, *adv.*, eagerly, resolutely: 455.

ansȳn, *f.*, sight, face: *n.s.*, 483; ansȳnu *a.s.*, 578.

Aprilis, *noun (Latin)*, April: 896; Aprelis, 897.

ārǣran, *wv.1*, raise up: ārǣrde *pret.ind.3s.*, 340G.

āreccan, *wv.1*, relate, tell: *inf.*, 136, 428, 548; ārecce *pres. ind.1s.*, 355; āreccenne *infl. inf.*, 369, 405.

ārfæst, *adj.*, gracious, merciful: ~an *a.s.f.*, 543; *g.s.f.*, 523.

ārian, *wv.2*, pardon: āra *imp.s.*, 642.

ārīsan, *sv.1*, arise: ārās *pret. ind.3s.*, 802, 814; ārisan *3p.*, 303.

arn: *see* yrnan.

ārwurðe, *adj.*, worthy, deserving of respect: ārwurða *n.s. m.wk.*, 5; ārwurðan *g.s.f. wk.*, 3.

āscēofan, *sv.2*, thrust, shove: āsceofen *pp.*, 472*.

ascunian, *wv.2*, reject, exclude: ascunod *pp.*, 501*.

āsecgan, *wv.3*, say, tell: *inf.*, 429; āsecge *pres.sbj.2s.*, 715.

āsecgendlic, *adj.*, speakable: *n.s.f.*, 433.

āsendan, *wv.1*, send: āsend *pp.*, 930.

āstandendnyss, *f.*, continuation, perseverance: ~e *d.s.*, 329G.

āstīgan, *sv.1*, ascend, go up, board: *inf.*, 398, 646; āstāh *pret.ind.1s.*, 577.

āstreccan, *wv.1*, stretch out, prostrate: *inf.*, 712; āstrehte *pret.ind.1s.*, 647; *3s.*, 276, 277 etc.; *pret.sbj.3s.*, 705; āstreht *pp.*, 337G.

āstyrian, *wv.2*, stir, excite: āstyrede *pret.ind.1s.*, 424, 524.

āsyndrian, *wv.2*, separate: āsyndrede *pret.ind.3s.*, 166

āþenian, *wv.2*, stretch out, extend, apply: āþenede *pret. ind.3s.*, 119*; āþenedum *pp. (d.p.m.)*, 321G.

āðolian, *wv.2*, endure: āðolode *pret.sbj.3s.*, 436.

āþringan, *sv.3*, push away: āþrungen *pp.*, 465.

āwendan, *wv.1*, avert, turn aside, divert: āwende *pret. ind.3s.*, 42*.

āweorpan, *sv.3*, throw away, cast off/out: āwyrpð *pres. ind.3s.*, 239; āwyrp *imp.s.*, 258; āwearp *pret.ind.1s.*,

414; *3s.*, 212; āwurpe *2s.*, 544; āworpen *pp.*, 501.

ax, *f.*, ash: *n.s.*, 345G.

āxian, *wv.2*, ask: āxast *pres. ind.2s.*, 608; āxode *pret.ind. 1s.*, 390, 567; *3s.*, 177, 865.

āxung, *f.*, enquiry, question: ~a *a.s.*, 570.

Æ

æ, *f.*, law, rule: *d.s.*, 184.

æfen, *m.*, evening: *d.s. (endingless locative?)*, 775; ~ne *d.s.*, 730.

æfenrepsung, *f.*, nightfall: *n.s.*, 190; ~a *d.s.*, 574.

æfre, *adv.*, ever: 689.

æfst, *m.*, malice: *n.s.*, 351G.

æfter, *prep.w.d./inst.*, after *(temporal)*: 8, 9 etc.; in accordance with: 494.

æfterfylgednyss, *f.*, sequel, continuation: ~e *a.s.*, 410.

æfterfyligan, *wv.1*, follow after, succeed: æfterfyligendan *pres.part. (d.s.nt.wk.)*, 865.

æghwanon, *adv.*, on every side, all around: 925.

æghwilc, (i) *adj.*, every, each, any, all: ~ne *a.s.m.*, 166; æghwylcne, 107; ~re *g.s.f.*, 654; *d.s.f.*, 127; ~um *d.s.nt.*, 685; (ii) *pron.*, each one: *n.s.m.*, 155, 174, 180; æghwylc *n.s.m.*, 161.

ægþer (. . .) ge . . . ge, *conj.*, both . . . and: 1, 406 etc.;

ægðer ge . . . and, 431, 687.

ælc, (i) *adj.*, each, any: ~es *g.s.m.*, 505; ~ere *d.s.f.*, 463, 472; (ii) *pron.*, each one: *n.s. m.*, 111, 145.

ælmihtig, *adj.*, almighty: ~um *d.s.m.*, 546.

ælðēodig, *adj.*, foreign: ~e *a.p.m.*, 450.

ǣmerge, *f.*, dust: *n.s.*, 344G.

ǣnig, (i) *adj.*, any: *n.s.m.*, 62, 65, 94; ~es *g.s.m.*, 374; *g.s. nt.*, 693; ~um *d.s.m.*, 380; *d. p.nt.*, 63, 375; ~a þinga, in any respect: 856, 857; (ii) *pron.*, anyone, anything: *n.s. m.*, 396.

ǣnlīpig, *adj.*, alone, solitary: ~u *n.s.f.*, 466.

ǣnne: *see* ān.

æppel, *m.*, fruit, apple: æppla *a.p.*, 157.

ǣr, (i) *prep.w.d.*, before *(temporal)*: 172, 445 etc.; (ii) *adv.*, before, beforehand: 28, 180 etc.; ǣrest *sp.*, first, at first: 79, 208 etc.; (iii) *conj.*, before: 649, 738; ǣr þan þe, 715; ǣr þām þe, 747.

ǣrist, *f.*, resurrection: ~es *g.s.*, 125, 172.

ǣrnemergen, *m.*, early morning, daybreak: *d.s (endingless locative?)*, 191, 455; ǣrnemorgen, 583.

ǣsce, *f.*, asking, enquiry: ǣscan *d.s.*, 571.

æt, *prep.w.d.*, at: 283, 747 etc.; from: 568.

ǣt, *m./nt.*, food: ~e *d.s.*, 598.

ætēowan, *wv.1*, show, reveal: *inf.*, 208, 879; ætēowe *pres. ind.1s.*, 718; *pres.sbj.3s.*, 71; ætēowdest *pret.ind.2s.*, 543, 708 etc.; ætēowde *3s.*, 222, 226; *pret.sbj.3s.*, 761; ætēowdon *3p.*, 117; ætēowod *pp.*, 552.

ætēowednyss, *f.*, revelation, manifestation: ~e *a.s.*, 47.

ætgædere, *adv.*, together: 101, 142 etc.

ætstandan, *sv.6*, stand near: *inf.*, 648; ætstōd *pret.ind.3s.*, 68.

B

bām: *see* būtū.

bæclincg, *adv.*, backwards: on bæclincg gewend, with one's back turned: 267-68.

be, *prep.w.d.*, about, concerning, by, with respect to: 19, 49 etc.

bēan, *f.*, bean: ~a *a.p.*, 157.

bearn, *nt.*, child, son: *a.s.*, 514.

bebēodan, *sv.2*, command, direct, entrust, commit: bebēode *pres.ind.1s.*, 513, 719; *pres.sbj.3s.*, 748; bebēad *pret.ind.3s.*, 79, 266; beboden *pp.*, 776, 910.

bebod, *nt.*, commandment, requirement, order: ~u *a.p.*, 31; ~um *d.p.*, 93.

bebrūcan, *sv.2*, enjoy, make use of, consume: **bebrēac** *pret.ind.3s.*, 42.

bebyrigan, *wv.1*, bury: **bebyrig** *imp.s.*, 893.

becuman, *sv.4*, arrive, come to: *inf.*, 458, 797; **becumaδ** *pres.ind.3p.*, 610; **becōm** *pret.ind.1s.*, 461, 539 etc.; *3s.*, 77, 198 etc.; **becōmon** *3p.*, 243; **becuman** *pp.*, 758.

bedǣlan, *wv.1*, deprive of: **bedǣled** *pp.*, 505.

bedīglian, *wv.2*, conceal, keep secret: **bedīglige** *pres.sbj. 3s.*, 14; **bedīglode** *pret.ind. 3s.*, 951.

befædmian, *wv.2*, encircle, encompass: **befædmaδ** *pres. ind.3s.*, 683.

befæstan, *wv.1*, entrust, commit: **befæste** *pres.ind.1s.*, 399; *pres./pret.sbj.2s.*, 931; **befæston** *pres.sbj.1p.*, 937; **befæst** *pp.*, 57.

befeallan, *sv.7*, fall, befall: **befēoll** *pret.ind.3s.*, 795.

befōn, *sv.7*, surround, embrace: **befēhδ** *pres.ind.3s.*, 683.

beforan, *prep.w.d.*, before, in front of: 66, 541 etc.; ~ **gesegnesse**, beyond expression, 89.

beforhtian, *wv.2*, dread, fear:

beforhtige *pres.ind.1s.*, 609.

begangan, *sv.7*, traverse: **begangende** *pres.part.*, 192; attend to, carry out: **begangenne** *infl.inf.*, 94, 933G.

begytan, *sv.5*, obtain: **begytanan** *pp. (a.p.nt.wk.)*, 152.

behealdan, *sv.7*, consider, pay attention to, look at: **behealde** *pres.sbj.3s.*, 96; **behealdende** *pres.part.*, 118, 219 etc.; **behēold** *pret.ind. 3s.*, 205, 786.

behealdnyss, *f.*, attention, regard, gaze: ~e *d.s.*, 204.

behelian, *wv.2*, cover up: **beheligenne** *infl.inf.*, 270.

belimpan, *sv.3*, concern, relate to: **belimpeδ** *pres.ind.3s.*, 734; **belumpon** *pret.ind.3p.*, 890.

belūcan, *sv.2*, lock, shut, *(of breath)* impede, restrict: **beluce** *pret.sbj.3s.*, 374; **belucen** *3p.*, 486; **belocen** *pp.*, 127, 228, 530.

bēn, *f.*, prayer, request: ~a *a.s.*, 544; ~e *a.s.*, 740; *g.s.*, 835, 843.

bend, *m.*, bond, fetter: ~um *d.p.*, 716.

bēon, *anom. v.*, be: *inf.*, 46, 501 etc.; **eom** *pres.ind.1s.*, 254, 343G etc.; **eart** *2s.*, 259, 281 etc.; **is** *3s.*, 7, 11 etc.; **bist** *2s.*, 744; **biδ** *3s.*, 295; **synd** *3p.*, 74, 89 etc.; **syndon** *3p.*,

849; **bēoð** *3p.*, 50; **sȳ** *pres.*
sbj.3s., 18, 62 etc.; **sīe**, 290;
sȳo, 787; **sīh** *pres.sbj.1s.*,
433; **sēo**, 545, *3s.*, 726; **bēo**
pres.sbj.1s., 421; *3s.*, 96;
imp.s., 435, 551; **wæs** *pret.*
ind.3s., 11, 24 etc.; **wære**
2s., 498, 930; *pret.sbj.3s.*, 8,
46 etc.; **wæron** *pret.ind.3p.*,
114, 139 etc.; *pret.sbj.3p.*,
147.
beorðor, *nt.*, birth: **beorðrum**
d.p., 56 *(see Commentary)*.
beran, *sv.4*, bear, carry: **berende** *pres.part.*, 793; **bær**
pret.ind.3s., 156.
berēafian, *wv.2*, deprive of,
bereave: **berēafod** *pp.*, 255.
besencan, *wv.1*, cause to sink,
plunge: **besencte** *pret.ind.*
3s., 438.
besēon, *sv.5*, look *(refl.)*: **beseah** *pret.ind.3s.*, 920.
besmēagan, *wv.1*, consider
about: **besmēage** *pres.sbj.*
3s., 745.
besmītan, *sv.1*, defile, pollute:
besmīte *pres.ind.1s.*, 515;
besmāt *pret.ind.1s.*, 366,
451; **besmitenum** *pp. (d.p.*
f.), 497; **besmitenre** *(d.s.f.)*,
500.
beswǣlan, *wv.1*, burn, sear:
beswǣled *pp.*, 669.
beswīcan, *sv.1*, seduce, deceive:
beswīcende *pres.part.*, 451.
besylian, *wv.2*, defile, sully:

besylede *pret.ind.1s.*, 384.
beþurfan, *pret.pres.v.*, need,
want *(w.g.)*: **beþorfest** *pret.*
ind.2s., 660; **beþorfte** *pret.*
sbj.3s., 61.
bewǣfan, *wv.1*, clothe, cover:
bewǣfde *pret.ind.3s.*, 946;
bewǣfed *pp.*, 259, 267.
bewendan, *wv.1*, turn: **bewende**
pret.ind.3s., 213, 339G.
bewerian, *wv.2*, hinder, prevent, block *(w.g. of access
or passage)*: **bewerede** *pret.*
ind.3s., 464, 475, 527.
bewitan, *pret.pres.v.*, be in
charge of, keep, watch over:
bewiste *pret.ind.3s.*, 80.
bīdan, *sv.1*, await *(w.g.)*: **bīð**
pres.ind.3s., 443.
biddan, *sv.5*, ask: *inf.*, 584;
bidde *pres.ind.1s.*, 252, 297
etc.; **biddende** *pres.part.*,
542, 653 etc.; **biddenne** *infl.*
inf., 280; **bæd** *pret.ind.1s.*,
636; *3s.*, 277, 278 etc.; **bǣd-
on** *3p.*, 146.
bīgan, *wv.1*, bend: **bīgenne** *infl.*
inf., 809.
bindan, *sv.3*, bind: **band**
pret.ind.3s., 162.
binnan, *prep.w.d.*, within: 717.
bismerlicum, *adv.*, shamefully:
423.
biterlīce, *adv.*, bitterly: 359,
487, 789.
bletsian, *wv.2*, bless: **bletsa**
imp.s., 297, 816; **bletsig-**

enne *infl.inf.*, 281; **bletsigende** *pres.part.*, 949; **blætsigende**, 754; **bletsode** *pret.
ind.3s.*, 805; **gebletsod** *pp.*,
300, 706, 707.

bletsung, *f.*, blessing: ~a *a.s.*,
146, 276, 277; *d.s.*, 348G;
~an *a.s.*, 238.

blōd, *nt.*, blood: *a.s.*, 510; ~es
g.s., 733, 737 etc.

bōc, *f.*, book: ~a *g.p.*, 687.

borhhand, *f.*, surety, guarantor:
~a *d.s.*, 652.

brēost, *f.*, breast: *a.s.*, 348G,
488 etc.

bringan, *wv.1*, bring, offer:
bringe *pres.sbj.2s.*, 740;
bringanne *infl.inf.*, 935G;
brōhte *pret.ind.1s.*, 601,
845, 847; *3s.*, 827.

broga, *m.*, danger, terror: ~n
d.s., 589.

brōðor, *m.*, brother: *n.s.*, 84,
397; *a.s.*, 362.

brūcan, *sv.2 (w.g.)*, partake of,
consume, use, enjoy: *inf.*,
622, 842; **brūcende** *pres.
part.*, 189; **brēac** *pret.ind.1s.*,
603, 624, 739.

bryne, *m.*, burning, fire: *a.s.*,
370; *a.s.*, 607; *d.s.*, 373;
byrne, 670.

būgan, *sv.2*, bend, turn away:
bēah *pret.ind.3s.*, 169.

burh, *f.*, city: **byrig** *d.s.*, 365,
596.

burna, *m.*, stream: *n.s.*, 242,

882; ~n *a.s.*, 243; *g.s.*, 245;
d.s., 837.

būtan, (i) *prep.w.d.*, without:
18, 120 etc.; but, apart from:
būton, 183, 693, 994; *w.a.*,
except: **būton**, 158. (ii)
conj., unless, except that:
336G; **būton**, 95, 129, 248
(cf. DOE, **būtan**, III.C.1);
būton þæt, except that: 264.

būtū, *adj.*, both: *n.m.*, 303; **bām**
d.m., 514.

bycgan, *wv.1*, buy: **bohte** *pret.
ind.1s.*, 568.

byfian, *wv.2*, tremble: **byfigende** *pres.part.*, 286, 529;
byfiende, 326G.

byrgan, *wv.1*, bury: **byrgenne**
infl.inf., 940.

byrgenn, *f.*, burial: ~e *g.s.*, 889.

byrhtnyss, *f.*, brightness: *n.s.*,
806˙.

byrne: *see* **bryne**.

bysen, *f.*, example: **bysne** *d.s.*,
38; **bysene** *g.s.*, 61.

bysmerglēow, *nt.*, shameful
lust: *a.s.*, 516.

bysmor, *nt.*, shamefulness, disgrace: *a.s.*, 413.

C

cafertūn, *m.*, courtyard: ~es
g.s., 481; ~e *d.s.*, 466, 475,
564.

calic, *m.*, chalice: *a.s.*, 776.

caric, *noun (found only here)*:

dried fig: ~**um** *d.p.*, 779.

cāsere, *m.*, emperor: ~**s** *n.p.*, 310G.

ceahhetung, *f.*, repeated laughter, bout of sniggering: ~**um** *d.p.*, 423.

cealdnyss, *f.*, cold: ~**e** *g.s.*, 668; *d.s.*, 671.

cēap, *m.*, payment: ~**e** *d.s.*, 377.

ceaster, *f.*, town, city: **ceastre** *d.s.*, 446.

ceastergewara, *m.*, townsperson, inhabitant of a city: **ceastergewarena** *g.p.*, 450.

cennestre, *f.*, mother: *n.s.*, 659; **cennestran** *g.s.*, 481, 523 etc.

cildhād, *m.*, childhood: ~**e** *d.s.*, 26, 77.

clǣne, *adj.*, clean, pure: *a.s.m.* *(undecl.)*, 499; **clǣnan** *d.s.f.* *wk.*, 500.

clǣnheort, *adj.*, pure in heart: ~**an** *n.p.m.wk.*, 50.

clǣnnyss, f., purity, chastity: ~**e** *g.s.*, 655.

clǣnsian, *wv.2*, cleanse, purify: **clǣnsiað** *pres.ind.3p.*, 820.

clǣnsung, *f.*, cleansing, purifying: ~**a** *d.s.*, 124.

clifer, *m.*, claw: **clifrum** *d.p.*, 936, 938.

clypian, *wv.2*, call out, cry: *inf.*, 810; **clypigende** *pres.part.*, 244, 555 etc.; **geclypode** *pp.* *(a.s.f.)*, 558.

clypung, *f.*, shouting, clamour:

~**a** *d.s.*, 235.

cnēow, *nt.*, knee: ~**a** *a.p.*, 103, 541, 809; ~**um** *d.p.*, 144, 203, 704.

cnyssan, *wv.1*, press, strike, oppress: *inf.*, 488; **cnyssende** *pres.part.*, 631, 639; **gecnyssed** *pp.*, 59.

corn, *nt.*, grain: ~**a** *g.p.*, 850.

coss, *m.*, kiss: *a.s.*, 827.

costnung, *f.*, temptation: ~**um** *d.p.*, 675.

Crīst, *proper name*, Christ: *a.s.*, 754; ~**es** *g.*, 98, 141, 211 etc.; ~**e** *d.*, 959.

crīsten, *adj.*, Christian: ~**um** *d.p.m.*, 123.

cucu: *see* **cwic**.

cuman, *sv.4*, come: **cymð** *pres. ind.3s.*, 796; **cume** *pres. sbj.1s.*, 735; *2s.*, 838; **cum** *imp.s.*, 75, 836; **cumende** *pres.part.*, 787; **cōmon** *pret. ind.3p.*, 37; **cōme** *2s.*, 83, 100, 305G; *pret.sbj.1s*, 87.

cunnan, *pret.pres.v.*, know, be aware of: **cūðe** *pret.ind.3s.*, 195, 724.

cwēn, *f.*, queen: *n.s.*, 561.

cweðan, *sv.5*, say, speak: **cweðende** *pres.part.*, 320G, 340G etc.; **cwæðende**, 361, 521 etc.; **cwæð** *pret.ind.1s.*, 28, 180 etc.; *3s.*, 11, 49 etc.; **cwǣde** *2s.*, 98; **gecweden** *pp.*, 893; **gecwedenum** *pp.* *(d.p.nt.)*, 102*.

cwyc, *adj.*, alive, living: ~e *a.s.f.*, 438; **cucu** *n.s.n.*, 697.

cwyde, *m.*, saying, sentence: *a.s.*, 16; ~as *a.p.*, 687.

cynn, *nt.*, kin, family, people, race: ~es *g.s.*, 12, 693; ~e *d.s.*, 561.

cyrice, *f.*, church: **cyrcan** *g.s.*, 6, 507; *d.s.*, 456, 575 etc.

cyrr, *m.*, time, occasion: ~e *d.s.*, 747.

cyrran, *wv.1*, turn, return, go: **cyrrende** *pres.part.*, 862; **cyrdon** *pret.ind.3p.*, 172, 774, 947.

cyssan, *wv.1*, kiss: **cyssende** *pres.part.*, 752.

cyðan, *wv.1*, reveal, make known: *inf.*, 360; **cyðe** *pres. sbj.2s.*, 747; **cyð** *imp.s.*, 743.

D

dæd, *f.*, deed: ~a *a.p.*, 164, 450; *g.p.*, 1; ~um, *d.p.*, 66, 105 etc.

dædbōt, *f.*, penitence, atonement: ~e *g.s.*, 547; *d.s.*, 553, 654.

dæg, *m.*, day: *a.s.*, 108, 138 etc.; ~es *g.s.*, 202, 571, 572; ~e *d.s.*, 137, 172, 357; **dagas** *a.p.*, 445; **daga** *g.p.*, 196; **dagum** *d.p.*, 223, 393 etc.

dæl, *m.*, part, portion: *a.s.*, 582, 732 etc.; ~e *d.s.*, 269, 291.

dælnimend, *m.*, participator,

sharer: ~e *a.p.*, 743.

dēad, *adj.*, dead: *n.s.m.*, 112; *n.s.f.*, 292*.

dēað, *m.*, death: *a.s.*, 442.

delfan, *sv.3*, dig: *inf.*, 915, 933; **delfe** *pres.sbj.1s.*, 912.

dēoflic, *adj.*, devilish, of the devil: ~an *a.p.nt.wk.*, 628.

dēopnyss, *f.*, depths, bottom: ~e *d.s.*, 919.

dēorwurðe, *adj.*, precious: **dēorwurðan** *a.s.f.wk.*, 573; *g.s.m.wk.*, 841; *g.s.f.wk.*, 452, 507, 535; *g.s.nt.wk.*, 778.

derigendlic, *adj.*, injurious, harmful: *n.s.nt.*, 11.

diacon, *m.*, deacon: *n.s.*, 5.

dīgol, (i) *adj.*, secret, hidden: **dīgle** *n.s.f.*, 130; (ii) *nt.*, secret: **dīgle** *a.p.*, 12.

dīgollīce, *adv.*, secretly: 913.

dōm, *m.*, judgement: ~es *g.s.*, 357.

dōn, *anom.v.*, do, carry out, perform: **dō** *pres.ind.1s.*, 319G; *imp.s.*, 719, 845, 936*; **dēst** *pres.ind.2s.*, 811; **dōnde** *pres.part.*, 753; **dyde** *pret. ind.3s.*, 266, 743 etc.; **gedōne** *pp. (n.p.nt.)*, 139, 361.

drencan, *wv.1*, plunge, submerge: **drencte** *pret.ind.3s.*, 807.

drēogan, *sv.2*, endure: **drēah** *pret.ind.1s.*, 667.

drīge, *adj.*, dry: **on drīgum**, on

dry land: 808.

Drihten: *m.*, Lord: *n.s.*, 707, 820 etc.; *a.s.*, 714, 754; **Drihtne** *d.s.*, 106, 297 etc.; **Drihtnes** *g.s.*, 141, 580, 778; **Dryhten** *n.s.*, 49.

drihtenlic, *adj.*, of the Lord, divine: ~e *a.s.nt.wk.*, 826; ~an *a.s.m.wk.*, 765; *d.s.m. wk.*, 137, 172 etc.

drihtlic, *adj.*, of the Lord, divine: ~an *g.s.m.wk.*, 737.

drohtnian, *wv.2*, conduct oneself, live, behave: **drohtnigende** *pres.part.*, 58, 957; **drohtnode** *pret.ind.3s.*, 29, 77, 773.

dropa, *m.*, drop: **dropum** *d.p.*, 287.

Dryhten, *see* **Drihten.**

duru, *f.*, door: *a.s.*, 475, 513; **dura** *a.s.*, 462; *g.s.*, 470, 527, 531; *d.s.*, 461, 530.

dust, *nt.*, dust: *a.s.*, 894; ~e *d.s.*, 895.

E

ēa, *f.*, river: *a.s.*, 165, 577 etc.; *d.s.*, 569.

ēac, *adv.*, also: 33, 45 etc.

ēadig, *adj.*, happy, blessed: ~e *n.p.m.*, 50; ~an *g.s.m.wk.*, 736; *g.s.f.wk.*, 954.

ēadignyss, *f.*, blessedness, happiness: ~e *d.s.*, 55.

ēadmōd, *adj.*, humble-minded:

~ne *a.s.m.*, 99; ~um *d.s.nt.*, 144; *d.p.m.*, 85.

ēadmōdlīce, *adv.*, humbly: 145, 790.

ēage, *nt.*, eye: **ēagan** *n.p.*, 833; *a.p.*, 213, 330G etc.; **ēagena** *g.p.*, 8, 872; **ēagum** *d.p.*, 320G, 877.

ēalā, *interj.*, O: 69, 289 etc.

eald, *adj.*, old, ancient: ~a *n.s.m.wk.*, 352G, 359 etc.; ~an *a.s.m.wk.*, 711; *a.s.f. wk.*, 227; *g.s.m.wk.*, 299, 927; *d.s.m.wk.*, 304G, 749 etc.; ~um *d.p.f.*, 133.

ealdor, *m.*, leader, source: *n.s.*, 552, *a.s.*, 654.

ealdung, *f.*, age, process of growing old: ~e *d.s.*, 666.

eall, (i) *adj.*, all: *n.s.nt.*, 531; *a.s.nt.*, 758, 906; ~es *g.s.m.*, 509, 560; ~e *n.p.m.*, 143, 471, 952; *n.p.f.*, 610; *a.p.m.*, 422, 441 etc.; *a.p.nt.*, 31, 100 etc.; *a.p.f.*, 42; **ealra** *g.s.f.*, 805; *g.p.nt.*, 78, 293, 951; **ealre** *g.p.nt.*, 923; ~um *d.s.nt.*, 465, 561; *d.p.m.*, 30, 36 etc.; *d.p.nt.*, 60, 518, 657; (ii) *adv.*, all, completely: 345G, 360, 529.

ealle, *adv. (instr.s. of **eall**)*, entirely, all, completely: 40, 716; *see also* **eall.**

eallunga, *adv.*, entirely, altogether: 254, 288 etc.; **eallinga,** 323G, 327G.

ēara, *nt.*, ear: *n.s.*, 429.

eard, *m.*, country, land: ~e *d.s.*, 74.

eardian, *wv.2*, dwell, live: eardodost *pret.ind.2s.*, 593.

earfeðe, *nt.*, hardship: earfeðu *a.p.*, 667.

earm, *adj.*, wretched, miserable: *n.s.f.*, 548; ~re *d.s.f.*, 257; ~an *a.s.f.wk.*, 637, 677; *a.p. m.wk.*, 431, 432.

earm, *m.*, arm, fore-legs: ~um *d.p.*, 321G, 939.

earmincg, *m.*, unfortunate wretch: *n.s.*, 910.

earmlic, *adj.*, wretched, miserable: ~re *d.s.f.*, 701.

Ēasterdæg, *m.*, Easter Day: ~e *d.s.*, 731*.

Ēastergewuna, *m.*, Easter observance: *n.s.*, 757.

eastweardes, *adv.*, facing east, eastwards: 200, 886.

ēce, *adj.*, eternal, perpetual: ēcan *d.s.f.wk.*, 55.

edlēan, *nt.*, reward: ~es *g.s.*, 237.

efstan, *wv.2*, hasten, hurry: *inf.*, 214, 222 etc.; efste *pret.ind.3s.*, 750, 868; geefst *pp.*, 111.

eft, *adv.*, again, moreover, on the other hand: 9, 12 etc.

eftcyrran, *wv.1*, turn gack, go back: eftcyrrende *pres.part.*, 753, 755, 788.

efthwyrfan, *wv.1*, return: eft-

hwyrfende *pres.part.*, 720.

ēge, *m.*, fear, dread: *n.s.*, 261; *a.s.*, 212, 285; *d.s.*, 863, 922.

Egypte, *proper name (p.)*, Egypt, Egyptian: ~a *g.*, 388; ~um *d.*, 361, 620.

Egyptisc, *adj.*, Egyptian: ~an *g.s.f.wk.*, 3.

ēhtan, *wv.1*, pursue *(w.g.)*: ēhtende *pres.part.*, 231.

ellenlic, *adj.*, brave: *a.s.nt.* 2.

elles, *adv.*, else: 724.

eln, *f.*, forearm: ~e *d.s.*, 331G.

emnwyrhta, *m.*, co-worker, fellow-worker: emnwyrhtum *d.p.*, 119; emwyrhtena *g.p.*, 402.

ende, *m.*, end: *n.s.*, 212, 699.

endebyrdnyss, *f.*, order, succession: ~e *d.s.*, 615.

engel, *m.*, angel: *n.s.*, 69, 79.

ēode: *see* gān/gangan.

eorðe, *f.*, earth, ground: *n.s.*, 437, 915; eorðan *a.s.*, 276, 326G etc.; *d.s.*, 18, 62 etc.

ēow: *see* þū.

ēower, *poss.adj.*, your *(p.)*: ēowrum *d.p.nt.*, 721.; *see also* þū.

ēð, *cp.adv.*, more easily: 378.

ēðel, *m.*, homeland: *a.s.*, 362.

F

faran, *sv.2*, go: *inf.*, 392, 395 etc.; fare *pres.ind.1s.*, 519; far *imp.s.*, 74, 717; farenne

infl.inf., 402; **fōr** *pret.ind.*
1s., 564*, 584, 596; *3s.*, 76,
187, 870; **fōron** *1p.*, 445,
767; *3p.*, 151; **fōre** *pret.sbj.*
3s., 130, 197.

fæc, *nt.*, space of time, period:
~e *d.s.*, 279, 602.

fæder, *m.*, father: *n.s.*, 86, 815;
a.s., 194.

fægen, *adj.*, glad, joyful: *n.s.m.*,
221.

fægnian, *wv.2*, fawn: *inf.*, 927.

fæmne, *f.*, virgin: *n.s.*, 498, 510,
517; **fēmne**, 509.

fæmnhād, *m.*, maidenhood,
virginity: *a.s.*, 366, 374.

færeht, *nt.*, passage-money: *a.s.*,
396, 397; ~e *d.s.*, 400.

færeld, *nt.*, journey, way: *a.s.*,
196, 421.

færlic, *adj.*, sudden, rapid: ~e
n.s.f.wk., 474.

færlīce, *adv.*, suddenly: 863.

færunga, *adv.*, suddenly, quickly: 389.

fæsten, *nt.*, fasting, fast: *a.s.*,
171; ~e *d.s.*, 917; ~um *d.p.*,
171.

fæstenwuce, *f.*, week of fasting:
fæstenwucan *g.s.*, 38.

fæstlīce, *adv.*, firmly, unhesitatingly: 266; **fæstlīcor** *cp.*,
147.

fæt, *nt.*, vessel: ~e *d.s.*, 732.

fēawa, *indecl.pron.* *(w.g.)*, few:
781.

fēdan, *wv.1*, feed, be nourished:

fēde *imp.s.*, 101; **fēddest**
pret.ind.2s., 598; **fēddon**
3p., 115; **gefēdde** *pp.*
(n.p.m.), 159.

fela, *indecl.pron.* *(w.g.)*, many:
88, 92.

feor, *adv.*, far: 166.

feorr, *adj.*, far, distant: ~um
d.p.f., 37.

feorran, *adv.*, from afar: 168,
554.

feorran, *wv.2*, keep apart: **feorrode** *pret.ind.1s.*, 588.

fēower, *num.*, four: 476.

fēowertig, *num.*, forty: ~um
d.p.m., 595.

fēran, *wv.1*, go, come: **fērde**
pret.ind.3s., 757.

fīftigða, *num.adj.*, fiftieth: **fīf-
tigðe** *a.s.nt.*, 57.

findan, *sv.3*, find: *inf.*, 598*,
876; **funde** *pret.sbj.1s.*, 664;
3s., 194.

finger, *m.*, finger: **fingrum** *d.p.*,
848.

fingeræppla, *n.p.*, finger-
shaped fruits, dates: *a.p.*,
781.

fisc, *m.*, fish: **fixa** *g.p.*, 620.

flæsc, *nt.*, flesh, body: *n.s.*,
345G; *a.s.*, 34; ~es *g.s.*, 494,
716.

flæsclic, *adj.*, fleshly, bodily:
~an *g.s.f.wk.*, 607.

flæscmete, *m.*, meat: **flæscmettas** *n.p.*, 619.

flēon, *sv.2*, flee: **flīhst** *pres.*

ind.2s., 235, 353; **flēo** *pres. sbj.3s.*, 354; **flēonde** *pres. part.*, 231, 588; **flēah** *pret. ind.3s.*, 230, 250.

flōr, *m.*, floor: *a.s.*, 538; ~as *a.p.*, 752.

folc, *n.*, people, folk, crowd: *n.s.*, 309G; ~es *g.s.*, 460; ~e *d.s.*, 459, 465; ~a *g.p.*, 372.

for, *prep.w.d.*, for, because of, on account of, for the sake of: 14, 84 etc.

fōr, *f.*, course, going: ~e *d.s.*, 192; *see also* **faran**.

forbēodan, *sv.2*, forbid, restrain: *inf.*, 811.

forbernan, *wv.1*, burn up: **forbernde** *pret.sbj.3s.*, 645.

fordrūwian, *wv.2*, dry out: **fordrūwod** *pp.*, 242.

fore, *adv.*, beforehand: 632.

forealdian, *wv.2*, grow very old: **forealdodne** *pp. (a.s. m.)*, 236.

foregān/foregangan, *anom. v./sv.7*, go forth, go about: **foregēode** *pret.ind.1s.*, 453.

foregehāt, *nt.*, vow, promise: ~es *g.s.*, 631.

forene, *adv.*, beforehand: 711.

forerynel, *m.*, forerunner, precursor: ~es *g.s.*, 737; **forryeles**, 581.

forescēawung, *f.*, foresight, foreknowledge: ~e *d.s.*, 265.

foresecgan, *wv.3*, mention before: *inf.*, 264; **foresæde**

pret.ind.3s., 956.

foresettan, *wv.1*, put forward, propose: **foresettende** *pres. part.*, 328G.

forfōn, *sv.7*, anticipate, forestall: **forfēng** *pret.ind.3s.*, 711.

forgangan, *sv.7*, go, proceed: **forgangende** *pres.part.*, 191.

forgyfan, *sv.5*, grant, give: **forgif** *imp.s.*, 506; **forgeaf** *pret.ind.3s.*, 302; **forgyfen** *pp.*, 313G.

forhabban, *wv.3*, avoid, refuse: **forhæbbe** *pres.sbj.2s.*, 838.

forhæfednyss, *f.*, abstinence, self-restraint: ~e *d.s.*, 29, 162; *g.s.*, 39.

forhælan, *sv.4*, cover up, conceal: **forhælende** *pres.part.*, 355.

forhtian, *wv.2*, fear, be frightened of: **forhtige** *pres.ind. 1s.*, 406.

forhycgan, *wv.1*, spurn, disdain: *inf.*, 364.

forlætan, *sv.7*, leave, grant, allow: *inf.*, 257; **forlætest** *pres.ind.2s.*, 710; **forlætað** *3s.*, 440; **forlæt** *imp.s.*, 410, 505 etc.; **forlēton** *pret.ind. 3p.*, 151; *pret.sbj.3p.*, 154.

forlætnyss, *f.*, loss: ~e *d.s.*, 8.

forlegen, *m.f. (pp. of* **forlicgan**, fornicate*)*, fornicator: ~re *d.s.(f.)*, 702.

forlēosan, *sv.2.*, lose, destroy:

forlēas *pret.ind.1s.*, 373.

forliger, *nt.*, promiscuity, fornication: ~es *g.s.*, 373, 379, 383.

forma, *adj.*, first: ~n *g.s.f.*, 138.

fornēah, *adv.*, almost, very nearly: 672.

foroft, *adv.*, very often: 671.

forrynel: *see* **forerynel.**

forsēon, *sv.5*, refuse, reject: **forseoh** *imp.s.*, 740.

forspillednyss, *f.*, perdition: ~e *g.s.*, 439, 454.

forstig, *adj.*, frosty: ~an *d.s.f. wk.*, 670.

forsuwian/forsweogian, *wv.2*, conceal by silence, pass over: **forsuwige** *pres.ind.1s.*, 15; *pres.sbj.1s.*, 22; **forsweogode** *pret.ind.3s.*, 759.

forð, *adv.*, forth, forwards: 234, 251 etc.; **forð heonon,** henceforth: 54.

forðāgoten, *adj.*, poured forth: ~um *d.p.m.*, 941.

forþan: *see* **forþon.**

forðgān, *anom.v.*, go forth: **forðgǣð** *pres.ind.3.s.*, 695.

forðbringan, *wv.1*, bring forth: *inf.*, 489; **forðbrōhte** *pret.ind.3s.*, 687.

forðencan, *wv.1*, despair of: **forðōht,** *pp.*, 548.

forðfōr, *f.*, departure, death: ~e *g.s.*, 954.

forðgangan, *sv.7*, go forth, advance: **forðgangende** *pres.*

part., 245*.

forðgewītan, *sv.1*, go forth, pass: **forðgewītendum** *pres. part. (d.p.f.)*, 10; **forðgewitene** *pp (n.s.nt.)*, 72.

forþon, (i) *adv.*, for that reason, therefore: 499, 739; (ii) *conj.*, because, since: 88, 252 etc.; **forþan þe:** 34, 50 etc.; **forþām þe:** 230, 294 etc.

forþȳ, *adv.*, for that reason, therefore: 100, 225, 503.

forwurðan, *sv.3*, perish, wear out: *inf.*, 441; **forwurdon** *pret.ind.3p.*, 666.

forwyrcan, *wv.1*, do wrong, sin: **forworht** *pp.*, sinner, criminal: *(n.s.f.)*, 496; **forworhte** *(d.s.f.)*, 257; **forworhtra** *(g.p.m.)*, 547.

forwyrnan, *wv.1*, prevent, hinder: **forwyrnþ** *pres.ind.3s.*, 396; **forwyrned** *pp.*, 483.

fōt, *m.*, foot: **fēt** *n.p.*, 752; *a.p.*, 854, 887, 941.

fōtlāst, *m.*, sole of foot: ~es *a.s.*, 922.

fracodlic, *adj.*, lewd, shameful, base: ~um *d.p.nt.*, 424.

fracodlicnyss, *f.*, obscenity, vileness: ~e *g.s.*, 433.

fram, (i) *prep.w.d.*, from: 17, 26 etc.; (ii) *adv.*, away, out: 501.

frætewian, *wv.2*, adorn: **gefrætewod** *pp.*, 25.

frēcednyss, *f.*, danger, harm: ~e
n.p., 610; ~um *d.p.*, 10, 656.

frecendlic, *adj.*, terrible: ~an
a.s.f.wk., 626.

fremde, *adj.*, strange, alien:
n.s.f., 507.

fremdian, *wv.2*, estrange, alienate: fremda *imp.s.*, 791.

fremman, *wv.1*, make, engage
in, accomplish: fremme
pres.ind.3s., 342G; fremanne *infl.inf.*, 477; gefremed *pp.*, 46, 221 etc.;
gefremod, 503; gefremede
(n.p.f.), 430; *(n.p.nt.)*, 699.

fremsumesta, *sp.adj.*, most benign: *n.s.f.wk.*, 542.

frēogan, *wv.1*, think lovingly
of: frēode *pret.sbj.2s.*, 606.

fruma, *m.*, beginning, instig-
ation: *n.s.*, 434; ~n *d.s.*, 366.

frymþ, *f.*, origin, beginning: ~e
d.s., 29.

fugel, *m.*, bird: ~a *g.p.*, 224.

ful, *adv.*, very, fully: 418.

fūl, *adj.*, foul, impure: ~an
a.p.m.wk., 637.

fulfremed, *adj.*, perfect, perfected: *n.s.m.*, 60; fulfremod, 35; ~ne *a.s.m.*, 71.

fulfremednyss, *f.*, perfection,
completeness: ~e *a.s.*, 32;
g.s., 298; *d.s.*, 118; fulfremodnysse *g.s.*, 823.

fulfremodlīce, *adv.*, completely, perfectly: 180, 712.

fūllic, *adj.*, foul, dirty, base:

~um *d.p.nt.*, 424, 446.

fulluht, *nt.*, baptism: ~e *d.s.*,
344G.

fulluhtere, *m.*, Baptist, baptizer:
~s *g.s.*, 581; fulwihteres,
576.

fultum, *m.*, help: ~e *d.s.*, 658.

fultumian, *wv.2*, help: fultum-
igende *pres.part.*, 956.

furðon, *adv.*, even: 110.

fyligan, *wv.1*, follow *(w.d.)*:
inf., 841.

fyllo, *f.*, fullness, satiety: fylle
g.s., 680.

fylst, *m.*, help: ~es *g.s.*, 505.

fȳr, *nt.*, fire: *n.s.*, 644.

fyrhtu, *f.*, fear, trembling: *n.s.*,
261; *a.s.*, 286; fyrhto *n.s.*,
528; *d.s.*, 333G.

fyrst, *m./n.*, time, period: ~e
d.s., 718.

G

gaderian, *wv.2*, assemble: gegaderode *pp.* *(n.p.m.)*, 143.

gān/gangan, *anom.v./sv.7*, go:
gangen *inf.*, 462; gang *imp.
s.*, 835; gangende *pres.part.*,
552, 808; ēode *pret.ind.1s.*,
563, 577; *3s.*, 78, 807, 861.

gang, *m*, passage, way: ~es *g.s.*,
464.

gangan: *see* gān.

gāst, *m.*, spirit, soul: *n.s.*, 338G,
342G, 344G; ~es *g.s.*, 101,
209, 306G; ~e *d.s.*, 35, 106

etc.

gāstbrūcan, *sv.2*, use in a spiritual manner: **gāstbrūc-ende** *pres.part.*, 43.

gāstlic, *adj.*, holy, spiritual: ~e *n.s.f.*, 289, 409 etc.; ~**an** *g.s. f.wk*, 48; ~**ra** *g.p.m.*, 88*; **gāstlicum** *d.p.nt.wk.*, 533.

ge . . . ge, *conj.*, both . . . and: 872-73; *see also* **ǣgþer**.

geanbidian, *wv.2*, wait for *(w.g.)*: **geanbida** *imp.s.*, 236, 734; **geanbidode** *pret. ind.3s.*, 763.

gēar, *nt.*, year: *a.s.*, 57, 758; *n.p.*, 592; *a.p.*, 662; ~**es** *g.s.*, 717, 720 etc.; ~**e** *d.s.*, 363, 866; *g.p.*, 655; ~**um** *d.p.*, 284.

geara, *adv.*, well, fully: 494.

geare, *adj.*, ready: *n.s.m.*, 536.

geat, *nt.*, gate: *n.s.*, 125; *a.s.*, 80; ~**u** *n.p.*, 148.

geaxian, *wv.2*, find out about, discover: **geaxode** *pret.ind. 1s.*, 20, 89.

geǣscwician, *wv.2*, be offended with: **geǣswicianne** *infl.inf.*, 341G.

gebǣdhūs, *nt.*, chapel, oratory: *a.s.*, 143, 153.

gebǣra, *nt.(p.)*, behaviour, demeanour: *a.p.*, 426; **gebǣrum** *d.*, 418.

gebed, *nt.*, prayer, blessing: ~**es** *g.s.*, 212, 238 etc.; ~**e** *d.s.*, 82, 103, 144; ~**u** *a.p.*, 257,

342G; ~**a** *g.p.*, 260; ~**um** *d.p.*, 170, 206 etc.; **gebǣd** *a.s.*, 298, 525 etc.

gebētan, *wv.1*, amend, improve: **gebetenne** *infl.inf.*, 746.

gebīdan, *sv.1*, wait for: **gebād** *pret.ind.3s.*, 783.

gebiddan, *sv.5 (often refl.)*, pray: *inf.*, 203, 318G etc.; **gebidde** *pres.sbj.1s.*, 497; *2s.*, 702; *imp.s.*, 895; **gebide**, 852; **gebǣd** *pret.ind. 3s.*, 200, 577, 877; **gebǣde** *pret.sbj.3s.*, 339G, 855; **gebeden** *pp.*, 726, 881.

gebīgan, *wv.1*, bend: **gebīgde** *pret.ind.1s.*, 541; *3s.*, 103; **gebīgedum** *pp. (d.p.nt.)*, 144, 203, 704.

geblǣdfǣstnyss, *f.*, blessing: ~**e** *d.s.*, 567.

gebletsian, *wv.2*, bless: **gebletsode** *pret.ind.3s.*, 346G.

gebōd, *n.*, requirement, command: *a.s.*, 319G, 770.

gebringan, *wv.1*, bring: **gebrōhton** *pret.ind.3p.*, 285, 628.

gebrōþru, *m.p.*, brothers, monks: *n.*, 766.

gebycgan, *wv.1*, buy: **gebohte** *pret.ind.1s.*, 566.

gebyrd, *f.*, birth, childbirth: ~**e** *d.s.*, 494.

gecēosan, *sv.2*, choose: **gecēose** *pres.ind.1s.*, 514; **gecēas** *pret.ind.1s.*, 632.

geclǣnsian, *wv.2*, cleanse, purify: **geclǣnsiað** *pres. ind.3p.*, 52.

gecȳgan, *wv.1*, summon, call: **gecȳgede** *pret.sbj.3s.*, 504.

gecynd, *nt.*, nature: ~es *g.s.*, 160, 188, 386.

gecyrran, *wv.1*, turn: *inf.*, 260; **gecyrrað** *pres.ind.3p.*, 590.

gecyssan, *wv.1*, kiss: **gecyste** *pret.ind.1s.*, 539.

gecȳðan, *wv.1*, reveal, make known, relate: *inf.*, 642; **gecȳðe** *pres.ind.1s.*, 369; *pres.sbj.2s.*, 614; **gecydde** *pret.ind.3s.*, 15, 81.

gedafenian, *wv.2*, befit: **gedafenað** *pres.ind.3s.*, 280; **gedafenodon** *pret.ind.3p.*, 885.

gedafenlic, *adj.*, fitting, proper: *n.s.n.*, 495.

gedōn, *anom.v.*, make, cause: **gedēð** *pres.ind.3s.*, 441, 589.

gedrēfan, *wv.1*, agitate,, disturb, vex: **gedrēfest** *pres. ind.2s.*, 340G; **gedrēfedon** *pret.ind.3p.*, 611, 627; **gedrēfed** *pp.*, 335G, 487, 529; **gedrēfedu** *(n.s.f.)*, 608; **gedrēfedan** *(a.p.m.wk.)*, 650.

gedrēfednyss, *f.*, disturbance, trouble: ~e *d.s.*, 127.

gedryncnyss, *f.*, dipping, immersion: ~e *d.s.*, 859.

geēacnian, *wv.2*, conceive: **geēacnodost** *pret.ind.2s.*, 509.

geearnian, *wv.2.*, earn, merit: **geearnige** *pres.sbj.1s.*, 356.

geednīwian, *wv.2*, renew, restore: **geednīwodon** *pret. ind.3s.*, 121.

geetan, *sv.5*, eat: **geæt** *pret. ind.1s.*, 582.

gefaran, *sv.6*, obtain, experience, come (upon): **gefærst** *pres.ind.2s.*, 556; **gefōr** *pret. ind.3s.*, 817.

gefæstnian, *wv.2*, fasten, fix: *inf.*, 202; **gefæstnod** *pp.*, 508.

gefēa, *m.*, joy: ~n *d.s.*, 801, 862.

gefeallan, *sv.7*, fall, fall headlong: **gefealle** *pres.sbj. 1s.*, 16.

gefēra, *m.*, fellow, companion: **gefērum** *d.p.*, 167.

geflǣscod, *adj.*, incarnate, made flesh: ~e *a.s.nt.wk.*, 701.

gefremman, *wv.1*, carry out, exercise, succeed: **gefremme** *pres.sbj.2s.*, 910; **gefremmanne** *infl.inf.*, 275; **gefremmane**, 549; **gefremode** *pret.ind.1s.*, 478.

gefultumian, *wv.2:* help, aid *(w.d.):* *inf.*, 63; **gefultuma** *imp.s.*, 504; **gefultumode** *pret.sbj.3s.*, 653.

gefyllan, *wv.*, fill, complete, fulfil, succeed: *inf.*, 279; **gefyllende** *pres.part.*, 171; **gefyllenne** *infl.inf.*, 549; **gefyl** *imp.s.*, 835; **gefyll**,

931; **gefylde** *pret.ind.1s.*,
65, 572; *3s.*, 4, 178, 907;
gefyldest *2s.*, 70; **gefyldon**
3p., 128*; **gefylled** *pp.*, 213,
533, 863; **gefylledne** *(a.s.
m.)*, 779; **gefylledum** *(d.p.
nt.)*, 147, 827.

gefyrht, *adj.*, afraid, terrified:
n.s.m., 922.

gegaderian, *wv.2*, gather, assemble: **gegaderigende**
pres.part., 451*.

gegearwian, *wv.2*, do, make
ready: **gegearwige** *pres.sbj.
2s.*, 308G; **gegearwode** *pret.
ind.3s.*, 532.

gegrīpan, *sv.1*, seize, take hold
of, catch: *inf.*, 875; **gegrāp**
pret.ind.3s., 261, 528;
gegripen *pp.*, 333G.

gegyrla, *m.*, clothing, apparel:
n.s., 665; **~n** *a.s.*, 159.

gegyrnian, *wv.2*, strive, seek:
gegyrnode *pret.ind.1s.*, 573.

gegyrwan, *wv.1.*, dress, put on:
gegyrede *pret.ind.3s.*, 269.

gehālgian, *wv.2*, consecrate,
make holy: **gehālgodum** *pp.
(d.s.nt.)*, 732.

gehātan, *sv.7*, promise, vow:
gehāte *pres.ind.1s.*, 515; **ge-
hēt** *pret.ind.3s.*, 819.

gehæftan, *wv.1*, detain, confine:
gehæft *pp.*, 769.

gehǣlan, *wv.1*, heal: **gehǣleð**
pres.ind.3s., 92.

gehealdan, *sv.7*, keep, preserve,

care about: **gehealt**
pres.ind.3s., 91; **geheold**
pret.ind.3s., 33, 678, 852;
gehealden *pp.*: **gehealden
on**, satisfied with, assured
of: 435.

gehihtan, *wv.1*, hope, trust in:
gehihtende *pres.part.*, 589;
gehihte *pret.ind.1s.*, 648.

gehrīnan, *sv.1*, touch: **gehrān**
pret.ind.1s., 470.

gehwanon, *adv.*, from everywhere, everywhere: 640.

gehwyrfednyss, *f.*, conversion,
inclination: **~e** *a.s.*, 1; *g.s.*,
443, 607.

gehȳdan, *wv.1*, hide: **gehȳdde**
pp. (a.s.nt.wk.), 878.

gehȳran, *wv.1*, hear: *inf.*, 234;
gehȳrende *pres.part.*, 686;
gehȳrde *pret.ind.1s.*, 19, 502
etc.; *3s.*, 262, 264 etc.; **ge-
hȳrdest** *2s.*, 713; **gehȳred**
pp., 248, 323G.

gehȳðe, *adj.*, suitable: **~s** *g.s.nt.*,
933.

gehyðoo, *nt.*, subsistence: *a.s.*,
566.

geīcan, *wv.1*, add, increase:
geīc *imp.s.*, 895*; **geīhte**
pret.ind.3s., 34.

gelǣdan, *wv.1*, lead: **gelǣdde**
pret.ind.1s., 439; *3s.*, 81, 99
etc.; **gelǣd** *pp.*, 521.

gelēafa, *m.*, faith, belief: **~n**
g.s., 522.

geleornian, *wv.2*, learn: **ge-**

leornode *pret.ind.1s.*, 629.

gelīc, *adj. (w.d.)*, like: ~e
a.p.m., 819; ~**um** *d.p.nt.*
(mistakenly for a.), 68.

gelīcnyss, *f.*, likeness, form: ~e
d.s., 207.

gelīffæst: *see* **gelȳffæst**.

geliger, *n.*, sexual depravity,
promiscuity, fornication:
~**es** *g.s.*, 371, 516; **geligre**
d.s., 643.

gelimpan, *sv.3 (impers.)*,
happen: **gelumpe** *pret.sbj.*
3s., 367.

gelōmlīce, *adv.*, often, constantly: 95.

gelustfullian, *wv.2*, enjoy, rejoice in: **gelustfullode** *pret.*
ind.1s., 621.

gelȳfan, *wv.1*, believe: **gelȳfað**
pres.ind.3p., 441; **gelȳf**
imp.s., 616, 692; **gelȳfanne**
infl.inf., 134; allow, grant:
gelȳfed *pp.*, 840.

gelȳffæst, *adj.*, life-giving: ~**an**
g.s.nt.wk., 733; **gelīffæstan**
g.s.f.wk., 535.

gemang, *prep.w.d.*, among: 119,
459, 571.

gemænigfealdian, *wv.2*, mult-
iply: **gemænigfealdode**
pret.ind.3s., 247.

gemǣnsumian, *wv.2 (w.g.)*,
partake of, participate in:
gemǣnsumode *pret.ind.1s.*,
579, 738; **gemǣnsumedon**
3p., 140.

gemedemian, *wv.2*, deem
worthy, condescend: **ge-
medemige** *pres.sbj.2s.*, 844;
gemedemodest *pret.ind.2s.*,
879; **gemedemod** *pp.*, 534.

gemengan, *wv.1*, mingle, mix:
gemengde *pret.ind.1s.*, 420,
447*, 525.

gemet, *nt.*, measure, manner,
degree: *a.s.*, 623; ~**e** *d.s.*,
354, 822.

gemētan, *wv.1*, meet, find:
gemētst *pres.ind.2s.*, 556;
gemēte *pres.sbj.1s.*, 357;
gemētte *pret.ind.1s.*, 389,
564; *3s.*, 190, 944.

gemunan, *pret.pres.v.*, remember: **gemunde** *pret.ind.*
3s., 769.

gemundian, *wv.2*, protect: **gemunde** *imp.s.?*, 853.

gemynd, *nt.*, memory, mind: ~**e**
d.s., 610.

genēalǣcan, *wv.1*, draw near,
approach: **genēalǣhte** *pret.*
ind.3s., 122, 575.

genihtsum, *adj.*, abundant:
~**estan** *sp.d.p.m.*, 680.

genihtsumian, *wv.2*, suffice, be
satisfied with: **geniht-
sumigende** *pres.part.*, 448;
genihtsumode *pret.ind.3s.*,
851, 939.

genihtsumnyss, *f.*, sufficient
supply: ~**e** *a.s.*, 156.

geniman, *sv.4*, take, put: **genim**
imp.s., 731; **genam** *pret.ind.*

3s., 779.

genōh, *adv.*, enough, sufficiently: 417, 499, 566.

genȳdan, *wv.1*, force, compel: *inf.*, 643; **genȳde** *pres.sbj.2s.*, 404; **genȳdde** *pret.ind.1s.*, 431.

genyrwan, *wv.1*, oppress, beset: **genyrwed** *pp.*, 919.

genyðrian, *wv.2*, abase, bring low: **genyðredan** *pp. (a.s. m.)*, ignominious: 16.

genyðrung, *f.*, disgrace, abasement: *n.s.*, 13.

gēomerung, *f.*, groaning, lamentation: *n.s.*, 249.

gēomorlic, *adj.*, sorrowful: ~an *a.p.f.wk.*, 489.

gēomrian, *wv.2*, sorrow, grieve: **gēomrigende** *pres.part.*, 830; **gēomrode** *pret.ind.3s.*, 919.

geond, *prep.w.a.*, through, throughout, over: 187, 632.

geondfēran, *wv.1*, traverse, roam through: **geondfērde** *pret.ind.1s.*, 373.

geondgēotan, *sv.2*, pour over, suffuse: **geondgoten** *pp.*, 286.

geong, *adj.*, young: ~e *a.p.m.*, 416; ~an *a.p.m.wk.*, 453; ~um *d.p.m.wk.*, 448.; ~ran *cp.d.s.m.wk.*, 291.

geonglincg, *m.*, youth: *n.s.*, 412.

geopenian, *wv.2*, reveal, open:

geopenige *pres.sbj.3s.*, 12; **geopenigenne** *infl.inf.*, 128, 506; **geopenod** *pp.*, 126; **geopenode** *(n.p.nt.)*, 148.

georne, *adv.*, keenly, intently: 219, 478* etc.

geornful, *adj.*, eager, keen: ~lan *d.s.f.wk.*, 204.

geornlīce, *adv.*, eagerly, zealously: 118, 225 etc.

gereccan, *wv.1*, tell, direct: *inf.*, 360; **gerecce** *pres.sbj.3s.*, 93; **gerece** *imp.s.*, 550; **gereccenne** *infl.inf.*, 365; **gereht** *pp.*, 836.

gerecednyss, *f.*, story, narrative: ~e *g.s.*, 411*; ~um *d.p.*, 21; **geræcednyssa** *a.s.*, 15.

gerēdan, *wv.1*, guide, advise: **gerēdst** *pres.ind.2s.*, 520.

gereord, *m.*, food, meal: ~es *g.s.*, 188, 730 etc.

gereordan, *wv.1*, take food: **gereordende** *pres.part.*, 142.

gereorddæg, *m.*, day of banquet, feast-day: ~e *d.s.*, 898.

gerihtan, *wv.1*, direct, guide, correct: **gerihtenne** *inf.inf.*, 746; **gerihtanne**, 955; **gerihte** *pret.ind.3s.*, 307G, 956*; *pret.sbj.3s.*, 585.

gerȳne, *nt.*, sacrament, sacramental rite, mystery: **gerȳnu** *n.p.*, 139, 282; *a.p.*, 534, 536 etc.; **gerȳnum** *d.p.*, 533, 580, 828.

gesamnian, *wv.2*, congregate,

assemble: **gesamnodon** *pret. ind.3p.*, 775.

gesamnung, *f.*, congregation, assembly: ~a *a.s.*, 855; *g.s.*, 311G.

gescēawung, *f.*, estimation: ~e *d.s.*, 822.

gescyndnyss, *f.*, confusion, shame: ~e *a.s.*, 405.

gesēcan, *wv.1*, seek: **gesēcað** *pres.ind.3p.*, 710; **gesēcenne** *infl.inf.*, 99; **gesōhte** *pret. ind.1s.*, 88.

gesegness, *f.*, expression: ~e *d.s.*, 89.

gesēon, *sv.5*, see, behold: *inf.*, 573; **gesihst** *pres.ind.2s.*, 255, 718, 839*; **gesēoð** *1p.*, 545*; *3p.*, 50; **gesēo** *pres. sbj.1s.*, 517; **gesēonde** *pres. part.*, 426, 800; **gesēonne** *infl.inf.*, 273, 477; **geseah** *pret.ind.1s.*, 416, 490; *3s.*, 104, 168 etc.; **gesāwon** *3p.*, 833; **gesāwe** *2s.*, 294; *pret. sbj.3s.*, 925; **gesewen** *pp.*, 215, 246.

gesetnysse, *f.*, law, ordinance, tradition: *n.s.*, 137 *(see Commentary)*.

gesihþ, *f.*, vision, sight, faculty of seeing: ~e *a.s.*, 224, 759; *g.s.*, 48, 221 etc.; *d.s.*, 290, 508 etc.; ~um *d.p.*, 497.

gespræc, *nt.*, speech, discourse: ~u *n.p.*, 114; ~um *d.p.*, 425.

gesprecan, *sv.5*, speak: **ge-**

spræcon *pret.ind.1p.*, 837.

gestandan, *sv.6*, stand: **gestōd** *pret.ind.1s.*, 481.

gestrangian, *wv.2*, confirm, strengthen: **gestrangige** *pres.sbj.3s.*, 93; **gestrangode** *pp. (n.p.m.)*, 147.

gestrēon, *nt.*, treasure, valuable: *a.p.*, 152; ~a *g.p.*, 109.

geswinc, *nt.*, toil, effort, work: *n.s.*, 315G; *a.s.*, 228, 274*, 612; ~es *g.s.*, 175, 178; ~e *d.s.*, 460, 906, 918; ~a *g.p.*, 177.

geswincan, *sv.3*, struggle for, strive for: **geswunce** *pret. ind.2s.*, 238.

geswutelian, *wv.2*, show, reveal; *inf.*, 253; **geswutelað** *pres.ind.3s.*, 292; **geswutela** *imp.s.*, 289, 614, 878.

gēt, *adv.*, yet: 328G.

getācnian, *wv.2*, mark out, indicate: **getācnigenne** *infl. inf.*, 296; **getācnod** *pp.*, 242, 882, 892.

getæcan, *wv.1*, teach: *inf.*, 63.

getēorian, *wv.2*, tire of, become weary of: **getēorige** *pres.sbj.2s.*, 356; **getēorod** *pp.*, 44.

getimbrian, *wv.2*, edify, uplift: *inf.*, 95; **getimbrede** *pret.sbj.3s.*, 195.

getrymman, *wv.1*, strengthen: **getrymmede** *pret.ind.3s.*, 211; **getrymede**, 348G.

getȳðian, *wv.2*, grant *(w.g. of thing)*: getȳðige *pres.sbj.2s.*, 843.

geþafian, *wv.2*, allow, permit: geþafode *pret.ind.3s.*, 712.

geþanc, *m.*, thought: *n.s.*, 109, 795; ~es *a.p.*, 637, 642; ~a *g.p.*, 611; ~um *d.p.*, 59.

geþencan, *wv.1*, think: *inf.*, 548.

geþēodan, *wv.1*, associate,join: *inf.*, 230; geþēodde *pret. ind.1s.*, 530; *3s.*, 167, 181; geðēoddest *2s.*, 84.

geþēode, *nt.*, language: *d.s.*, 4.

geþingian, *wv.2*, intercede *(w. d.)*: geþinga *imp.s.*, 291.

geþoht, *m./nt.*, thought: *a.s.*, 633; ~as *a.p.*, 341G, 646, 651; ~um *d.p.*, 612.

geþring, *nt.*, pressure, pushing: ~es *g.s.*, 480.

geþringan, *sv.3*, push, press: *inf.*, 469.

geþrȳstlæcan, *wv.1*, dare, presume: geðrȳstlæcende *pres.part.*, 759; geþrȳstlæhte *pret.ind.3s.*, 335G, 856, 887.

geþyncan, *wv.1 (impers.w.d.)*, seem, seem good: geþūhte *pret.ind.3s.*, 163.

gewæcan, *wv.1*, weaken: gewæced *pp.*, 288, 917; gewæht, 932.

gewæpnian, *wv.2*, arm: gewæpnode *pret.ind.3s.*, 926.

geweald, *nt.*, power, control: ~e *d.s*, 400; covering, protection: ~an *d.p.?*, 944.

geweaxnyss, *f.*, growth, increase, interest: ~e *d.s.*, 18.

gewemman, *wv.1*, defile, besmirch: gewemmað *pres. ind.3p.*, 407.

gewendan, *wv.*, turn, translate: gewenden *inf.*, 253; gewende *pret.ind.3s.*, 5; *pp.*, 886.

gewilnian, *wv.2*, desire, wish *(w.g.)*: gewilnode *pret.ind. 1s.*, 377, 402, 621; *3s.*, 34, 193 etc.; gewilnodan *pp. (a. s.m.wk.)*; gewilnedan *(g.s.f. wk.)*, 870; *(d.s.f.wk.)*, 220.

gewilnung, *f.*, desire, wish: ~a *d.s.*, 623; *a.p.*, 379, 382; *g.p.?*, 617; ~um *d.p.*, 619.

gewinn, *nt.*, struggle, conflict: *n.s.*, 72; *a.s.*, 3; gewin, 178; ~e *d.s.*, 146.

gewislīce, *adv.*, certainly, exactly: 723.

gewiss, *nt.*, certainty, surety; ~e *d.s.*: mid ~e, purposefully: 197.

gewita, *m.*, adviser, guide, witness: ~n *d.s.*, 97, 328G.

gewitan, *pret.pres.v.*, get to know, learn: gewiste *pret. sbj.3s.*, 866.

gewītan, *sv.1*, depart, go away: gewāt *pres.ind.1s.*, 480; *3s.*, 413, 905, 948.

gewitnyss, *f.*, witness, knowledge: ~e *a.s.*, 176.

gewrit, *nt.*, writing, scripture: *n.s.*, 892; ~u *a.p.*, 690; ~a *g.p.*, 41, 45.

gewrīðan, *sv.1*, bind, attach: **gewriðon** *pret.sbj.3p.*, 38.

gewuna, (i) *m.*, practice, custom: *n.s.*, 296; (ii) *adj.* *(indecl.)*, wonted, accustomed: *n.s.f.*, 420; *n.p.m.*, 721.

gewunelic, *adj.*, traditional, usual: ~an *d.s.f.wk.*, 184; *d.p.nt.wk.*, 766.

gewunelīce, *adv.*, in the usual way, according to custom, traditionally: 139, 174 etc.

gewunian, *wv.2*, be accustomed to: **gewunode** *pret.ind.1s.*, 414; *3s.*, 201, 768.

gewurðan, *sv.3*, come to be, happen: **gewurðe** *pres.ind.* *3s.*, 20.

gewyrcan, *wv.1*, make, perform: **geworhte** *pret.ind.3s.*, 889, 939.

gewyrde, *nt.*, amount: *a.s.*, 850.

gewyrht, *f.nt.*, merit, desert: ~um *d.p.*, 545.

gewyrpan, *wv.1*, recover from illness *(refl.)*: **gewyrpte** *pret.ind.3s.*, 773.

geyppan, *wv.1*, utter, bring out: **geypte** *pret.ind.3s.*, 240.

geyrnan, *sv.3*, run: **geurnon** *pret.sbj.3p.*, 380.

gif, *conj.*, if: 100, 167 etc.

gifan, gifu; *see* **gyfan, gyfu.**

glēaw, *adj.*, skilful, clever: ~esta *sp.n.s.m.wk.*, 874.

God, *m.*, God: *n.s.*, 91, 134 etc.; *a.s.*, 50, 97 etc.; ~es *g.s.*, 13, 107 etc.; ~e *d.s.*, 47, 89 etc.

gōd, *adj.*, good: *n.s.m.*, 819; ~a *n.s.m.wk.*, 100; ~an *g.s.f.* *wk.*, 634.

godcund, *adj.*, divine: ~a *n.s.* *nt.wk.*, 464; ~e *n.s.f.wk.*, 293; ~an *a.s.m.wk*, 120; *g.s.m.wk.*, 732; *g.s.f.wk.*, 46, 51 etc.; *d.s.f.wk.*, 265, 936G; *d.s.nt.wk.*, 146; *n.p.nt.wk.*, 114, 139; *a.p.nt.wk.*, 741, 812, 903; *d.p.f.wk.*, 154; ~um *d.p.nt.*, 93.

godcundlic, *adj.*, godly, divine: ~e *n.s.nt.wk.*, 678; ~an *g.s.m.wk.*, 742; *g.p.nt.*, 283.

gōdnyss, *f.*, benefit, good thing: ~a *a.p.*, 42.

gōdspell, *nt.*, gospel: ~e *d.s.*, 688.

gold, *nt.*, gold: ~es *g.s.*, 109.

goldhord, *nt.*, treasure of gold: *a.s.*, 878.

Grecisc, *adj.*, Greek: *d.s.nt. (undecl.)*, 4.

grētan, *wv.1*, greet: **grētte** *pret.ind.3s.*, 145, 928.

grēting, *f.*, greeting: ~e *d.s.*, 512.

grim, *adj.*, fierce, terrible: ~e *a.s.nt.*, 516.

grimlic, *adj.*, terrible, dire: ~e

n.s.f., 495.

grimlīce, *adv.*, terribly: 669.

grin, *nt.*, trap, snare: *a.s.*, 439, 454.

gyfan, *sv.5*, give: *inf.*, 375; **gyfest** *pres.ind.2s.*, 709; **gifað** *3s.*, 726.

gyfu, *f.*, gift, grace: *n.s.*, 295, 306G; **gyfum** *d.p.*, 283, 374; **gifu** *d.s.*, 101; **gyfe** *g.s.* (but with *m./nt. article*), 851.

gȳman, *wv.1*, notice, observe: **gȳme** *pres.sbj.3s.*, 788.

gyrnan, *wv.1*, yearn for, long for (*w.g.*): **gyrnde** *pret.ind. 1s.*, 620.

H

habban, *wv.3*, have, keep, be devoted to: **hæbbe** *pres.ind. 1s.*, 933; **hæfst** *2s.*, 395; **hæfð** *3s.*, 313G; **habbað** *1p.*, 319G; **hæbben** *pres.sbj.3p.*, 399; **hæbbende** *pres.part.*, 40, 97 etc.; **habbende**, 175; **hæbbenne** *infl.inf.*, 273, 415; **hafa** *imp.s.*, 733; **hæfde** *pret.ind.1s.*, 361, 371 etc.; *3s.*, 43; *pret.sbj.1s.*, 402; **hæfdon** *pret.ind.3p.*, 113, 165.

hāl, *adj.*, safe, well: ~**e** *a.p.m.*, 441, 589*.

hālig, *adj.*, holy: **hāligra** *g.p.f.*, 687; *g.p.nt.*, 41, 45; **hālga** *n.s.m.wk.*, 404; **hālige**

a.p.nt., 690; *n.s.f.wk.*, 312G, 517 etc.; *n.s.nt.wk.*, 924; **hālgan** *a.s.m.wk.*, 138, 765, 937; *a.s.f.wk.*, 15, 458 etc.; *g.s.m.wk.*, 101, 581, 730; *g.s.f.wk.*, 392, 452 etc.; *g.s.nt.wk.*, 122, 884; *d.s.m. wk.*, 729, 730, 775; *d.s.f. wk.*, 541, 596; *d.s.nt.wk.*, 283, 344G etc.; *a.p.nt.wk.*, 536; **hālgum** *d.p.f.wk*, 21; *d.p.nt.wk.*, 313G, 828; **hāligan** *g.s.m.wk.*, 306G: **hālgestan** *sp.d.s.nt.*, 78.

hāligdōm, *m.*, sacrament: ~**es** *g.s.*, 739.

hālsian, *wv.2*, beseech, implore: **hālsige** *pres.ind.1s.*, 714; **hālsigende** *pres.part.*, 700.

hālwende, *adj.*, healing, salutary: **hālwendre** *g.s.f.*, 411; **hālwendan** *a.p.nt.wk.*, 257.

hām, *adv.*, home: 717, 774.

hand, *f.*, hand: *a.s.*, 779; ~**a** *d.s.*, 415; *a.p.*, 578, 885; ~**um** *d.p.*, 631, 829.

hangian, *wv.2*, hang: **hangiende** *pres.part.*, 332G.

hātan, *sv.7*, name, call, command: **hātað** *pres.ind. 1p.*, 780; **hāt** *imp.s.*, 511; **gehāten** *pp.*, 27.

hātheortnyss, *f.*, passion, heat: ~**e** *d.s.*, 376.

hāwian, *wv.2*, gaze, look: **hāwigende** *pres.part.*, 559, 872.

hæbban (= **hebban**), *sv.6*, raise up: **hæbbende** *pres.part.*, 790.

Hǣlend, *m.*, Saviour: *n.s.*, 509, 742; ~**ne** *a.s.*, 714, 754; ~**es** *g.s.*, 141, 580, 778; ~**um** *d.s.*, 959.

hǣlo, *f.*, salvation: *n.s.*, 561; *a.s.*, 833; *g.s.*, 74, 485, 551; **hǣlu** *a.s.*, 301; **hǣle** *g.s.*, 682.

hǣman, *wv.1*, have sexual intercourse: **hǣmdon** *pret. ind.3p.*, 449.

hǣmet, *nt.*, sexual intercourse: ~**es** *g.s.*, 645.

hǣs, *f.*, bidding, command: ~**e** *d.s.*, 936G.

hǣto, *f.*, heat: *g.s.*, 669; *d.s.*, 216; **hǣtu** *d.s.*, 522.

hē, hēo, hit, *pers. pron.*, he, she, it: **hē** *n.s.m.*, 10, 25 etc.; **hēo** *n.s.f.*, 3, 131 etc.; *n.p.m.*, 140, 946; *n.p.f.*, 885; **hit** *n.s.nt.*, 7, 11 etc.; *a.s.nt.*, 73; **hine** *a.s.m.*, 71, 81 etc.; **hī** *a.s.f.*, 227*, 277* etc.; *n.p. m.*, 37, 45 etc.; *a.p.m.*, 38, 39 etc.; **his** *g.s.m.*, 17, 25 etc.; **hyre** *g.s.f.*, 3, 437, 635; *d.s.f.*, 519, 636; **hire** *g.s.f.*, 217, 231 etc.; *d.s.f.*, 268, 269 etc.; **him** *d.s.m.*, 33, 37 etc.; *d.p.m.*, 132; **heora** *g.p. m.*, 52, 111 etc.; *g.p.nt.*, 405; **heom** *d.p.m.*, 111, 399 etc.

hēafod, *nt.*, head: **hēafdes** *g.s.*, 217.

hēahengel, *m.*, archangel: *n.s.*, 7.

hēahnyss, *f.*, height: ~**e** *a.s.*, 321G.

healdan, *sv.7*, hold, keep, guard: **healdende** *pres.part.*, 137; **hēoldon** *pret.sbj.3p.*, 152; **gehealden** *pp.*, 133, 180.

healf, (i) *f.*, side, half: ~**e** *a.s.*, 169, 206 etc.; *d.s.*, 245, 800, 883; (ii) *adj.*, ~**ne** *a.s.m.*, 582; ~**a** *a.p.m.*, 600.

hēalīce, *adv.*, highly, profoundly: 26.

heard, *adj.*, hard: *n.s.f.*, 916.

heardlīce, *adv.*, hard, vigorously: 639.

hell, *f.*, hell: ~**e** *a.s.*, 438.

hēof, *m.*, grief, mourning: ~**es** *g.s.*, 249.

hēofan, *sv.7*, lament: **hēofende** *pres.part.*, 488, 856.

heofon, *m.*, sky: *a.s.*, 205; *a.p.*, 830; ~**e** *d.s.*, 790.

heonon, *adv.*, hence, from here: 54; **heonone**, 793.

heord, *f.*, flock, herd: *n.s.*, 310G; ~**e** *a.s.*, 745.

heorte, *f.*, heart: **heortan** *g.s.*, 485, 651, 919; *d.s.*, 488, 913.

hēr, *adv.*, here: 88, 100 etc.

hergung, *f.*, praise, praising: ~**e** *g.s.*, 107.

herian, *wv.2*, praise: **herigende**

pres.part., 754, 949.

herigendlic, *adj.*, praiseworthy, laudable: ~**estan** *sp. a.s.f.*, 1.

hider, *adv.*, hither, here: 84, 601, 787 etc.; **hyder**: 99, 258, 694.

Hierusalem, *proper name*, Jerusalem: *d.s. (undecl.)*, 391, 444.

hiht, *m.*, hope: ~**e** *d.s.*, 237, 681.

hingrigan, *wv.2 (impers.)*, hunger: *inf.*, 618.

hīw, *nt.*, appearance, form: *a.s.*, 224.

hīwung, *f.*, appearance, form, pretence: *n.s.*, 433; ~**a** *d.s.*, 338G.

hlāf, *m.*, bread, loaf: ~**e** *d.s.*, 116, 684; ~**es** *g.s.*, 582; ~**as** *a.p.*, 565, 600; ~**a** *g.p.*, 663.

hlāford, *m.*, lord: ~**e** *d.s.*, 17.

hlǣfdige, *f.*, lady: *n.s.*, 493, 511 etc.; **hlǣfdig** *n.s.*, 542.

hlēoran (= **lēoran**), *wv.1*, depart, die: **hlēorende** *pres. part.*, 896; **hlēorde** *pret.ind. 3s.*, 907, 958.

hlihhan, *sv.6*, laugh: **hlihhende** *pres.part.*, 413.

hlūd, *adj.*, loud: ~**dre** *d.s.f.*, 235.

hlūde, *adv.*, loudly: 705.

hlystan, *wv.1*, listen, hear: **hlyste** *pret.ind.1s.*, 696.

hnappian, *wv.2*, doze, slumber: **hnappode** *pret.ind.3s.*, 785.

hnesce, *adj.*, soft, gentle: **hnescan** *a.p.f.*, 807, 860.

hopian, *wv.2*, expect, trust: **hopige** *pres.ind.1s.*, 439; **hopode** *pret.ind.3s.*, 865.

hraðor, *adv. (cp. of* **hraðe***)*, more quickly, more readily: 369.

hræd, *adj.*, quick, rapid: ~**estan** *sp.d.s.m.wk.*, 229.

hrædlīce, *adv.*, quickly, readily: 750; **hrædlīcor**, *cp.*: 401.

hræglung, *f.*, clothing: ~**e** *g.s.*, 661.

hrēafigende, *adj.*, eagerly, rapaciously: *n.s.f.*, 633; *but see Commentary.*

hrēowsian, *wv.2*, repent: **hrēowgigende** *pres.part.*, 864; **hrēowsigendan** *pres. part. (a.p.m.wk.)*, 536.

hrēowsung, *f.*, repentance, penitence, sorrow: ~**a** *a.s.*, 2, 440; *d.s.*, 504; ~**e** *g.s.*, 547.

hrepsung, *f.*, evening, night: ~**e** *d.s.*, 782.

hrōwan (= **rōwan**), *sv.7*, go by water, row, sail: **hrēowan** *pret.ind.3p.*, 427.

hū, *adv.*, how: 3, 73 etc.

hūmeta, *adv.*, in what way, how: 437.

hund, *nt.*, hundred: *a.s.*, 957.

hunta, *m.*, hunter: *n.s.*, 874.

hūru, *adv.*, indeed, even: 719, 740, 792.

hūslgang, *m.*, partaking in the eucharist: ~**e** *d.s.*, 898.

hwā, *m.f.*, **hwæt**, *nt.*, *interrog.*

pron., who, what: **hwā** *n.s.*
m., 900; **hwæt** *n.s.nt.*, 226,
289; *a.s.nt.*, 176, 547 etc.;
hwæs *g.s.nt.*, 273; **hwȳ** *inst.*
s.nt., 340G; **hwī**, 911.

hwanon, *adv.*, whence, from
where: 87.

hwænne, *adv.*, when: 83.

hwǣr: *conj.*, where: 799; *see
also* **swā hwǣr swā**.

hwæs, hwæt: *see* **hwā**.

hwæthwegu, *indecl.pron.*, a
little, something: 844.

hwæðer, (i) *pron.*, one of two,
each: **hwæðra** *g.p.m.*, 232;
(ii) *conj.*, whether: 394, 891;
hweðer, 65; (iii) *conj. introducing a direct question*, is it
that . . .?: 62, 787.

hwega, *adv.*, some, somewhat:
185.

hweorfan, *sv.3*, turn, depart:
hwearf *pret.ind.3s.*, 788.

hwī, *adv.*, why: 235, 271; *see
also* **hwā**.

hwider, *adv.*, whither, where:
390*, 519.

hwīl, *f.*, time, while: ~**e** *d.s.*,
199, 604.

hwilc, (i) *interrog.adj.*, what,
which: *n.s.m.*, 428, 568; ~**e**
a.s.f., 178; ~**ra** *g.p.n.*, 176;
~**um** *d.p.m.*, 482; *d.p.n.*, 84,
598; **hwylcre**, *d.s.f.*, 305G;
(ii) *indef. adj.*, some: *n.s.m.*,
129; *n.s.f.*, 473; **hwylc**,
341G; **hwilcere** *d.s.f.*, 129;

hwylcere, 338G; **hwylce** *a.
s.f.*, 307G; (iii) *indef. pron.*,
anyone, anything: *n.s.m.*,
168; ~**es** *g.s.nt.*, of any kind:
901.

hwilchwugu, *adj.*, a little, some:
hwilcehwugu *a.s.f.*, 357.

hwīlum, *adv.*, at times: 667,
668.

hwīt, *adj.*, white: ~**e** *n.p.m.*,
217.

hwomm, *m.*, corner: ~**e** *d.s.*,
481.

hwōn, *adv.*, a little, somewhat,
at all: 142, 189, 338G.

hwyrfan, *wv.1*, turn, depart:
hwyrfe *pres.sbj.1s.*, 793.

hyder: *see* **hider**.

hyderes, *adv.*, hither: 869.

hȳran, *wv.1*, hear: **hȳrende**
pres.part., 352G.

hyrde, *m.*, shepherd: *n.s.*, 101.

hȳrsumian, *wv.2*, obey *(w.d.)*:
hȳrsumigende *pres.part.*,
814.

hȳðnyss, *f.*, benefit, advantage:
~**e** *d.s.*, 308G.

I

ic, *pers. pron.*, I: *n.s.*, 14, 15
etc.; **me** *a.s.*, 236, 252 etc.;
d.s., 15, 18 etc.; **mīn**, *g.s.*,
236, 734; **wē** *n.p.*, 138, 173
etc.; **ūs** *a.p.*, 92, 93 etc.; *d.p.*,
99, 100; **wit** *n. dual*, 937;
wytt, 837; **unc** *d. dual*, 837.

īdel, (i) *adj.*, empty, vain: *n.s.m.*, 792; (ii) *nt.*, uselessness: **on īdel**, in vain, 469.

Idus, *Latin noun*, Ides: 897.

in, *prep.w.a.d.*, in, into: 577, 832, 947; *see also* **inn**.

inc: *see* **þū**.

ingān/ingangan, *anom.v./sv.*7, go in, enter: **ingangan** *inf.*, 463; **ingangendum** *pres. part. (d.p.m.)*, 525, 528; **inēode** *pret.ind.1s.*, 527; **inēodon** *3p.*, 462.

ingang, *m.*, entry, entrance: *n.s.*, 530; *a.s.*, 473, 486 etc.; ~**es** *g.s.*, 531.

ingehȳd, *m.*, conscience, mind: ~**e** *d.s.*, 174.

inn, *adv.*, in, inside: 243, 469 etc.; **in**, 462.

innan, *adv.*, from within: 644, 697.

inneweard, *adj.*, inner, inward, deep: ~**re** *d.s.f.*, 488.

innon, *prep.w.d.*, inside, in: 78, 533.

inra, *cp.adj.*, inner: ~**n** *a.s.nt.*, 947; *d.s.nt.*, 750.

intinga, *m.*, cause, reason: ~**n** *d.s.*, 87; **intingum** *d.p.*, 483.

Iohannes, *proper name*, John: *n.s.*, 954; *g.s.*, 575, 582; **Iohanne** *d.s.*, 743.

Iordane, *proper name*, Jordan: *a.*, 165, 185 etc.; *d.*, 75, 77 etc.; ~**n** *a.s.*, 576, 694, 738; *g.s.*, 734; ~**s**, 782, 803, 804;

~**m** *a.s.*, 601, 665 etc.

īsiht, *adj.*, icy: *g.s.f.wk.*, 667.

L

lā, *interj.*, O: 272, 435, 713.

lāf, *f.*, what is left, remnant: **tō lāfe**, alone: 767; **tō lǣfe**, 466.

lamb, *nt.*, lamb: *n.s.*, 948.

landlēod, *m.*, inhabitant, native: ~**um** *d.p.* 132.

lang, *adj.*, long, long-lasting: ~**an** *d.s.nt.wk.*, 918.

lange, *adv.*, long, for a long time: 674, 869.

langsumlīce, *adv.*, patiently, 442.

lār, *f.*, teaching: ~**e** *g.s.*, 61, 87; *d.s.*, 282; ~**um** *d.p.*, 38.

lāttēow, *m.*, guide: *n.s.*, 551.

lǣdan, *wv.1*, lead: **lǣt** *pres.ind. 3s.*, 553.

lǣden, *nt.*, Latin: *a.*, 5.

lǣf: *see* **lāf**.

lǣg: *see* **licgan**.

lǣran, *wv.1*, teach, train: **lǣrende** *pres.part.*, 434, 697; **gelǣred** *pp.*, 27.

lǣst, *adj. (sp.of* **lȳtel**), least: ~**ra** *g.p.nt.*, 759.

lǣswian, *wv.2*, graze, feed, look after: **gelǣswod** *pp.*, 310G.

lǣtnyss, *f.*, slowness: ~**e** *a.s.*, 763.

lǣttewestre, *f.*, guide: **lǣttewestran** *a.s.*, 585.

lēaf, *f.*, leave, permission: ~e *a.s.*, 505.

leahtor, *m.*, sin, vice: leahtra *g.p.*, 370; leahtrum *d.p.*, 367, 423

lencgu, *f.*, length: *a.s.*, 606.

Lenctenfæsten, *n.*, Lenten fast, Lent: ~es *g.s.*, 123, 764; ~e *d.s.*, 720.

lenticula, *Latin noun (f.)*, lentil: 781, 849.

lēo, *m./f.*, lion, lioness; *n.s.(f.)*, 927, 938, 947; ~n *a.s.*, 921; *d.s.(m.)*, 929.

lēoht, *n.*, light: *a.s.*, 639.

leornian, *wv.2*, learn: leornode *pret.ind.1s.*, 695; *3s.*, 901; leornodest *2s.*, 689.

leoð (= lið), *nt.*, limb: leoðum *d.p.*, 928.

lēoþ, *nt.*, song, poem: *a.p.*, 628.

lettan, *wv.1*, hinder: lettenne *infl.inf.*, 857; gelet *pp.*, 857.

letting, *f.*, hindrance, impediment: ~a *d.s.*, 472; lættinge *d.s.*, 463.

libban, *wv.3*, live: leofað *pres. ind.3s.*, 684, 959; libbende *pres.part.*, 112; libbendan *(g.s.m.)*, 140; leofode *pret. ind.1s.*, 387, 664; *3s.*, 170; lyfde *1s.*, 381.

liccian, *wv.2*, lick: liccode *pret.ind.3s.*, 922.

licgan, *sv.5*, lie: licgende *pres.part.*, 373, 885, 914; licgendan *(g.s.f.wk.)*, 926;

læg *pret.ind.1s.*, 368, 673; *3s.*, 337G.

līchama, *m.*, body: *n.s.*, 250, 479; ~n *a.s.*, 158, 269 etc.; *g.s.*, 141, 156 etc.; *d.s.*, 112, 208 etc.; *n.p.*, 114; *a.p.*, 52.

līchamlic, *adj.*, bodily: ~re *d.s.f.*, 768; ~um *d.p.m.*, 254.

līcian, *wv.2*, please, be pleasing to: līcie *pres.sbj.3s.*, 94; līcode *pret.sbj.3s.*, 891; līc- odon *3p.*, 182.

līcwurðe, *adj.*, pleasing, worthy: *a.p.m.*, 418; *n.p.m.*, 89; ~an *g.s.f.wk.*, 550.

līcwyrðlīce, *adv.*, pleasingly, in a praisworthy manner: 70.

līf, *nt.*, life: ~es *g.s.*, 4, 25; ~e *d.s.*, 385.

līffæst, *adj.*, life-giving: ~an *g.s.nt.wk.*, 483; *a.p.nt.wk.*, 741; *d.p.nt.wk.*, 579; lȳf- festan *a.p.nt.wk.*, 735.

locc, *m.*, lock, hair: ~as *n.p.*, 217.

lōcian, *wv.2*, look, gaze: lōc- igende *pres.part.*, 830; loc- ode *pret.ind.3s.*, 205.

lof, *n.*, praise: ~um *d.p.*, 949.

lufian, *wv.2*, love: lufiað *pres. ind.3p.*, 66, 726.

lufu, *f.*, love: *n.s.*, 98, 293; *a.s.*, 364; *d.s.*, 117; lufe *d.s.*, 371.

lust, *m.*, pleasure, desire, lust: *n.s.*, 627 ~e *d.s.*, 419; ~as *a.p.*, 436; ~um *d.p.*, 618.

lȳffest: *see* līffæst.

lyft, *f.*, air: ~e *a.s.*, 407; *d.s.*, 332G.

lȳtel, (i) *adj.*, little: *a.s.nt.*, 914; ~ne *a.s.m.*, 776, 779; ~re *g.s.f.*, 843; **lȳtlan** *d.s.m.wk.*, 307G; (ii) *nt.*, a little: **lȳtles** *g.s.*, 185, 843.

lȳthwōn, *adv.*, a little: 330G.

M

mā, (i) *nt., indecl. (w.g.)*, more: 402; (ii) *cp.adv.* more: 51.

magan, *pret.pres.v.*, be able, can: **mæg** *pres.ind.1s.*, 252, 428 etc.; *3s.*, 94, 428; **miht** *2s.*, 729; **mæge** *pres.sbj.1s.*, 259; *2s.*, 73, 370; *3s.*, 797; **mage** *3s.*, 63; **mihtest** *pret. ind.2s.*, 597; **mihtst**, 605; **mihte** *3s.*, 155, 233, 270 etc.; *pret. sbj.1s.*, 378; *3s.*, 771, 803, 874.

man, (i) *m.*, man, person, sir: *n.s.*, 19, 70, 304G etc.; *a.s.*, 214, 564, 693; **mann**, *n.s.*, 94, 254, 713; ~nes *g.s.*, 331G, 374; **menn** *d.s.*, 197, 715; **men** *a.p.*, 416; ~num *d.p.*, 123, 182, 726; (ii) *indef. pron.*, one: 12, 323G, 354 etc.; **mon**, 13.

māndǣd, *f.*, wicked deed, sin: ~a *a.p.*, 429.

mānful, *adj.*, wicked, evil: ~lum *d.p.m.*, 423; ~lan *g.s. m.wk.*, 383; *g.s.nt.wk.*, 516.

manig, *adj.*, many: **manega** *a.p.f.*, 438; *g.p.f.*, 279; **mænige** *n.p.nt.*, 592; *a.p.m.*, 445; **mænga**, 450; **menegra** *g.p.f.*, 605; **manegum** *d.p. m.*, 393; *d.p.f.*, 688; *d.p.nt.*, 284, 424; **mænegum** *d.p.m.*, 772.

manðwǣre, *adj.*, gentle, placid: **manðwǣra** *g.p.nt.*, 617.

māra, *cp.adj.*, greater, more: **māre** *n.s.nt.*, 71; *a.s.nt.*, 548; **māran** *g.s.f.*, 60.

Maria, *proper name*, Mary: *n.s.*, 906, 945; *g.s.*, 893; ~n *a.*, 585, 824; *g.*, 3.

mattuc, *m.*, mattock: *n.s.*, 912.

mæg, *m.*, kinsperson: ~um *d.p.*, 363.

mægen, *nt.*, power, force: *n.s.*, 464, 531, 678; ~e *d.s.*, 926*.

mægþ, *f.*, race, country, region: ~e *d.s.*, 25.

mæncgan, *wv.1*, mingle, mix: *inf.*, 468.

mænigfeald, *adj.*, various, in many ways: *a.p.nt.*, 667; ~an *a.p.nt.wk.*, 706; ~um *d.p.f.*, 497, 656 etc.

mænigfealdlīce, *adv.*, in various ways, numerously, abundantly: 942; **mænigfeald-līcor** *cp.*, 378, 725.

mærsian, *wv.2*, celebrate, proclaim: **mærsigenne** *infl.inf.*, 124; **mærsodon** *pret.ind.3p.*, 953.

mǣrsung, *f.*, exaltation, celebration, observance: *n.s.*, 44; ~e *d.s.*, 187.

mǣrð, *f.*, glory: ~a *a.p.*, 953.

mǣst, (i) *sp.adj.*, most: *n.s.f.*, 270; ~e *n.s.nt.wk.*, 929; (ii) *adv.*, especially, most: 270.

mēd, *f.*, reward: ~e *a.s.*, 54.

medemnyss, *f.*, rank, dignity: ~e *d.s.*, 295.

meniu, *f.*, multitude, crowd: *n.s.*, 473; *a.s.*, 372, 388; **mæniu**, *n.s.*, 390.

mennisc, *adj.*, human: ~e *a.s.nt. wk.*, 697; *d.s.f.*, 207; ~um *d.s.nt.*, 561.

mennisclic, *adj.*, human: ~e *a.s.f.*, 223.

mete, *m.*, food: *a.s.*, 113*.

metsian, *wv.2*, provide with food: **metsode** *pret.ind.3s.*, 155.

mettrumnyss, *f.*, weakness, infirmity: ~e *d.s.*, 769; ~a *g.p.*, 92.

miccle, *adv.*, much: 51, 71; *see also* **micel**.

micclum, *adv.*, much, greatly: 237; *see also* **micel**.

micel, (i) *adj.*, great, much: *n.s.f.*, 13, 272; *a.s.nt.*, 274, 939; ~e *a.s.f.*, 387; ~ne *a.s.m.*, 286; **miccle** *a.p.m.*, 753; **micclan** *a.s.f.wk.*, 2; *d.s.m.wk.*, 670, 862, 863; *d.s.f.wk.*, 670; *d.s.nt.wk.*, 602; **micclum** *d.s.m.*, 801,

888; *d.s.nt.*, 444 *(but with f. noun)*, 460, 906; *d.p.nt.*, 679; miccle *n.p.m.*, 74; **mycel** *n.s.m.*, 351G; **myccles** *g.s.m.*, 935G; *g.s.nt.*, 316G; **mycelre** *d.s.f.*, 333G; (ii) *adv.*, much: 821.

micelnyss, *f.*, great size, largeness: ~e *g.s.*, 920.

mid, *prep.w.d.*, with, by means of: 53 etc.; with, among: 82, 100 etc.; **mid þām**, *adv.*, at that time, at the same time: 113, 517, 630; **mid þām þe**, *conj.*, when: 469.

middaneard, *m.*, world, earth: ~es *g.s.*, 509, 560; ~e *d.s.*, 309G, 314G, 905.

middæg, *m.*, mid-day: ~es *g.s.*, 198.

milde, *adj.*, gentle, meek: **mildeste** *sp.n.s.nt.wk.*, 948.

mildheortnyss, *f.*, pity, mercy: ~e *a.s.*, 357, 543; *d.s.*, 523.

miltsian, *wv.2*, have pity on: **miltsa** *imp.s.*, 252, 371 etc.

mīn, *poss.adj.*, my: *n.s.f.*, 591; *a.s.nt.*, 484, 633; ~ne *a.s.m.*, 354, 366 etc.; ~e *a.s.f.*, 405, 440 etc.; *d.s.f.*, 853; *n.p.nt.*, 406, 833; *a.p.m.*, 436, 642; *a.p.f.*, 578, 658; *a.p.nt.*, 426; ~es *g.s.m.*, 403, 419; *g.s.nt.*, 379, 567, 631; ~re *g.s.f.*, 363, 484 etc.; *d.s.f.*, 511, 652; ~ra *g.p.m.*, 371, 451; *g.p.f.*, 486; *g.p.nt.*, 413; ~um

d.s.nt., 482; *d.p.m.*, 362; *d.p.*
f., 630; *d.p.nt.*, 275, 557;
~on *d.s.m.*, 307G; *see also*
ic.

misdǣd, *f.*, misdeed: ~a *g.p.*,
486.

mislic, *adj.*, various, diverse:
~um *d.p.f.*, 674.

mōd, *nt.*, mind: *a.s.*, 41, 484; ~e
d.s., 53, 61 etc.

mōdor, *f.*, mother: *n.s.*, 289,
312G etc.

mōdorlic, *adj.*, maternal: ~um
d.p.nt., 56.

mon: *see* man.

mōna, *m.*, moon: ~n *g.s.*, 806.

mōnað, *m.*, month: mōnðe *d.s.*,
896.

mōtan, *pret.pres.v.*, be permitted, may: mōste *pret.sbj.*
1s., 841.

mundbyrdnyss, *f.*, protector,
advocate; advocacy, surety:
~e *g.s.*, 550, 632; *d.s.*, 514,
520.

munuc, *m.*, monk: *n.s.*, 62, 129;
a.s., 339G; munece *d.s.*, 80;
muneces *g.s.*, 314G; munecas *n.p.*, 36, 774; munecum
d.p., 83, 85.

munuclic, *adj.*, monastic,
monkish: ~um *d.p.m.*, 26,
31 etc.; ~an *g.s.m.wk.*, 32.

mūð, *m.*, mouth: *a.s.*, 437, 849;
~e *d.s.*, 685.

myngian, *wv.2*, remind of
(something *(g.)*): myngode

pret.ind.1s., 631.

mynster, *nt.*, monastery: *a.s.*,
57, 134; mynstres *g.s.*, 80,
126 etc.; mynstre *d.s.*, 24,
28 etc.; mynstrum *d.p.*, 37,
722.

mynsterwīse, *f.*, monastic
practice: mynsterwīsan *a.p.*,
955.

N

nā, *adv.*, not, not at all: 152, 217
etc.; nā þæt ān, not only:
130.

nabban, *wv.3*, not have: næbbe
pres.ind.1s., 397.

nacod, *adj.*, naked: ~e *a.f.s.*,
943.

nāht, (i) *nt.*, nothing: *a.s.*, 355,
901 etc.; (ii) *adv.*, not, not at
all: 335G, 393 etc.

nāhwider, *adv.*, nowhere: 245.

nama, *m.*, name: *n.s.*, 110; ~n
a.s., 864, 902; *d.s.*, 262, 294.

nān, (i) *adj.*, no: *n.s.m.*, 18, 70,
344G; *n.s.f.*, 432; *n.s.nt.*, 48,
153 etc.; *a.s.nt.*, 158, 324G
etc.; nǣnne *a.s.m.*, 692; ~e
a.s.f., 223;~re *g.s.f.*, 60, 660;
g.p.nt., 224; ~um *d.s.m.*,
715; (ii) *pron.*, none, no one,
nothing: *n.s.m.*, 163, 167,
177; *n.s.nt.*, 323G; *a.s.nt.*,
345G?, 888; nǣnne *a.s.m.*,
239, 440, 709; ~um *d.s.m.*,
696.

nǣddre, *f.*, snake, serpent, adder: ~n *a.s.*, 354.

nǣfre, *adv.*, never: 41, 44 etc.

nǣnig, (i) *adj.*, no: *a.s.nt.*, 922; (ii) *pron.*, no one, none; ~e þinga, not at all, on no account: 14, 785.

nǣs, *adv.*, not, not at all: 152; *see also* **nesan**.

ne, (i) *adv.* not: 14, 18 etc.; (ii) *conj.*, nor: 20, 48 etc.

nēadþearfnysse: *see* **nȳdþearfnyss**.

nēah, (i) *adv.*, near: 233; **nēar** *cp.*, 232; (ii) *prep.w.d.*, near, close to: 75.

Neapolis, *proper name*, Naples: *g.*, 5.

nēdbehǣfednyss, *f.*, necessity: ~um *d.p.*, 186*.

nellan, *anom.v.*, will not, not wish to: *pres.sbj.3p.*, 398; **nelle** *pres.ind.1s.*, 746; *3s.*, 442.

nemnian, *wv.2*, name, call: **nemniað** *pres.ind.1p.*, 138, 765; **nemnað** *pres.ind.1p.*, 174; **nǣmdest** *pret.ind.2s.*, 294; **nǣmnede** *3s.*, 262.

nēod, *f.*, need: *n.s.*, 86, 270, 272.

neorxnewang, *m.*, paradise: *a.s.*, 120.

nerian, *wv.2*, preserve, save: **genered** *pp.*, 10.

nesan, *anom.v.*, be not: **nis** *pres. ind.3s.*, 70, 86 etc.; **nys**, 796;

nǣs *pret.ind.1s.*, 447; *3s.*, 110, 128 etc.; **nǣron** *3p.*, 108.

nigeþa, *num.adj.*, ninth: ~n *d.s.f.*, 897.

niht, *f.*, night: *a.s.*, 189, 583; ~e *g.s.*, 805; *d.s.*, 897; ~es *g.s.*, by night, at night: 108.

niman, *sv.4*, take: **nimað** *imp. p.*, 421; **nāmon** *pret.ind.3p.*, 427.

nīwe, *adj.*, new: **nīwes** *g.s.nt.*, 63.

notian, *wv.2*, use *(w.g.)*: **notigende** *pres.part.*, 603; **notode** *pret.ind.1s.*, 663.

nū, (i) *adv.*, now: 136, 289 etc.; (ii) *conj.*, now that, since: 796, 912.

nȳd, *nt.*, force, violence: ~e *d.s.*, 479.

nȳdþearf, *f.*, need, necessity: ~e *d.s.*, 129*.

nȳdþearfnyss, *f.*, necessity, need: ~e *a.s.*, 626; *g.s.*, 188; *d.s.*, 652; ~um *d.p.*, 115, 675; **nēadþearfnysse** *n.s.*, 160 *(see Commentary, 159)*.

nȳdwrǣclīce, *adv.*, violently, forcefully: 459.

nytan, *pret.pres.v.*, not know: **nāt** *pres.ind.1s.*, 911; **nyte** *pres.sbj.1s.*, 64; *2s.*, 73; **nyste** *pret.ind.3s.*, 163.

nȳten, *nt.*, beast, animal: *a.s.*, 693; ~a *g.p.*, 224.

O

of, *prep.w.d.*, from: 4, 10 etc.

ofdūne, *adv.*, down: 671.

ofer, *prep.w.a.*, over, beyond, against: 351G, 478 etc.; after: 515.

ōfer, *m.*, bank, shore: **ōfrum** *d.p.*, 782.

oferbrǣdels, *m.*, covering, garment: ~e *d.s.*, 682.

oferdruncennyss, *f.*, drunkenness: ~e *d.s.*, 622.

oferfaran, *sv.6*, cross, go over, pass: *inf.*, 606, 796, 803; **oferfærst** *pres.ind.2s.*, 555; **oferfar** *imp.s.*, 721; **oferfōr** *pret.ind.1s.*, 601, 666; *3s.*, 185*, 906; **oferfōre** *pret.sbj. 1s.*, 738; **oferfaren** *pp.*, 165; **oferfarenum** *(d.s.m.)*, 867.

oferfēran, *wv.1*, cross: **oferfērde** *pret.ind.1s.*, 694.

oferflōwendlīce, *adv.*, overwhelmingly: 638.

ofergēotan, *sv.2*, pour over, suffuse, cover: **ofergēotende** *pres.part.*, 408; **ofergēat** *pret.ind.1s.*, 647; *3s.*, 909; **ofergoten** *pp.*, 334G, 359; **ofergotene** *(case unclear)*, 781.

ofergetilian, *wv.2*, overcome: **ofergetiligende** *pres.part*, 228.

oferlīhtan, *wv.1*, shine on, illuminate: **oferlīhte** *pret.sbj.*

3s., 650.

oferwrēon, *sv.1/2*, cover up: *inf.*, 260; **oferwrēah** *pret. ind.3s.*, 269, 943; **oferwrigen** *pp.*, 682.

ofgēotan, *sv.2*, soak: *inf.*, 877; **ofgotene** *pp. (a.p.f.)*, 158.

ofgifan, *sv.5*, render, give over: **ofgif** *imp.s.*, 894.

ofst, *f.*, haste, speed: ~e *d.s.*, 444.

ofstlīce, *adv.*, speedily, quickly: 221, 564.

oft, *adv.*, often: 45, 611.

on, (i) *prep.w.acc.*, into, onto, in, at, in respect of: 4, 16 etc.; *w.d.inst.*, among, on, in: 4, 18 etc.; **an**, 817*; (ii) *adv.*, on, forward: 16; within: 646.

onǣlan, *wv.1*, inflame, set on fire: **onǣled** *pp.*, 376.

onbīdan, *sv.1*, remain, wait: **onbīd** *imp.s.*, 727.

oncnāwan, *sv.7*, understand, know, recognize: *inf.*, 73, 370; **oncnāwenne** *infl.inf.*, 225; **oncnāwen** *pp.*, 110, 295; **oncnāwan** *pp.*, 498; **oncnāwenne** *(n./a.p.nt.)*, 716.

ondrǣdan, *wv.1*, fear, dread: **ondrǣdendum** *pres.part. (d. p.m.)*, 708; **ondrǣde** *pret. ind.1s.*, 643.

ondrincan, *sv.3*, drink *(w.g.)*, **ondranc** *pret.ind.1s.*, 582.

onemnþrōwigan, *wv.2*, sympathize with: *inf.*, 299.

onfōn, *sv.7*, receive, accept *(may take g.,d.)*: *inf.*, 260; **onfēhð** *pres.ind.3s.*, 546; **onfōnne** *inf.inf.*, 736; **onfēng** *pret.ind.3s.*, 268, 828, 904; **onfēnge** *pret.sbj.1s.*, 375; **onfangenan** *pp. (a.s.m. wk.)*, 17; **onfangenum** *(d.s. nt.)*, 82, 103; **onfangene** *(n. p.m.)*, 471.

ongēan, (i) *prep.w.a.*, against, in front of: 473; (ii) *adv.*, in turn, back again: 278.

ongēanweardes, *prep.w.d.*, towards: 253, 809.

onginnan, *sv.3*, begin: **ongan** *pret.ind.1s.*, 364, 456 etc.; *3s.*, 79, 234 etc.; **ongunnon** *3p.*, 463; **ongunne** *pret.sbj. 3s.*, 824.

ongyrwan, *wv.1.*, take off, unclothe: **ongyrede** *pret.ind. 3s.*, 267.

ongytan, *sv.5*, perceive, grasp: *inf.*, 73, 325G; **ongyten** *inf.*, 323G; **ongeat** *pret.ind.1s.*, 558; *3s.*, 264, 903, 954.

onhrīnan, *sv.1*, touch, lay hold of *(w.a.,g.)*: **onhrān** *pret.ind. 3s.*, 484, 849.

onhyring, *f.*, imitation, emulation: ~**e** *d.s.*, 39.

onlīhtan, *wv.1*, light up, enlighten: **onlīhte** *pret.ind.3s.*, 806; **onlīht** *pp.*, 265.

onlīhtnyss, *f.*, enlightenment,

illumination: ~**e** *g.s.*, 47, 52; *d.s.*, 9.

onuppan, *prep.w.a.*, above, on top of: 807.

openlīce, *adv.*, openly: 372.

opennyss, f., manifestation: ~**e** *a.s.*, 51.

oreð, *nt.*, breath: ~**e** *d.s.*, 288.

orsāwle, *adj.*, lifeless: *a.s.m.*, 884.

oþ, *prep.w.a.*, until, to: 57, 218 etc.

ōþer, (i) *adj.*, other: *n.s.m.*, 794; *a.s.nt.*, 835, 888; **ōþre** *a.s.f.*, 169, 244; *d.s.f.*, 245, 799, 883; *n.p.m.*, 74; *a.p.nt.*, 689; **ōþra** *g.p.nt.*, 109; **ōþrum** *d.p.nt.*, 424, 890; (ii) *pron.*, other, other one: **ōþerne** *a.s.m.*, 95, 145 etc.; **ōþres** *g.s.m.*, 163; **ōþra** *g.p.m.*, 822; **ōþrum** *d.p.f.*, 688; *d.p.m.*, 166, 468.

oþhrīnan, *sv.1*, touch: *inf.*, 860*, 888; **oþrān** *pret.ind. 3s.*, 854; **oþhrinon** *pp.*, 522.

oþstandan, stand fixed, remain: **oþstōd** *pret.ind.1s.*, 466; *3s.*, 198.

oþþæt, *conj.*, until: 870, 936; **oððe,** 465, 475, 735.

oþþe, *conj.*, or: 21, 64 etc.; *see also* **oþþæt.**

P

Palestina, *proper name*, Palestine: *d.*, 24, 28.

Palmdæg, *m.*, Palm Day, Palm Sunday: *a.s.*, 173.

palmtrēow, *m.*, palm-tree: ~a *g.p.*, 157, 780.

Paulus, *proper name*, Paul: *n.*, 5.

peneg, *m.*, penny, coin: ~as *a.p.*, 565.

pyse, *f.*, pea: **pysan** *n.p.*, 849.

R

Raphahel, *proper name*, Raphael: *n.*, 7.

rǣdan, *wv.1*, read: **rǣdde** *pret.ind.3s.*, 899; **rǣddon** *3p.*, 696; **gerǣd** *pp.*, 7.

rægel (= **hrægel**), *nt.*, garment, clothing: ~es *g.s.*, 945.

reccan, *wv.1*, recount, relate, direct, control: **reccende** *pres.part.*, 658; **rehte** *pret. ind.3s.*, 950; **rehton** *3p.*, 46; **gereht** *pp.*, 309G.

regol, *m.*, rule, regulation: *n.s.*, 132, 179; *a.s.*, 724; ~es *g.s.*, 31, 187; ~e *d.s.*, 58; ~um *d.p.*, 31.

restan, *wv.1*, rest: **restende** *pres.part.*, 189; **reste** *pret. ind.1s.*, 583.

riht, *adj.*, proper, right: ~re *d.s.f.*, 654.

rihtgelēafful, *adj.*, true-believing, orthodox: ~an *g.s.f.wk.*, 311G.

rihtgelēaffulnyss, *f.*, true faith: ~e *g.s.*, 825.

rihtlic, *adj.*, right, proper: *n.s.nt.*, 500.

rihtlicost, *sp.adv.*, most directly: 569.

rihtwīslic, *adj.*, righteous: ~re *d.s.f.*, 798.

rīxian, *wv.2*, reign, rule: **rīxað** *pres.ind.3s.*, 959.

rōd, *f.*, cross: ~e *a.s.*, 458, 517 etc.; *g.s.*, 211, 347G etc.

ryne, *m.*, course, routine: *a.s.*, 128*, 202; ~s *g.s.*, 763; *d.s.*, 229, 867, 907; **rynu** *d.s.*, 837; **ryna** *g.p.*, 232; **rynum** *d.p.*, 655.

S

sācerd, *m.*, priest: *n.s.*, 812.

sācerdlic, *adj.*, priestly, sacerdotal: ~an *d.s.f.*, 282.

samnian, *wv.2*, gather, assemble: **gesamnode** *pp.* (*n. p.m.*), 416.

samod, *adv.*, together: 457.

sancte, *adj.*, holy: *g.s.f.*, 5; **sanctes** *g.s.m.*, 575; **sancta** *a.s.f.*, 585.

sāwan, *sv.7*, sow: **sāwende** *pres.part.*, 177.

sāwol, *f.*, soul: **sāwla** *a.s.*, 637; *g.s.*, 296; *a.p.*, 438; *g.p.*, 301; **sāwle** *a.s.*, 677; *g.s.*, 851; *d.s.*, 12.

sǣ, *f.*, sea: *n.s.*, 436; *d.s.*, 389,

415, 448.

sǣd, *nt.*, seed: ~e *a.p.*, 177.

sceamian, *wv.2*, shame: **sceam-aθ** *pres.ind.3s.*, 365.

sceamu, *f.*, shame, modesty: **sceame** *a.s.*, 255.

sceandlic, *adj.*, shameful, lewd: ~ra *g.p.nt.*, 627.

scearp, *adj.*, sharp, keen: *n.s.nt.*, 697; ~ran *cp.a.p.m.*, 116.

scearpnyss, *f.*, sharpness, keenness: ~um *d.p.*, 872.

scēawian, *wv.2*, see, behold, gaze upon: **scēawiaθ** *pres. ind.3p.*, 51; **scēawige** *pres. sbj.1s.*, 496.

sceoplēoθ, *nt.*, song, poem: ~a *g.p.*, 627.

sceortlīce, *adv.*, briefly, shortly: 368.

scēotan, *sv.2*, dart, shoot: **scēat** *pret.ind.3s.*, 243.

scīnan, *sv.1*, shine: **scīnende** *pres.part.*, 105, 640, 884.

scinhīw, *nt.*, phantom, illusion: *n.s.*, 210.

scip, *nt.*, ship: *n.s.*, 796; *a.s.*, 427; **scypa** *g.p.*, 398.

scipfæreld, *nt.*, voyage: ~e *d.s.*, 430.

scræf, *nt.*, pit, hole: *a.s.*, 939.

sculan, *pret.pres.v.*, shall, must, ought to: **sceall** *pres.ind.3s.*, 796; **sceolde** *pret.ind.1s.*, 462; *3s.*, 393.

scyccels, *m.*, cloak: *a.s.*, 258; ~e *d.s.*, 267.

scyld, *m.*, sin, iniquity: ~a *g.p.*, 451.

scyldful, *adj.*, sinful, disgraceful: ~lan *a.p.f.wk.*, 379.

scyp: *see* **scip**.

se, sēo, þæt, (i) *def. art.*, the: **se** *n.s.m.*, 5, 7 etc.; **sēo** *n.s.f.*, 122, 130 etc.; **þæt** *n.s.nt.*, 71, 126 etc.; *a.s.nt.*, 57, 143 etc.; **þone** *a.s.m.*, 16, 17 etc.; **þā** *a.s.f.*, 2, 15 etc.; *n.p.m.*, 309G; *n.p.nt.*, 114; *a.p.m.*, 246, 431 etc.; *a.p.nt.*, 13, 93 etc.; *a.p.f.*, 42, 219 etc.; **þæs** *g.s.m.*, 16, 31 etc.; *g.s.nt.*, 80, 122 etc.; **þære** *g.s.f.*, 3, 6 etc.; *d.s.f.*, 12, 24 etc.; *g.p. m.*, 322G, 663; *g.p.f.*, 848; *g.p.nt.*, 617; **þām** *d.s.m.*, 34, 58 etc.; *d.s.nt.*, 4, 75 etc.; *d.p.m.* 30, 119 etc.; *d.p.f.*, 10, 21 etc.; *d.p.nt.*, 14, 19 etc.; **ðan** *inst.s.m.*, 172; **þon**, 729; **þī** *inst.s.nt.*, 354, 719; **þȳ**, 865; **þǣra** *g.s.f.*, 470, 805; *g.p.m.*, 157, 367 etc.; *g.p.f.*, 686; *g.p.nt.*, 8, 283, etc.; **þāra** *g.p.m.*, 620; (ii) *dem. adj.*, that: **þæt** *a.s.nt.*, 57, 134; **þǣre** *d.s.f.*, 348G; **þǣra** *g.p.m.*, 822; (iii) *dem. pron.*, that (one), he, etc.: **sē** *n.s.m.*, 15, 26 etc.; **þæt** *n.s.nt.*, 44, 72 etc.; *a.s.nt.*, 96, 336G etc.; **þone** *a.s.m.*, 389, 567; **þā** *a.s.f.*, 648, 654; *n.p.m.*, 51, 89; *n.p.f.*, 217;

a.p.m., 819; þæs *g.s.m.*, 268; *g.s.nt.*, 64, 195; þām *d.s.nt.*, 113, 142 etc.; *d.p.m.*, 461, 726; ðǣm *d.s.nt.*, 49; þon *inst.s.nt.*, 503; þan, 532, 715; þȳ, 378; þē *inst.s.nt.*, *w.cp.*, the: 116, 146 etc.; þǣra *g.p.m.*, 603, 696, 710; *g.p.nt.*, 9, 66, 398; (iv) *rel. pron.*, who, which, that: sē *n.s.m.*, 17; þone *a.s.m.*, 294, 509; þǣre *d.s.f.*, 241, 508, 539; þā *a.p.m.*, 566; þām *d.s.nt.*, 621; *d.p.m.*, 565; *containing its own antecedent*, that which: þæt *n.s.nt.*, 222; (v) se þe, *rel.pron.*, who: *n.s.m.*, 91, 300 etc.; þone þe *a.s.m.*, 263; þā þe *n.p.m.*, 590.

sealm, *m.*, psalm: ~as *a.p.*, 690.

sealmsang, *m.*, psalm, singing of psalms: *n.s.*, 44; *a.s.*, 149; ~e *d.s.*, 889; ~um *d.p.*, 766.

sēcan, *wv.1*, seek, look for: **sēcende** *pres.part.*, 870; **sōhte** *pret.ind.3s.*, 440, 899.

secgan, *wv.3*, say, tell: *inf.*, 760; **secgenne** *infl.inf.*, 87; **sege** *imp.s.*, 308G, 409; **sǣde** *pret.ind.1s.*, 382, 663; *3s.*, 55, 193 etc.

seldon, *adv.*, seldom: 414.

sendan, *wv.1*, send, put: *inf.*, 234; **sende** *pret.ind.3s.*, 251, 777, 850.

sēo: *see* se, sēo, þæt; bēon.

sēocnyss, *f.*, sickness: ~e *g.s.*, 773.

seofon, *num.*, seven: 594.

seofontȳne, *num.*, seventeen: 616, 655, 662.

seolfor, *n.*, silver: **seolfres** *g.s.*, 109.

setl, *n.*, setting: ~e *d.s.*, 574.

settan, *wv.1*, set, situate, place: **geset** *pp.*, 123; **gesæt**, 75; **geseted**, 192; **gesette** *(d.s.f.)*, 576; **gesettum** *(d.p. f.)*, 201.

sibb, *f.*, peace: ~e *a.s.*, 314G; *g.s.*, 827; *d.s.*, 717, 832, 836.

siccetung, *f.*, sighing, sigh: ~a *a.p.*, 489; ~um *d.p.*, 248.

sīd, *adj.*, ample, extensive: ~dran *cp.n.p.f.*, 218.

sîe, sîh: *see* bēon.

singal, *adj.*, constant, continuous: ~um *d.p.n.*, 170.

singan, *sv.3*, sing: *inf.*, 203; **singanne** *infl.inf.*, 629; **sang** *pret.ind.3s.*, 204; **sungon** *3p.*, 149.

sittan, *sv.5*, sit, rest: **sittende** *pres.part.*, 189.

sīþ, *m.*, time, occasion: ~um *d.p.*, 476.

siþþan: *see* syþþan.

sīðfæt, *m.*, path, way: *n.s.*, 905; *a.s.*, 571, 755; ~es *g.s.*, 202, 316G etc.; ~e *d.s.*, 169, 199 etc.; **sȳðfætes** *g.s.*, 228.

six, *num.*, six: 195.

slāw, *adj.*, slow, lazy: ~an

g.s.m.wk., 16.

slāwian, wv.2, to be slow, slacken: slāwedest pret.ind. 2s., 274.

slǣpan, sv.7, sleep: slēp pret. ind.3s., 190.

smēagan, wv.1, consider, think: smēagende pres.part., 679, 786; smēade pret.ind.1s., 382; smēadon 3p., 696.

smēagung, f., meditation, reflection, thought: n.s., 45; ~um d.p., 41.

smearcian, wv.2, smile: smearcode pret.ind.3s., 691.

smyltnyss, f., peace, tranquillity: n.s., 641.

sōna, adv., immediately, at once: 76, 168 etc.; sōna swā, conj., as soon as: 227, 665 etc.

sorgian, wv.2, sorrow, lament: sorgigende pres.part., 638, 783.

sōð, adj., true: ~e n.s.f.wk., 98; ~an a.s.m.wk., 493; d.s.f.wk, 117; d.s.nt.wk., 648.

sōðfæst, adj., truthful, righteous: ~a n.s.f.wk., 819.

sōðfæstnyss, f., truthfulness: ~e g.s., 552.

sōðlīce, adv., certainly, indeed, truly: 11, 35 etc.

spadu, f., spade: n.s., 912.

specan, sv.5 (= sprecan), speak, say: inf., 335G.

sprǣc, f., speech, narrative,

telling: ~e a.s., 21; n.p., 108.

sprecan, sv.5, speak, say: inf., 80, 304G; sprecende pres. part., 8, 62, 327G; sprǣc pret.ind.1s., 558; 3s., 913; sprǣcon 3p., 882.

stān, m., stone: n.s., 602.

standan, sv.6, stand: inf., 921; stand imp.s., 238; standende pres.part., 202, 417 etc.; stōd pret.ind.1s., 490; 3s., 207, 245 etc.; stōdon 3p., 752; stōde pret.sbj.3s., 473.

staðol, m., condition, state: a.s., 851.

staðolfæst, adj., firm, stable: ~e a.s.f., 313G.

staþolfæstlic, adj., secure, stable: n.s.f., 641.

staðolfæstnys, f., stability, steadfastness: n.s., 107; ~e a.s., 300.

stæf, m., letter, writing: ~as a.p., 899.

stæfcyst, f., letters, learning from books: ~e a.s., 695.

stemn, f., voice: n.s., 650; stefne a.s., 554; stemne a.s., 233, 234 etc.; g.s., 323G.

sticmǣlum, adv., little by little, gradually: 232.

stilness, f., stillness, silence: ~e d.s., 322G.

stōw, f., place: n.s., 130; ~e g.s., 871; d.s., 241, 490 etc.; ~um d.p., 37.

strang, adj., strong: n.s.f., 473.

swy̆ðe, 623; swīðost *sp.*, especially, most: 111, 293,
923.
swīðlic, *adj.*, intense, violent:
n.s.m., 261, 627; *n.s.f.*, 817;
~re *d.s.f.*, 666; swȳðlice *n.s.*
nt.wk., 644
swīðlīce, *adv.*, very much, severely: 335G, 863.
swīðra, *adj. (cp. of* swīð,
strong*)*, right (hand, side
etc.): ~n *a.s.f.*, 206, 873.
swōrettan, *wv.1*, sigh: *inf.*, 287.
swōretung, *f.*, groan, sigh: ~a
a.p., 247; sworettungum *d.*
p., 763, 918.
swūra, *m.*, neck: ~n *a.s.*, 218.
swutellīce, *adv.*, clearly: 265.
swutol, *adj.*, clear: *a.s.nt.*, 870.
swutole, *adv.*, clearly: 903.
sȳ: *see* bēon.
sȳfre, *adj.*, abstinent, clean:
sȳfrum *d.s.nt.*, 96; *d.p.m.*,
53.
sylf, *adj.*, self: *n.s.m.*, 33, 49
etc.; *n.s.f.*, 503, 609 etc.;
~ne *a.s.m.*, 95, 118 etc.; ~e
a.s.f., 382, 399 etc.; *a.p.m.*,
124, 820; ~re *d.s.f.*, 485,
678; ~um *d.s.m.*, 162, 170
etc.; *d.p.m.*, 132.
syllan, *wv.1*, give: syle *imp.s.*,
238; syllanne *infl.inf.*, 397;
syllendan *pres.part. (a.p.*
m.wk.), 432; sealde *pret.*
ind.3s., 565.
symbeldæg, *m.*, feast-day: ~e

d.s., 173.
symbelnyss, *f.*, feast, solemnity:
n.s., 452; ~e *d.s.*, 446; ~um
d.p., 154.
symle, *adv.*, always, ever: 52,
126 etc.
synd, syndon, sȳo: *see* bēon.
synful, *adj.*, sinful: *n.s.nt.*,
343G; *a.s.nt.*, 272; ~lum
d.s.m., 315G; ~re *d.s.f.*,
305G; ~le *n.p.m.*, 545; ~ra
g.p.m., 546; ~lan *g.s.m.wk.*,
442; *a.p.m.wk.*, 504.
syngian, *wv.2*, sin: syngigenne
infl.inf., 431.
syngiga, *m.*, sinner: ~n *a.s.*,
236.
synlust, *m.*, desire for sin: ~es
g.s., 377; ~a *g.p.*, 368.
synn, *f.*, sin: ~a *a.p.*, 793.
syrwian, *wv.2*, plot, deceive:
syrwiende *pres.part.*, 342G.
sȳðfæt: *see* sīðfæt.
syþþan, (i) *adv.*, afterwards,
then, from then on: 143, 519
etc.; sippan, 676; (ii) *conj.*,
since, after: siððan, 694,
736.

T

tācn, *nt.*, sign: *a.s.*, 806, 870; ~e
d.s., 211, 347G, 804 etc.
talent, *m.*, talent: *a.s.*, 17.
tænel, *m.*, wicker basket: *a.s.*,
779, 846.
tēar, *m.*, tear: ~as *a.p.*, 246;

~**um** *d.p.*, 240, 247 etc.

tellan, *wv.1*, tell, count, fathom: **tellende** *pres.part.*, 282; **tealde** *pret.ind.1s.*, 385.

tempel, *nt.*, temple: **temples** *g.s.*, 461, 475 etc.; **temple** *d.s.*, 457, 534.

teolian, *wv.2*, strive, try: **teoligende** *pres.part.*, 809; **teolode** *pret.ind.1s.*, 357.

tēon, *sv.2*, draw, entice: **tēonde** *pres.part.*, 452.

tēona, *m.*, injury, wrong: ~**n** *a.p.*, 386.

tīd, *f.*, time, hour: *n.s.*, 122, 168 etc.; ~**e** *g.s.*, 907; *d.s.*, 188, 387 etc.; ~**a** *a.p.*, 4; *g.p.*, 279, 606; ~**um** *d.p.*, 133, 201.

tihtan, *wv.1*, incite, provoke: **tihtende** *pres.part.*, 434.

tilian, *wv.2*, work for, strive after: **tiligende** *pres.part.*, 301.

tō, (i) *prep.w.d./inst.*, to: 8, 37 etc.; at, on *(time)*: 729, 730, 741; for, as, as a, a cause of: 97, 384 etc.; *w.infl.inf.*, 87, 94 etc.; **tō þām** (. . .) **þæt**, to the extent that, with the intention/purpose that: 116, 152, 306G; **tō þon þæt**, 503, 704, 930; **tō þȳ þæt**, in order to: 378; **tō hwȳ**, why: 340G; **tō sōðan**, in truth: 648, 709; (ii) *adv.*, too: 19; *expressing sense of arrival*, (came) along: 198 *(see* BT, **tō**, V*)*.

Tobie, *proper name*, Tobit, Tobias: *d.*, 8.

tōcyme, *m.*, arrival: *a.s.*, 783.

tōdæge, *adv.*, today: 308G.

tōēacan, *adv.*, in addition, besides: 34.

tōforan, *prep.w.d.*, in front of, before: 357, 633.

tōgædere, *adv.*, together: 149, 388, 758.

tōgeȳcan, *wv.1*, add to: **tōgeihte** *pret.ind.3s.*, 246.

tōmiddes, *prep.w.g.*, in the midst of, amongst: 420; *see* BT, **tōmiddes**, II.

tōteran, *sv.4*, tear to pieces: **tōtorene** *pp. (n.p.m.)*, 666.

tōweard, *adj.*, approaching, to come, coming: *n.s.nt.*, 72; ~**an** *a.s.f.wk.*, 54; *g.s.m.wk.*, 720.

tōwrīðan, *sv.1*, twist: **tōwrīðende** *pres.part.*, 571.

trēow, *nt.*, tree: *a.s.*, 914; ~**es** *g.s.*, 483.

trūwa, *m.*, faith, trust, belief: ~**n** *d.s.*, 522, 635.

tunga, *f.*, tongue: *n.s.*, 428.

twēgen, *num.*, two: *a.*, 151; **twǣgen**, 600.

twelfta, *adj.*, twelfth: ~**n** *d.s.nt.*, 363.

twēntig, *num.*, twenty: 196.

twēonian, *wv.2*, doubt, be uncertain: **twēonigende** *pres. part.*, 802.

tȳddernyss, *f.*, frailty: ~e *a.s.*, 259.

tȳn, *wv.1*, instruct, teach: **getȳd** *pp.*, 27.

tȳn, *num.*, ten: 416.

Þ/Ð

þā, (i) *adv.*, then: 76, 78 etc.; (ii) *conj.*, when: 204, 212 etc.; **þā þā**: 198, 233 etc.; *see also* **se, sēo, þæt**.

þanc, *m.*, thanks: ~as *a.p.*, 753.

þanone, *adv.*, thence, from there, from then: 480, 587.

ðægn, *m.*, thegn, follower: ~as *a.p.*, 742.

þǣr, (i) *adv.*, there: 3, 58, 106 etc.; (ii) *conj.*, where: 104, 206; **þǣr þǣr**, 415.

þǣræfter, *adv.*, after that, thereafter: 826.

þǣrmid, *adv.*, therewith: 915.

þæs, *g.s. of dem.pron.* **þæt** *(see also* **sē, sēo, þæt***)*: **þæs þe**, *conj.*, as, according as, of which, because: 45, 434 etc.

þæslic, *adj.*, agreeable, fitting: *n.s.nt.*, 495; ~e *a.m.*, 417.

þæt, (i) *conj.*, that: 7, 11 etc.; in order that, so that, to the extent that: 37, 73 etc.; (ii) *rel. particle*, who, which, that: 62, 72, 75 *(latter two could also be neuter rel. prons)* etc.; *see also* **se, sēo, þæt**.

þe, (i) *rel. particle*, who, which, that: 10, 19 etc.; (ii) *used to form conj. with* **forþan, þæs, mid þām**; *see also* **se, sēo, þæt**.

þē: *see* **se, sēo, þæt; þū**.

þēah, *conj.*, although: 72, 398 etc.

þēahhwæðere, *adv.*, however: 865, 895.

þearle, *adv.*, exceedingly, excessively: 609.

þēaw, *m.*, custom, *(in pl.)* morals, conduct, behaviour: *n.s.*, 83, 828; ~a *g.p.*, 2, 88; ~um *d.p.*, 25, 26 etc.

þencan, *wv.1*, think: *inf.*, 467, 891; **þencende** *pres.part. (d.s.f.)*, 485; **þencendum** *(d.s.m.)*, 68; **þōhte** *pret.ind. 1s.*, 482; *3s.*, 786, 799, 891.

þenian, *wv.2*, exert oneself: **þenigende** *pres.part.*, 229.

þēnung, *f.*, service, duty: ~e *g.s.*, 932; ~a *a.s.*, 307G.

þēostru, *nt (p.)*, darkness: *a.p.*, 806.

þēowtscipe, *m.*, service: ~s *g.s.*, 32.

þēow, *m.*, slave, servant: ~es *g.s.*, 17*.

þēowen, *f.*, slave, servant, handmaid: *n.s.*, 236; ~e *a.s.*, 821, 832; *g.s.*, 931.

þēowian, *wv.2*, serve: **þēowigende** *pres.part.*, 106, 284.

ðerscwold, *m.*, threshold: *a.s.*, 470.

þes, þēos, þis (i) *dem. adj.*, this:
þis *a.s.nt.*, 524, 633 etc.;
þisne *a.s.m.*, 149, 587 etc.;
þeosne, 676; ðās *a.s.f.*, 1,
132 etc.; *n.p.nt.*, 285, 406,
?716; *a.p.nt.*, 240, 713 etc.;
a.p.f., 40; þises *g.s.m.*,
315G; þyses *g.s.nt.*, 625;
þissa *d.s.f.*, 20; þissere
g.s.f., 590, 930; *d.s.f.*, 518;
þyssere *d.s.f.*, 292, 718, 896;
þysum *d.s.m.*, 747; *d.s.nt.*,
592, 653, 664; *d.p.nt.*, 541;
(ii) *dem. pron.*, this: þes *n.s.
m.*, 27; ðis *n.s.nt.*, 179, 368;
a.s.nt., 332G, 515 etc.; ðas
a.p.nt., 68, 117; þysum *d.s.
nt.*, 58, 122 etc.; *d.p.nt.*, 68,
102 etc.; þyssum *d.p.nt.*,
826.

þicgan, *wv.1*, receive, consume:
þigde *pret.ind.1s.*, 739.

þīn, *poss.adj.*, your *(s.)*: *n.s.m.*,
551; *a.s.nt.*, 514; ~ne *a.s.m.*,
258, 498; ~es *g.s.m.*, 517,
841; *g.s.nt.*, 238; ~re *g.s.f.*,
298, 506 etc.; *d.s.f.*, 500; ~e
a.s.f., 496, 543 etc.; *a.p.m.*,
341G; *a.p.nt.*, 257; ~um
d.s.m., 74; *d.s.nt.*, 832, 835,
880; *d.p.m.*, 936; *d.p.nt.*,
313G, 841; ~ra *g.p.nt.*, 260.

þincan, *wv.2* seem *(impers.
w.d.)*: þincð *pres.ind.3s.*,
595; þūhte *pret.ind.3s.*, 418.

þīnen, *f.*, servant, handmaid:
n.s., 291.

þing, *nt.*, thing, circumstance:
a.s., 324G, 326G; ~a *g.p.*,
14, 699 etc.; ~um *d.p.*, 14,
19 etc.; þincg, *n.s.*, 49, 153
etc.; *a.s.*, 158, 614 etc.; *a.p.*,
353, 360 etc.

þingian, *wv.2*, intercede: þingode *pret.sbj.3s.*, 942.

þonne, (i) *adv.*, then: 140, 142
etc.; (ii) *conj.*, when: 165,
618 etc.; (iii) *conj.w.cp.*,
than: 72, 218.

þrǣscan, *wv.1*, writhe, torment:
þrǣscende *pres.part.*, 645;
geþrēst *pp.*, 625.

þrēagan, *wv.1*, reproach:
þrēade *pret.ind.3s.*, 864.

þrēagung, *f.*, reproach, reproof:
~e *d.s.*, 793.

þrēo: *see* þrȳ.

þringan, *sv.3.*, press, push: *inf.*,
460.

þrōwian, *wv.2*, endure, attempt,
experience: þrōwige
pres.sbj.1s., 612; þrōwode
pret.ind.1s., 476.

þrōwung, *f.*, passion, suffering:
~a *g.s.*, 125; ~e *d.s.*, 403.

þrȳ, *num.*, three: 565; þrēo, 57;
þrēora *g.*, 850.

þrȳstlǣcan, *wv.1*, presume,
dare, become bold: þrȳst-
lǣcende *pres.part.*, 523.

þrywa, *adv.*, thrice, three times:
476.

þū, *pers. pron.*, you: *n.s.*, 69, 70
etc.; þē *a.s.*, 85, 92 etc.; *d.s.*,

72, 86 etc.; **ēow** *a.p.*, 87;
d.p., 88, 421, 422; **ēower**
g.p., 421; **inc** *d. dual*, 515.

þurh, *prep.w.a.*, through, by
means of: 47, 239 etc.

þurhtēon, *sv.*2, continue, carry
on, perpetrate: **þurhtēah**
pret.ind.3s., 196; **þurhtuge**
pret.sbj.1s., 385.

þurhwæccendlic, *adj.*, very
vigilant: ~**an** *d.s.nt.wk*, 53.

Þurresdæg, *m.*, Thursday: ~**e**
d.s., 731.

þus, *adv.*, thus, so: 11, 61 etc.

þwēan, *sv.*6, wash, cleanse:
þwōh *pret.ind.1s.*, 578; *3s.*,
887, 941.

þyder, (i) *adv.*, thither, there:
243, 471 etc.; (ii) *conj.*, to
where: 585.

þyderes, *adv.*, thither: 869.

þyderweardes, *adv.*, on the way
there: 861.

þyllic, *adj.*, such, such a: ~**e**
a.s.f., 234, 251; *a.p.m.*, 646.

U

unāblinnendlīce, *adv.*, unceasingly: 192, 367 etc.

unāfyllendlic, *adj.*, insatiable:
~**e** *a.p.f.*, 282.

unālȳfed, *adj.*, wrongful, illicit:
~**an** *a.s.m.wk.*, 270.

unālȳfendlīce, *adv.*, wrong-
fully, licentiously: 367.

unāsecgendlic, *adj.*, unspeak-

able: *n.s.f.*, 433.

unāstyrigendlic, *adj.*, motionless: *n.s.f.*, 672.

unberēafīgendlic, *adj.*, never to
be taken away, inalienable:
~**e** *a.s.nt.wk.*, 298.

unbesmiten, *adj.*, undefiled:
~**an** *g.s.m.wk.*, 141, 777;
~**um** *d.p.nt.wk.*, 579.

unblinnendlic, *adj.*, unceasing:
n.s.f., 107.

unc: *see* ic.

uncūð, *adj.*, unknown: *n.s.f.*,
131.

underfōn, *sv.*7, receive, obtain,
take, undertake: *inf.*, 394,
844*; *pres.sbj.3p.*, 401;
underfonde *pres.part.*, 54*;
underfonne *infl.inf.*, 537;
underfēng *pret.ind.3s.*, 635;
underfēnge *pret.sbj.1s.*, 380.

undergytan, *sv.*5, perceive:
undergeat *pret.ind.3s.*, 871.

underntīd, *f.*, morning-time,
morning: *n.s.*, 572.

understandan, *sv.*6, notice, pay
heed to: **understandende**
pres.part., 229.

underþēodan, *wv.*1, subject,
subjugate: *inf.*, 35; **under-**
ðēoddon *pret.sbj.3p.*, 39;
underþēoded *pp.*, 368.

underwreðian, *wv.*2, sustain,
uphold: **underwreðed** *pp.*,
281.

unēaðe, *adv.*, hardly: 625.

unfeormigende, *adj.*, inexpi-

able: **unfeormiganda** *n.p.nt.*,
486.
unforbūgendlīce, *adv.*, unswervingly: 492.
unforswīgod, *adj.*, unconcealed
by silence: *a.s.nt.*, 43.
ungelēafful, *adj.*, unbelieving,
disbelieving: *n.s.m.*, 19.
ungelȳfedlic, *adj.*, unbelievable, incredible: *n.s.nt.*, 49.
ungesǣlig, *sdj.*, unhappy: ~an
a.s.m.wk., 798.
ungesǣlignyss, *f.*, unhappiness:
~e *d.s.*, 853.
ungetēorod, *adj.*, unfailing: ~ne
a.s.m., 113.
ungewemmednyss, *f.*, spotlessness, purity: ~e *d.s.*, 500.
ungewunelic, *adj.*, uninhabited:
n.s.f., 131.
unlīcwyrðe, *adj.*, unpleasing,
displeasing: *n.s.f.*, 422.
unmǣte, *adj.*, great, excessive:
unmǣttre *g.s.f.*, 920; **un-
mǣtan** *g.s.m.wk.*, 668; *g.s.
nt.wk.*, 923; **unmǣtum**
d.p.f., 675.
unmedeme, *adj.*, unworthy, un-
fit: **unmedemre** *d.s.f.*, 512.
unmiht, *f.*, weakness: ~e *d.s.*,
467.
unnytt, *adj.*, idle, useless: ~e
n.p.f., 108.
unoferwrigen, *adj.*, uncovered:
~e *n.s.f.*, 256.
unrihtlic, *adj.*, wrongful,
wicked: ~an *a.p.m.wk.*, 436.

unsǣlig, *adj.*, wretched, unhappy: ~e *n.s.m.wk.*, 911;
n.s.f.wk., 461; ~an *a.s.m.
wk.*, 644.
unscēadwīs, *adj.*, irrational: ~ra
g.p.nt., 618.
unsceamlic, *adj.*, shameless.
immodest: ~an *a.p.nt.wk.*,
426.
unsceandlīce, *adv.*, shamelessly: 419*.
untǣllīce, *adv.*, blamelessly: 33.
untȳnan, *wv.1.* open: **untȳnde**
pret.ind.3s., 437; **untȳnede**
pp. (a.s.f.), 513.
unwemme, *adj.*, unstained: *a.s.
m. (undecl.)*, 851.
unwemmed, *adj.*, unstained:
a.s.m. (undecl.), 499.
unwīslic, *adj.*, foolish: ~ra
g.p.m., 611.
unwurð, *adj.*, unworthy: ~an
a.s.f.wk., 544; *d.s.m.wk.*,
797.
ūp, *adv.*, up: 205, 340G etc.;
upp: 244.
ūpāhebban, *sv.6*, raise up:
ūpāhōf *pret.ind.3s.*, 330G;
ūpāhafenum *pp. (d.p.nt.)*,
320G, 877; **ūpāhefene** *(a.s.
f.)*, 331G.
ūpāhefennyss, *f.*, exaltation: ~e
g.s., 453.
ūre, *poss.adj.*, our: **ūrne** *a.s.m.*,
714; **ūres** *g.s.m.*, 141, 580,
778; **ūrum** *d.s.m.*, 349G,
958.

ūt, *adv.*, out: 74, 129 etc.

ūtan, *adv.*, from without: 343G.

ūtgān, *anom.v.*, go out: **ūtēode** *pret.ind.1s.*, 539.

ūtscūfan, *sv.2*, push out: **ūt-sceofe** *pret.sbj.3s.*, 526.

W

wāfung, *f.*, astonishment: *n.s.*, 817.

wana, *adj. (undecl.)*, lacking: 912.

wang, *m.*, cheek: ~as *a.p.*, 647.

waruð, *nt.*, shore: ~e *d.s.*, 417.

wǣdlung, *f.*, poverty, begging: ~a *d.s.*, 381.

wǣfels, *m.*, garment: ~um *d.p.*, 254.

wǣg: *see* **weg**.

wǣgan, *wv.1*, falsify, deceive: **wǣge** *pres.sbj.1s.*, 21.

wǣs, wǣre, wǣron: *see* **bēon**.

wǣstm, *m.*, fruit: ~um *d.p.*, 780.

wǣter, *nt.*, water: *a.s.*, 185, 555, 694; ~es *g.s.*, 583, 782 etc.; ~e *d.s.*, 116, 158, 578; ~u *a.p.*, 803, 805; ~a *g.p.*, 78; ~um *d.p.*, 815; **wǣtru** *a.p.*, 807; **wǣttrum** *d.p.*, 810.

wǣterwǣdlnyss, *f.*, lack of water: ~e *d.s.*, 625.

weallende, *adj.*, ardent, enthusiastic: *a.p.m.*, 106.

weard, weardes: *see* **wið**.

weaxan, *sv.7*, grow: **wēoxon**

pret.ind.3p., 161.

weg, *m.*, way, road, path: *n.s.*, 316G; *a.s.*, 569; ~as *n.p.*, 74; **wǣg** *n.s.*, 567; *a.s.*, 551, 553.

wel, *adv.*, very, very much, well: 36, 45.

wela, *m.*, riches, wealth: ~n *d.s.*, 380.

weler, *m.*, lip: ~as *a.p.*, 347G; ~a *g.p.*, 322G.

wēnan, *wv.1*, think: *inf.*, 478; **wēnst** *pres.ind.2s.*, 394; **wēn** *imp.s.*, 380; **wēnde** *pret.ind. 3s.*, 209, 390.

wendan, *wv.2*, go, turn: **wend-ende** *pres.part.*, 200; **wende** *pret.ind.3s.*, 169, 271; **gewend** *pp.*, 268.

wēnunga, *adv.*, perhaps, perchance: 129.

wēofod, *nt.*, altar: ~e *d.s.*, 284.

weorc, *nt.*, work, act, task: *a.s.*, 43, 932 etc.; *a.p.*, 13, 94 etc.; ~um *d.p.*, 30, 65 etc.

weorpan, *sv.3*, throw, cast: **wearp** *pret.ind.1s.*, 537; *3s.*, 268, 945.

weorðan, *sv.3*, become, be: **wurðe** *pres.sbj.1s.*, 507; *3s.*, 315G; **wearð** *pret.ind.1s.*, 521; *3s.*, 333G, 335G etc.; **geworden** *pp.*, 30, 507.

wēpan, *sv.7*, weep: *inf.*, 359, 487; **wepende** *pres.part.*, 235, 558 etc.; **wēop** *pret. ind.1s.*, 638; *3s.*, 789.

wer, *m.*, man: *n.s.*, 24, 404.

wēste, *nt.*, waste, desert: *a.s.*, 633.

wēsten, (i) *nt.*, desert, wasteland: *a.s.*, 66*, 181 etc.; ~**es** *g.s.*, 625, 756; ~**e** *d.s.*, 4, 161 etc.; (ii) *adj.*, waste, desolate: *n.s.f.*, 130.

westweardes, *adv.*, westwards: 214.

wīdgill, *adj.*, expansive, vast: ~**e** *a.s.nt.wk.*, 868.

wīf, *n.*, woman: *n.s.*, 279, 304G etc.; *a.s.*, 272; ~**es** *g.s.*, 784, 884.

wīfhād, *m.*, female sex: ~**es** *g.s.*, 254.

wīflic, *adj.*, womanly, female: ~**an** *a.s.f.*, 259; *d.s.f.*, 467.

wīfman, *m.*, woman: *n.s.*, 215.

wildēor, *nt.*, wild beast: *n.s.*, 929; *a.s.*, 693, 875, 924; ~**es** *g.s.*, 923; ~**a** *g.p.*, 224, 226, 618.

willa, *m.*, will, wish: *n.s.*, 551, 586; ~**n** *a.s.*, 319G, 477.

willan, *anom.v.*, wish, be willing, will: **wille** *pres. ind.1s.*, 136, 395, 398; *2s.*, 256; *pres.sbj.2s.*, 729; **willan** *3p.*, 384; **wile** *pres. ind.3s.*, 839; **willendan** *pres. part. (a.p.m.)*, 432; **wolde** *pret.ind.3s.*, 156, 390; *pret. sbj.1s.*, 468; *3s.*, 771; **woldon** *pret.ind.3p.*, 376, 392.

wilnian, *wv.2*, desire, wish for

(w.g.): **wilnast** *pres.ind.2s.*, 273.

wilnung, *f.*, desire: ~**e** *g.s.*, 871.

wīn, *nt.*, wine: ~**es** *g.s.*, 621.

winnan, *sv.3*, strive, toil: **winnende** *pres.part.*, 657, 675; **wan** *pret.ind.1s.*, 617; **wunnon** *3p.*, 182.

winter, *m.*, winter, year: **wintres** *g.s.*, 668, 671; **wintre** *a.p.*, 617; **wintra** *g.p.*, 958; ~**um** *d.p.*, 372, 595.

wīse, *f.*, matter, affair, thing, practice: **wīsan** *a.s.*, 132, 171 etc.; *d.s.*, 20, 305G, 890; *n.p.*, 746; *a.p.*, 33, 40 etc.

wistmete, *m.*, food, sustenance: **wistmettum** *d.p.*, 681.

wit: *see* ic.

wita, *m.*, elder, wise man: ~**n** *g.s.*, 299; **witon** *a.p.*, 105.

witan, *pret.pres.v.*, know, learn: **wāt** *pres.ind.1s.*, 406, 494, 709; *3s.*, 405; **wite** *imp.s.*, 342G, 811; **witenne** *infl.inf.*, 274; **wiste** *pret.ind.1s.*, 569; *3s.*, 902.

witodlīce, *adv.*, certainly, indeed, truly: 7, 28 etc.

wið, *prep.w.a.*, against, facing, beside: 514, 921: *w.g.*, to, against: 460; **wið . . . weard(es)**, towards: 168, 691, 703 etc.; *w.d.*, to: 336G.

wiðerwinna, *m.*, enemy, adversary: ~**n** *d.s.*, 349G.

wiðsacan, *sv.6*, forsake, reject, deny *(w.d.)*: **wiðsace** *pres.ind.1s.*, 518.

wōp, *m.*, weeping: ~e *d.s.*, 889.

wōpig, *adj.*, sad, doleful: **wopegum** *d.p.m.*, 705.

word, *nt.*, word: *n.s.*, 697; *a.s.*, 701; *n.p.*, 285, 406; *a.p.*, 240, 352G; ~es *g.s.*, 683; ~e *d.s.*, 685, 832; ~a *g.p.*, 413; ~um *d.p.*, 102, 328G etc.

woruld, *f.*, world: ~e *g.s.*, 590; *d.s.*, 292, 518 etc.; **on worulda woruld**, world without end: 960.

wracu, *f.*, vengeance, punishment: *n.s.*, 474.

wraxlian, *wv.2*, wrestle, struggle: **wraxligende** *pres. part.*, 676.

wrītan, *sv.1*, write: **wrītende** *pres.part.*, 19; **write** *pret.sbj. 3s.*, 900.

wuldor, *nt.*, glory: *n.s.*, 545, 820, 958; *a.s.*, 544; **wuldre** *d.s.*, 818, 880.

wuldorfæst, *adj.*, glorious, magnificent: ~e *n.s.f.*, 493, 511; ~an *g.s.f.wk.*, 220; *d.s. nt.wk.*, 818; *a.p.nt.wk.*, 13; **wulderfæstan** *d.s.f.wk.*, 9.

wuldorfæstlicnyss, *f.*, glory: ~e *a.s.*, 708.

wuldorlic, *adj.*, glorious: ~an *d.s.f.wk.*, 869.

wuldrian, *wv.2*, glorify: **wuldrigende** *pres.part.*, 752,

801 etc.; **wuldrode** *pret.ind. 3s.*, 725, 908.

wull, *f.*, wool: *n.s.*, 217.

wundor, *nt.*, wonder, marvel: *n.s.*, 48; **wundru** *a.p.*, 707.

wundrian, *wv.2.* wonder, marvel: *inf.*, 723; **wundrige** *pres.ind.1s.*, 435.

wunian, *wv.2*, remain, dwell: **wuna** *imp.s.*, 100; **wunode** *pret.ind.1s.*, 363, 446; *3s.*, 104, 170.

wurðian, *wv.2*, honour, celebrate: *inf.*, 393; **wurþigenne** *infl.inf.*, 459; **wurðodon** *pret.ind.3p.*, 953.

wurðung, *f.*, honouring, honour, celebration: ~a *d.s.*, 124, 392.

wylm, *m.*, scorching, boiling: ~es *g.s.*, 668.

wynlust, *m.*, desire for pleasure: ~as *g.s.*, 403.

wynstre, *adj.*, left: **wynstran** *a.s.f.wk.*, 873.

wynsumian, *wv.2.* rejoice, make glad: **wynsumigende** *pres.part.*, 902; **wynsumigendum** *(d.s.m.)*, 801.

wyrcan, *wv.1*, perform, do, work: **wyrceað** *pres.ind.3s.*, 707; **wyrcende** *pres.part.*, 97, 176.

wyrsa, *adj.*, worse: **wyrsum** *d.p.nt.*, 447*.

wyrt, *f.*, plant: ~um *d.p.*, 161, 664.

wyrðe, *adj.*, worthy: *n.s.m.*, 46.
wytt: *see* ic.

Y

yfel, *nt.*, evil: ~um *d.p.*, 679.
ylca, *wk.adj.*, same: ~n *a.s.m.*,
     755; *d.s.f.*, 524, 581 etc.;
     d.p.m., 612.
yldo, *f.*, age: ylde *a.s.*, 228; *g.s.*,
     363; yldum *d.p.*, 932.
ymb, *prep.w.d.*, after: 836.
ymbsellan,   *wv.1*,   enclose,
     surround, protect: ymbseald
     pp., 343G.
ymbūtan, *prep.w.a.*, about: 640.
yrmð, *f.*, misery: ~e *d.s.*, 384.

yrnan, *sv.3*, run: *inf.*, 456, 456;
     yrnende   *pres.part.*,   241,
     388;   yrnendum   *(d.p.m.)*,
     456;   arn *pret.ind.1s.*, 415,
     570; *3s.*, 221, 225 etc.
ȳtemest, *sp.adj.*, uttermost, ex-
     treme: ~an *d.p.m.wk.*, 848.
ȳð, *f.*, wave: ~a *a.p.*, 807, 860.

Z

Zosimus, *proper name*, Zoz-
     imus (= Zosimas): *n.*, 27, 55
     etc; *a.*, 134, 261; Zosimam
     d., 271; Zosime *d.*, 280, 285,
     302.